IDOLS OF THE MARKET

Modern Iconoclasm and the Fundamentalist Spectacle

SVEN LÜTTICKEN

Sternberg Press

TABLE OF CONTENTS

PREFACE

This project was first conceived in 2005 as an exhibition; when I took it up again the following year, it met with massive institutional disinterest. It then morphed into a book, maintaining an essayistic and interventionist—rather than purely academic—character. This book seeks to surpass the now-dominant representation of iconoclasm as a pathological phenomenon grimly situated in the past, or in retrograde cultures. Rather than relegate it to history, my aim is to historicize iconoclasm to the point where its potential for the present situation becomes apparent.

That the study of art is intimately linked to that of religion was driven home in my student days, when Peter van Dael instructed me in medieval Christian theories of the image and Carel Blotkamp discussed Mondrian in the light of theosophy. Now circumstances have forced me to "theologize" to an unprecedented degree; no doubt I have stumbled from time to time, but I hope that I make good use of the authors who have guided me through this field, even when I immodestly beg to differ from them. A kind of expanded art history, this project also encroaches on philosophy and critical theory, creating an interdisciplinary montage that is born of necessity, not fashion. The most important interdisciplinary dialog here is with artists.

Over the past three years a number of people have supported me in significant ways, especially by allowing me to test—sometimes in quite rudimentary form—ideas and approaches that culminate in this book. In particular I would like to thank Susan Watkins and Tony Wood at *New Left Review*, and André Rottmann, Mirjam Thoma and Isabelle Graw at *Texte zur Kunst*; these publications have offered me something of a refuge in the world of criticism and theory. Related texts, which have to a greater or lesser degree turned up in this book, have also been published in *Open* (thanks to its benevolent editor Jorinde Seijdel), in *Grey Room* (with thanks in particular to Tom McDonough), and in the reader accompanying the Dutch presentation at the 2007 Venice Biennale, *Citizens and Subjects: The Netherlands* (edited by Maria Hlavajova, Charles Esche and Rosi Braidotti; Maria Hlavajova also helped me realize the exhibition part of the project after all, at BAK, Utrecht in late 2008).

Further thanks are due to Perry Anderson, Tom Holert, André Rottmann and Tony Wood for their comments; needless to say, I alone am responsible for the shortcomings of this book, which was produced under often hectic circumstances in the spare moments offered by academic and extra-academic life. Caroline Schneider and Kari Rittenbach at Sternberg Press were crucial in bringing the book into the light of day; if it débuts slightly later than anticipated, the changes in the economic and political landscape since most of it was written—the end of the Bush Era, world economic meltdown—emphasize the urgency of its attempts to rethink the dominant conditions of the decade that is drawing to an end.

Finally, I thank my colleagues and students at the Vrije Universiteit as well as my family—a blend of Catholic and Protestant influences without which this atheist would be nothing—for both enduring and inspiring me. My most profound and virtually idolatrous gratitude is reserved for Binna Choi, to whom this book is dedicated.

Introduction

WELCOME TO THE IMAGE WARS

All the merry little elves can go hang themselves
My faith is as cold as can be
Bob Dylan[1]

It has long been regarded as art's task to criticize the images produced by the culture industry—whether in the form of direct comments on such imagery, or by developing an autonomous realm of untainted visuality in opposition to it. Clement Greenberg's mid-century definition of Modernist art as an exercise in self-criticism, leading to even more restrictions and an even "purer" art, to the rejection of illusionism and the triumph of "flatness" in painting, was aimed against the "kitsch" of the culture industry.[2] In the end, it became obvious that was perfect for the modern apartments of wealthy collectors or corporate lobbies and offices. If modern art cannot help being both autonomous and a *fait social,* as Adorno argued, High Modernism's refusal to address its social context made it, paradoxically, less autonomous.[3] Artists associated with the neo-avant-garde of the late 1960s and 70s tried to remedy this by questioning the position of the institutions of art and the mass media as pillars of the bourgeois ideology supporting capitalism. Since then, criticality has been firmly established as the core business of art, part of the brand that is "advanced art." Today, however, both media images and "critical" art itself are increasingly contested by fundamentalist versions of the monotheistic religions.

OLD AND NEW IDOLS

In one way or another, most recent religious controversies revolve around images—some of them highly dramatic and violent. They range from the attack on the World Trade Center, that abstract double icon of capitalism and American power, to the cartoons published by the Danish paper *Jyllands-Posten*. Some of these were tailor-made for escalation, and it comes as no surprise that they were used by hardliners on both sides to create the impression of an irreconcilable opposition between "the West" (or "modernity") and Islam. The Danish caricatures not only represented the Prophet, thus breaking a widespread—though by no means universal—Muslim custom, but they caricatured him in ways that sometimes seemed racist and oddly reminiscent of anti-Semitic caricatures of old, while structurally resembling traditional Christian depictions of Muhammad in hell. (In 2002, an al Qaeda cell in Italy was reported to have planned the bombing of a church in Bologna, the location of a fifteenth-century fresco depicting this scene.[4]) Given that such images are met with outrage, monotheism—Islam, in particular—is often regarded as inherently intolerant, its iconoclastic ire presenting a danger to civilized society. Various atheist websites have posted an image of the Twin Towers with the Lennon-inspired caption: IMAGINE NO RELIGION (fig. 0.1).[5] But religion is too important to be left to fundamentalists; indeed, it is too important to be left to believers alone.

Many of the recent controversies revolve around images that are seen as both idolatrous and blasphemous—perceived as illicit representations of a deity or prophet who should not be represented, as well as offensive caricatures.[6] One of the Danish caricatures depicts Muhammad as a sinister-looking fellow whose turban hides a bomb; that image of Islam as backward and violent was effectively fortified by the preachers and masses engaged in violent protests against such caricatures. Certain Sudanese Muslim groups also actively embraced Western clichés about Islam in the absurd 2007 affair over an English school teacher, who had allowed her pupils to name the class teddy bear Muhammad, after one of the boys. She was sentenced to fifteen days in prison for insulting the prophet by seemingly representing him in the form of a soft toy. Clearly, one or more political factions were exploiting an imaginary offense by a western foreign national to further their political agenda, yet we should not treat the religious "surface" as a mere passive reflection of the "real" economic and political issues. Like cultural production in general, religion can develop a dynamic of its own, articulating political issues as well as interfering in them.

The interdiction of idolatry, of images that may come to be worshiped as false gods, is the founding act of monotheism. The seemingly secular "West" is seen by many Muslim fundamentalists as idolatrous, worshiping the false gods of material wealth and alluring images. It is, as the mid-twentieth century Egyptian radical Sayyd Qutb stated, the new jahiliyya—the term *jahiliyya* standing for the idolatrous "state of ignorance" of pre-

Muhammad Arabia.[7] Some scholars emphasize that, in distancing themselves from the jahiliyya, the Qur'an and the hadith did not in fact accord a central place to the question of the image.[8] However, a ban on images is implicit in the condemnation of *shirk*, or the polytheistic association of other gods with God. Furthermore, the Qur'an contains numerous references to the primal scene of idolatry in the Torah—the episode of the Golden Calf—when the Israelites relapsed into worshiping a material image as a divinity.[9] Such a practice had been explicitly forbidden by the Second Commandment, which states that Israel shall have no other gods than Yahweh, and which condemns graven images "or any likeness of any thing that is in heaven above, or that is in the earth beneath, or that is in the water under the earth." This commandment, given in Exodus 30:3–4 and in Deuteronomy 20:3–4, is elaborated upon in Deuteronomy 4:15–19, when the Israelites are reminded that they "saw no manner of similitude on the day that the LORD spoke unto [them] in Horeb out of the midst of the fire," and that representations of people and animals should be avoided because they might lead to "corruption"; to the worship of these images (a similar danger also existed in the case of the sun, moon, and stars).

These passages are anything but unambiguous; some elements clearly suggest a lingering belief in the reality of other gods. This means that originally, monotheism was not based on the ontological belief that there is only one God who is beyond representation, but on a much more personal, social relationship between Israel and a jealous, possessive God. Paradoxically, then, the belief that there is only one God is not as central to monotheism as the refusal to worship other gods, who may very well exist.[10] In time, of course "social" monotheism or monolatry became "ontological" monotheism.[11] Yet ontological monotheism is anything but monolithic or consistent; interpretations of the Second Commandment have varied widely over the centuries in all three "Abrahamic" religions.

The Christian doctrine of the Incarnation set Christianity apart from its monotheistic competition: by taking the form of a man, God abrogated the Second Commandment, paving the way for the reintroduction of images into religious cult. Of course, Byzantine iconoclasts and Protestants argued that such images could still be put to idolatrous use, sometimes claiming that images of Christ could only represent one of his two natures: the physical one, not his divinity. While no significant form of contemporary Christianity has a militantly anti-iconic agenda, Christians do attack individual representations of Christ or saints they consider to be blasphemous. In 2004, a Nativity scene at Madame Tussaud's in London, in which Joseph and Mary were represented by wax likenesses of David and Victoria Beckham—while an angel looked suspiciously like Kylie Minogue, one of the three wise men like George W. Bush—was roundly condemned by various church leaders, without effect. A 39-year old law lecturer then took matters into his own hands and staged his own private *Bildersturm,* during which he toppled the David Beckham waxwork and ran off with Victoria's head (which was smashed when he dropped it).[12] Again, idolatry and blasphemy are entangled when it comes to controversies about images: casting the Beckhams as Joseph and Mary could be seen both as incitement to worship worthless stars and as a blasphemous smear of Jesus's human parents. More recently, an Indian sheikh addressed the pressing problem of wax-based idolatry from an Islamic perspective, by issuing a fatwa condemning the Tussaud's statue of a popular Bollywood actor.[13]

Islam, of course, takes a particularly tough stance on (potentially) idolatrous images. It is possible that early Islam was radicalized by its confrontation with Christianity, since radical aniconism could function as a symbolic marker of difference in relation to Christianity.[14] Just as in the case of Judaism, a traditional and at first undogmatic aniconism may have been gradually converted into radical iconoclasm by its confrontation with Egyptian and other "visual" deities—a process that resulted in the biblical interdiction. Although some Islamic theologians have stated that only God may not be represented, in general, Islamic scholarship is far more rigorous in its interpretation of the Mosaic interdiction: humans and animals—beings that breathe—must not be depicted, while plants are allowed. In spite of this theoretical radicalism, even the Prophet Muhammad was not infrequently depicted by Islamic artists between the fourteenth and sixteenth centuries; while his face would often be veiled, this was not always the case.

It is crucial to note, however, that these depictions were miniatures in illustrated manuscripts made for various rulers, and *not* decorations in mosques. The Muslim fear of a relapse into *shirk,* the "association" of other deities or powers with God, manifests itself in a rather extreme ban on *tasweer*, images that might stimulate such idolatry, in houses of prayer. Outside the mosque, practices vary widely even now. That the Taliban went so far as to erase realistic faces depicted on the packaging of hair-care products as well as graphic representations of men and animals on traffic signs—both cases recorded in photographs by Thomas Dworzak—makes them eccentric rather than typical (fig. 0.2).

MONOTHEISM AND ENLIGHTENMENT

Since the attack on the World Trade Center on September 11, 2001, there has been no shortage of events that have been milked by the Islam-bashing authors who have hijacked the European and American public spheres with their insistence that Islam is structurally immune to reform and incompatible with the West, democracy, and the Enlightenment. These polemicists, including Ayaan Hirsi Ali, a Somali-Dutch author and politician currently residing in the US; Christopher Hitchens, also in the US; Pascal Bruckner in France; and Necla Kelek in Germany, have been dubbed "Enlightenment's fundamentalists."[15] They claim the problem is that Islam is intrinsically backward and evil; those who argue that Islam has been seized by fanatic groups that exploit the economic deprivation, political disenfranchisement, and symbolic humiliation experienced by various Muslim populations, are accused of being cowardly appeasers, squandering Western values. Even liberals who are seen as opponents of the Enlightenment fundamentalists, such as Ian Buruma, share some of their presuppositions when they reduce Islamic fundamentalism to a pathological, hysterical, and prudish Occidentalism.[16] In this climate, right-wing populists such as Dutch parliamentarian Geert Wilders can garner publicity (and votes) by comparing the Qur'an to *Mein Kampf* and demanding that it be banned. Meanwhile, the increasing importance of Christian fundamentalism in the United States in particular is downplayed, as are the close historical ties between Christianity, Judaism, and early Islam.

What makes the Enlightenment fundamentalists' writings deeply problematical is not primarily their manifest content. As the Enlightenment fundamentalists are keen to ask: How could anyone be against them criticizing the lack of democracy in Muslim societies, fundamentalist intolerance and anti-Semitism, the oppression of women, forced marriages, and female circumcision? The problem lies in the latent content of their discourse. By presenting all problems in Muslim societies and communities as an inevitable outcome of "Islam," they deflect attention from the West's destructive political, military, and economic operations—including support for various charming dictatorships. In the process, they disavow any link between religion and the "western values" they claim to represent. Given the Bush-style "let's bomb Iraq" stance taken by many Enlightenment fundamentalists while it seemed politically opportune, and given their reluctance to attack Christian-fundamentalist elements in the Republican party, their avowed secularism seems to be blind in one eye. That Hirsi Ali now works for the neoconservative American Enterprise Institute, which had a very cozy relationship with the Bush Administration, is one symptom of her and others' instrumental use of Enlightenment rhetoric.

The Enlightenment fundamentalists' avowed opponent is a type of Islam that attempts to put everything in the service of a transcendental God. There is a great interest in "Salafism" and "Wahhabism" as dangerous fundamentalist movements, which claim to go back to the origins of Islam, but even while those tendencies within Islam are criticized and accused of being at the root of Islamic terrorism, many authors effectively seem to agree with Salafist radicals' interpretation of Islam: yes, Islam indeed has a timeless essence, a core that is resistant to change and historical development, to critique. As Talal Asad puts it: "A magical quality is attributed to Islamic religious texts, for they are said to be both essentially univocal (their meaning *cannot* be subject to dispute, just as 'fundamentalists' insist), and infectious."[17] For Western Enlightenment fundamentalists, this timeless Islam is the perfect Professor Moriarty—an unyielding, tenacious, omnipresent threat. However, contrary to the Enlightenment fundamentalists, Judaism, Christianity, *and* Islam propelled secularization forward by attacking idolatry. As Marc De Kesel puts it, monotheism already revolves around the criticism of religion, even if this criticism in turn takes on the form of a religion.[18] Atheism is the continuation of monotheism with other means.

Moshe Halbertal and Avishai Margalit have proposed a "chain of the criticism of religion," in which the criticism of idolatry by the monotheistic religions is followed by that of folk religion by the religious Enlightenment, that of religion in general by the secular Enlightenment, and finally the criticism of ideology.[19] The first two criticisms are religious; the second two secular. The Enlightenment fundamentalists structurally ignore this sequence, and refuse to acknowledge that the "secular" Enlightenment is scarcely conceivable without the monotheistic questioning of idolatry. An important moment in this process of transforming the concept of idolatry is represented by Francis Bacon's *Novum Organum,* in which Bacon identified four types of "idols of the mind," or fallacies that hinder thinking. One category is constituted by the *idola fori,* or "idols of the market," which are "idols formed by the intercourse and association of men with each other, which I call Idols of the Market-place, on account of the commerce and consort of men there. For it is by discourse that men associate; and words are imposed according to the apprehension of the vulgar. And therefore the ill and unfit choice of words wonderfully obstructs the understanding."[20]

The Enlightenment would continue Bacon's appropriation and transformation of monotheistic concepts, thus effectively demonstrating the interdependence of dogma and critique—even if the intent was anti-Christian, and even if reason itself was turned into a fetish. The concept of the fetish is itself a prime example of the secularization of religious ideas, an anthropological take on the concept of idolatry. In his *Du Culte des dieux fétiches* from 1760, Charles de Brosses claims to unveil the most primitive form of religion, the embryonic stirrings of idolatry: fetishism, or the worship of random objects rather than statues or other man-made images.[21] Since Marx's commodity fetish was based on de Brosses's and later authors' theories on religious fetishism—an idol of the market, indeed—it comes as no surprise that Max Horkheimer, in a 1969 letter written just after Theodor W. Adorno's death, argued that their critical theory was based on the Second Commandment. In other words, critical theory analyzed and opposed the capitalist culture industry as a distinctly post-Baconian idolatry of the market.[22]

The same goes for another strand of Marxist theory, that of the Situationist International, which attacked capitalism as a society of the spectacle. Now that this spectacle seems to be ruled by opposing fundamentalisms, which block any prospect of change, it seems more urgent than ever to re-appropriate monotheistic iconoclasm in order to create cracks in the seamless surface of the fundamentalist spectacle. Against the kind of hysterical atheism that seeks to "imagine no religion," it should be maintained that it is more productive to *imagine,* or to *re-imagine religion* beyond the Manichaean opposition between Western Enlightenment on the one hand and evil monotheism—Islam in particular—on the other.

CETTE MAUVAISE RÉPUTATION: ON CRITIQUE

The presence of monotheistic elements in leftist discourse makes for an easy target: isn't Marxism, in particular, just a thinly disguised religion? Žižek rightly argues that the links between monotheism and Marxism should be affirmed rather than denied.[23] However, if Marxism is, in some ways, a repetition of monotheism, the differences in this repetition matter as much as the recurrence itself; one might argue that Marxism is a fundamental transformation of monotheism and rescues what was valuable about it for the criticism and critique of today's fundamentalist spectacle. Although the terms are often used synonymously, and the distinction does not exist in other languages, in English *critique* can stand for the sustained analysis of discourses and their ideological suppositions, rather than for "external" *criticism* imposing value judgments on the material. As Terry Eagleton has remarked, "'Criticism,' in its Enlightenment sense, consists in recounting to someone what is awry with their situation, from an external, perhaps 'transcendental' vantage-point. 'Critique' is that form of discourse which seeks to inhabit the experience of the subject from the inside, in order to inhabit those 'valid' features of that experience which point beyond the subject's present condition."[24]

Can monotheistic religion be anything other than a *criticism* of other religions? Could it possibly function as critique? One might say that the biblical Moses was engaged in "recounting to someone what is awry with their situation, from an external, perhaps 'transcendental' vantage-point," but hardly that he sought to "inhabit the experience of the subject from the inside." Would not a real *critique* of idolatry entail the secular deconstruction of the very concept of idolatry, which is, after all, a polemical (mis)representation of religious practices, one not recognized by those who engage in these practices? In spite or because of their polemical nature, monotheistic conceptualizations of idolatry nonetheless contain a truly critical dimension—perhaps more so than their contemporary enlightened critics, who smugly point out the dogmatism and crudeness of religious idolatry-bashers. For early Christians and Muslims, their adopted religion must have functioned as a true critique, instigating people to reëxamine and change their lives. This, after all, is how conversions work when they do not take place at gunpoint or under severe social or economic pressures. The monotheistic religions and their various and often conflicting tendencies have used the concept of idolatry to question cultural, social, and political practices; insofar as the authors spoke to their own people, one may in fact argue that they "sought to inhabit the experience of the subject from the inside, in order to inhabit those 'valid' features of that experience which point beyond the subject's present condition." Did not the Mosaic prohibition also aim at the implications of the deities and their images in an oppressive state religion, just as today's religious rejections of imperialist wars puts many liberals to shame?

Islam is often presented as the odd one out among monotheistic religions because it is said to be a fatally *uncritical* religion: its rejection of other faiths never seems to have been followed by an autocritique à la Luther, let alone later thinkers. The stagnation evident in Islamic culture after the decline of the Ottoman Empire and the end of al Andalus in Spain is seen as proof that Islam was, is, and always will be resistant to critique.[25] While this patently ahistorical essentialization must be rejected, it is true that Islam is lagging behind in this respect; it has, however, turned criticism into a powerful engine of active dissent. Hence western intellectuals' fascination with the Iranian Revolution; Michel Foucault noted that it impressed him "in its effort to politicize structures that are inseparably social and religious, in response to current problems."[26] If this may seem like a typical case of an intellectual falling under the spell of a totalitarian movement, it is easy to forget the liberatory role played by Islam at that moment, before Khomeini's theocracy took shape. Even if his own thinking often fell short of his stated ambition, it is noteworthy that Ali Shariati, the "leftist Islamist" who, next to Khomeini, had the most profound influence on the Iranian Revolution, dreamed of an Islam that "eliminates the spirit of imitation and obedience, which is the hallmark of the popular religion, and replaces it with a critical, revolutionary, aggressive spirit of independent reasoning (*Ijtihad*)."[27]

There is no single point where dogmatic criticism becomes critique; and sometimes, relentless criticism *is* the true critique. Up to a point, the most dogmatic forms of religion may in fact come to criticize more "advanced" and more "tolerant" positions, and criticism and critique may exchange places. From this perspective, it is not very surprising that certain left-wing (as well as right-wing) groups pursue alliances with Islamists. While these rapprochements cannot be condoned, they drive home the point that at times the most dogmatic religion can function as a criticism of "secular" theory: after all, is not such theory all too often complicit with the imperialist politics it frivolously deconstructs at international conferences and in peer-reviewed journals?

In recent years, the notion of critique has itself been criticized by authors such as Bruno Latour; so much so that critique is neutralized a priori, absorbed by the system, co-opted, and rendered powerless by the very profusion of criticism and critiques. In 2002, Latour co-curated the show *Iconoclash: Beyond the Image Wars in Science, Religion, and Art* at the Center for Art and Media (ZKM), Karlsruhe; in which he proposed an "archaeology of hatred and fanaticism" that traced the monotheistic tradition to its debased, devalued, banal afterlife in recent philosophy and theory—the ubiquity of "critique."[28] Having perfected the art of having his cake and eating it too, Latour criticized the "fanaticism and hatred" of "real" iconoclasm, while also bemoaning the devaluation of criticism into meaningless virtuoso performance. Considering religious criticism and secular critique of the same ilk, since one is based on the other, Latour goes so far as to say: "suspicion has rendered us dumb."[29] This is a perfect rationalization for academic quietism; if critique is ultimately a form of collaboration, then why not collaborate in a straightforward and more profitable way?

Of course, Latour is right in pointing out the inflation and instrumentalization of critique; ubiquitous criticism is indeed part of the system. However, in an age of clashing fundamentalisms, the answer to the abuse and inflation of readymade criticality surely cannot be to abandon critique as such. The true drama of contemporary culture lies in the fact that it has become almost impossible to imagine social change that is not cataclysmic. We may decide that criticism and critique do not work and that it is preferable to develop fatal strategies of over-affirmation and the like; but do these really offer chances for "thinking past terror," to quote Susan Buck-Morss's apt expression?[30] Critical thought is not enough, but it is a necessary condition for interventions in the course of events. One must battle the inefficiency of critique, not critique itself; critical projects must be pushed to the point where they become full-blown dissent—an actual contestation of the existing order. To achieve this, to think beyond the idols of the market, critique must preserve some of the force of the criticism of idolatry.

The most powerful forms of secular dissent, from the Enlightenment and its intellectual and political revolutions to Marx and the New Left of the 1960s and beyond, have always retained a connection with religious imagery, even while transforming it. Secular critique would do well to avoid espousing secularist ideology; if it were to rid itself of all traces of monotheistic motifs, critique would become unimaginable.

RE-IMAGINING THE IMAGE

Seeking to go "beyond the image wars in science, religion, and art," *Iconoclash* disparaged iconoclasm in favor of an "iconoclash" that amounts to a questioning of images, a suspension of the urge to smash them. However, iconoclasm was always more than mere image-smashing, and amid today's spectacular battle over images it is crucial to reclaim iconoclasm from its fundamentalist appropriators. Under current circumstances, it would be folly to leave iconoclasm to those who are hijacking both religion and visual culture—and, more than ever, the two must be considered together. If our approach to images is still shaped by monotheism, as Belting has persuasively argued, then what is needed is a re-imagining both of religion and of the image. If religion seeks to shape the ways in which we picture the world, this means that religion itself must also answer to worldly concerns, and that art and religion can enter into a dialogue—however testy at times—precisely in so far as both are visual practices and, to some extent, visual theories.[31]

In recent years, a number of prominent art historians have done important work relating to iconoclasm and the Christian visual tradition—as well as publishing books of their own, Hans Belting, Dario Gamboni, and Joseph Leo Koerner all contributed to *Iconoclash*.[32] Of these authors, Belting goes furthest in staging such as dialogue, yet in general his stance remains that of the expert; the detached specialist studying curious phenomena. It remains to be seen whether a more interventionist form of *Bildwissenschaft* is possible. Ever since the 1980s, it seemed that all left-wing scholars could do was go into refined, Adornian mourning for a lost revolutionary project. However, starting in the later 1990s, there have been two crucial developments: on the one hand, art history and theory recovered from abstract mourning over institutional recuperation of the avant-garde by investigating art spaces and publications as counter-media which can sustain a critical public presence; on the other hand, in the anti-globalist "movement of movements" there emerged new consciousness of a post-industrial multitude and shifting coalitions as proponents of activism.[33]

Although the former tended to fetishize the art context and its institutions, the latter was all too eager to succumb to old reflexes and declare "institutionalized" art irrelevant, opting instead for a romantic glorification of activism, without arriving at any fundamental theory of what exactly was being contested (capitalism as such, or just "neoliberalism"?) and often falling back on dated forms of spectacular protest that were perfect fodder for the media. It has become obvious that what is urgently needed is a coalition between different contexts—academic, artistic and activist. Under present conditions, such alliances are structurally unstable, possible only as a series of incidents or as in-between spaces. As one such incident, this book was written with one foot in the university and the other in the art world, purposefully occupying the increasingly deserted no-man's-land beyond the borders of art criticism and contemporary academia, both of which increasingly produce texts which are *not meant to be read*—in the case of criticism because the texts either report on the market or advertise certain artistic products, and in the case of academia because publications primarily exist in order to appear on publication lists.[34] Yet both systems still offer specific spaces for thought, and I attempt to rethink the image (in an age when its instrumentalization is continually reaching new heights) by creating overlaps between them—mapping possibilities for critical acts in art, theory, and elsewhere.

Today's fundamentalists fully participate in the Western spectacle they profess to abhor: the Taliban took care to document their destruction of the giant Buddha of Bamyan and to distribute this footage. While it is often remarked that iconoclasm generates new images, this says nothing about their nature and quality. Are there forms of contemporary iconoclasm that allow us to imagine a different kind of image than those produced by this fundamentalist version of the society of the spectacle? In this book, this question is addressed through the medium of contemporary art, which is framed in a way that is not purely art-historical, necessitating (for better or worse) not only philosophical and economical, but also theological excursions. If discussions of individual works or oeuvres rarely exceed one paragraph, this does not mean that they should be seen as mere illustrations of an overall argument; on the contrary, they function as flares that illuminate part of the way—an instable constellation of illuminations.

Soon after September 11, a Photoshopped image featuring Osama bin Laden in cahoots with *Sesame Street's* Bert (from one of the mirror sites of the curious "Bert is Evil" website) turned up on a placard in a pro-bin Laden demonstration in Bangladesh. Those who made the placard had evidently downloaded the image from the net without taking a closer look.[35] In this image, bin Laden, the idol of terror, is joined by an uncannily leering Bert, who is apparently the gray eminence pulling strings in the background. Regardless of whether the Photoshop *monteur* responsible for this picture was being ironic or displaying a peculiar pathological obsession, this transformation of the terrorist star into a Muppet's dummy is an oddly fitting emblem for a contemporary practice of secular iconoclasm that dares to imagine counter-histories to the myths of our fundamentalist spectacle.

NOTES

A note on the notes: Apart from some exceptions and inconsistencies that arise from reading in more than one language, I refer to the original editions of works by German or French authors. Translations are usually my own; if not, the source is indicated. Referenced web pages were accessed in July and August 2008 unless otherwise noted.

1 See Bob Dylan, *Huck's Song* on the eighth volume of Dylan's *Bootleg Series (Tell Tale Signs: Rare and Unreleased 1989–2006*, 2008).

2 For practical purposes, I here gloss over the differences between Greenberg's various phases, from the relatively complex portrayal of the relation between avant-garde and kitsch in 1939 ("Avant-Garde and Kitsch") to the much more simplistic characterization of Modernist self-criticism in "Modernist Painting" [1960], in *The Collected Essays and Criticism*, vol. 4: *Modernism with a Vengeance*, ed. John O'Brian (Chicago/London: University of Chicago Press, 1993), 85–93.

3 Theodor W. Adorno, "Ästhetische Theorie," in *Gesammelte Schriften*, vol. 7, ed. Gretel Adorno and Rolf Tiedemann (Frankfurt: Suhrkamp, 1972), 16, 335, 340.

4 Philip Willan, "Al-Qaida plot to blow up Bologna church fresco," in *The Guardian,* June 24, 2002,http://www.guardian.co.uk/world/2002/jun/24/arts.artsnews.

5 http://www.atheistsunited.org/images/ImagineNoReligion.jpg (accessed July 20, 2008).

6 For an extensive analysis of blasphemy, in particular in contemporary culture, see S. Brent Plate, *Blasphemy: Art That Offends* (London: Black Dog Publishing, 2006).

7 On the concept of jahiliyya in early Islam, see G. R Hawting, *The Idea of Idolatry and the Emergence of Islam: From Polemic to History* (Cambridge: Cambridge University Press, 1999); on the "new jahiliyya," see Ian Buruma and Avishai Margalit, *Occidentalism: The West in the Eyes of Its Enemies* (New York: Penguin, 2004), 116–122.

8 Silvia Naef, *Bilder und Bilderverbot im Islam: Vom Koran bis zum Karikaturenstreit*, trans. Christiane Seiler (Munich: C. H. Beck, 2007), 12–13.

9 For the most extensive re-telling, see Sura 20, verses 85 to 98.

10 The point is also made by Wouter J. Hanegraaff in "The Trouble with Images: Anti-Image Polemics and Western Esotericism," *Polemical Encounters: Esoteric Discourse and Its Others*, ed. Olav Hammer and Kocku von Stuckrad (Leiden/Boston: Brill, 2007), 107–136.

11 Jan Assmann, lecture given on February 1, 2009, as part of the project *The Return of Religion and Other Myths*, BAK, basis voor actuele kunst, Utrecht.

12 "Becks Waxwork Vandal Discharged," January 24, 2005, http://news.bbc.co.uk/2/hi/uk_news/england/london/4202821.stm.

13 Anil Sinanan, "Fatwa for Salman Khan aka the Fourth Dummy!" http://entertainment.timesonline.co.uk/tol/arts_and_entertainment/film/bollywood/article3279721.ece.

14 Naef, *Bilder und Bilderverbot* (see note 8), 3–32.

15 The term "Enlightenment fundamentalist" gained some prominence when Timothy Garton Ash called Hirsi Ali "a brave, outspoken, slightly simplistic Enlightenment fundamentalist" in his review of Ian Buruma's *Murder in Amsterdam* for the *New York Review of Books*, October 5, 2006; see http://www.nybooks.com/articles/article-preview?article_id=19371. Garton Ash followed a cue from Buruma himself, who uses the term in his book. Buruma's book and Garton Ash's review then sparked a debate on signandsight.com, begun by Pascal Bruckner, in which the term proved a bone of contention; see http://www.signandsight.com/features/1146.html. The term "Enlightenment fundamentalist" and variations thereof, however, predate this affair. In the Dutch media, for instance, a number of earlier instances of the use of the word *verlichtingsfundamentalisme* or *Verlichtingsfundamentalist* can be found.

16 For all its merits, this tendency mars Ian Buruma's and Avishai Margalit's *Occidentalism* (see note 7).

17 Talal Asad, *Formations of the Secular: Christianity, Islam, Modernity* (Stanford: Stanford University Press, 2003), 11.

18 Marc De Kesel, "Religion als Kritik, Kritik als Religion: Einige Reflexionen zur monotheistischen Schwäche der zeitgenössischen Kritik," in *Wieder Religion? Christentum im zeitgenössischen Denken—(Lacan, Žižek, Badiou u.a.)*, ed. Marc De Kesel and Dominiek Hoens, trans. Erik M. Vogt (Vienna: Turia + Kant, 2006), 15–39.

19 Moshe Halbertal and Avishai Margalit, *Idolatry*, trans. Naomi Goldblum (Cambridge, MA: Harvard University Press, 1992), 112.

20 Francis Bacon, *The New Organon* [1620], in *The Works of Francis Bacon*, vol. VIII, ed. James Spedding et al. (New York/Boston: Hurd and Houghton/Taggard and Thompson, 1864), 78.

21 On theories of the fetish and fetishism, see chapter 3.

22 Max Horkheimer, letter to Otto O. Herz, September 1, 1969, in *Briefwechsel 1949–1973*, vol. 18 of *Gesammelte Schriften*, ed. Alfred Schmidt and Gunzelin Schmid Noerr (Frankfurt am Main: S. Fischer, 1996), 743.

23 Slavoj Žižek, *The Fragile Absolute—or, Why Is the Christian Legacy Worth Fighting For?* (London/New York: Verso, 2000), 2.

24 Terry Eagleton, *Ideology: An Introduction* (London/New York: Verso, 1991), xiv.

25 Tariq Ali has argued that had al Andalus continued to exist, it would have produced a Reformation before long; in response to Ali's claim, Hans Küng argues that the absence of a Reformation—rather than local reforms, which did take place—is due to factors inherent in the organization of the Islamic religion and Muslim society. See Hans Küng, *Islam: Past, Present, and Future* (Oxford: Oneworld, 2007), 395–397.

26 Michel Foucault, "What Are the Iranians Dreaming About?" [1978], in Janet Afary and Kevin B. Anderson, *Foucault and the Iranian Revolution: Gender and the Seductions of Islamism* (Chicago/London: University of Chicago Press, 2005), 208.

27 Ali Shariati, "Where Shall We Begin?" http://www.iranchamber.com/personalities/ashariati/works/where_shall_we_begin.php. Buruma and Margalit rightly note that Shariati's attitude toward Marxism was complex: both tactical (instrumentalizing) and substantive (111).

28 Bruno Latour, "What Is Iconoclash? Or Is There a World Beyond the Image Wars?" in *Iconoclash: Beyond the Image Wars in Science, Religion, and Art*, exh. cat., ed. Bruno Latour and Peter Weibel (Karlsruhe: ZKM, 2002), 14, 25.

29 Ibid., 25. See also Bruno Latour, "Why Has Critique Run out of Steam? From Matters of Fact to Matters of Concern," in *Critical Inquiry* 30, no. 2 (2004), http://criticalinquiry.uchicago.edu/issues/v30/30n2.Latour.html.

30 Susan Buck-Morss, *Thinking Past Terror: Islamism and Critical Theory on the Left* (London/New York: Verso, 2003).

31 Hans Belting, *Das echte Bild: Bildfragen als Glaubensfragen* (Munich: C. H. Beck, 2005).

32 The first of these books, Gamboni's *The Destruction of Art: Iconoclasm and Vandalism since the French Revolution* (London: Reaktion Books, 1997), deals mostly with "secular" vandalism. Joseph Leo Koerner's *The Reformation of the Image* (London: Reaktion Books, 2004) is a masterful study of Lutheran approaches to religious imagery; Hans Belting has followed his essay on the Christian legacy in contemporary visual culture, *Das echte Bild* (see note 31), with a more extensive art historical study on Islamic and Christian (Renaissance) visual culture, *Florenz und Bagdad: Eine westöstliche Geschichte des Blicks* (Munich: C. H. Beck, 2008).

33 The former tendency encompasses the discourse on "new institutionalism," as well as the writings in my own book, *Secret Publicity: Essays on Contemporary Art* (Rotterdam: NAi Publishers, 2006), which, however, places greater emphasis on the need for a counterpublicness, than on institutions as such. The anti-institutional position has been defended most brilliantly by Brian Holmes and Gerald Raunig.

34 See also Peter Geimer, "Aufs offene Meer. Drei Kommentare zu Texten von Stefan Germer" in *Texte zur Kunst*, no. 70 (May 2008): 65–66.

35 The original "Bert is Evil" website was created by Dino Ignacio, who took his site down after the bin Laden incident; the Bert and Osama image was apparently created for a Dutch mirror site operated by a certain J-roen, who also removed the image. A statement to this effect can be found at http://web.archive.org/web/20011217110419/www.j-roen.net/bert/index.phtml.

Chapter One

MYTHS OF ICONOCLASM

I think the destructive element is too much neglected in art.
Piet Mondrian[1]

The concept of idolatry is often discussed primarily as the theoretical foundation of iconoclasm—for violent attacks on images of other religions or of "bad" forms of the iconoclasts' own religion—from Antiquity to the present, via the Byzantine image wars and the Reformation. In recent literature, it is often stressed that the accusation of idolatry says more about the accuser than the accused. People who are accused of idolatry do not, as a rule, recognize themselves in the behavior that anti-idolaters ascribe to them. And is not the anti-idolater someone who actually does what he accuses his opponent of, by taking the image literally?[2] Often, iconoclasm is presented as a symptom of monotheism's inherently intolerant nature, which is scarcely reconcilable with "modern values" such as tolerance and freedom of speech. Is the cost of what Jan Assmann has termed the "Mosaic distinction" between God and idols simply too high?

Assmann has sparked fierce debate with his assertion that this distinction created a previously unknown kind of intolerance and violence.[3] Until "Moses," gods and their cults had in general—or at least in principle—been compatible with one another; one god could be "translated" and fused with a similar god from a neighboring region. The Mosaic distinction rejects such assimilation; there is one true god, the others are idols. The one true God is invisible, manifesting himself perhaps in a burning bush, but allowing for no anthropomorphic or zoomorphic representation. Visibility is the realm of the false gods with their grotesque or all-too-human forms. Since it is clear that much religious violence has sprung from this distinction, which can be forever radicalized and refined (you claim to be a true monotheist, but you are in fact an idolater), it is tempting indeed to see Judaism, Christianity, and Islam as so many aberrations; as cultural diseases that must be fought.

It is the rise of fundamentalist Islam in particular that has once more fuelled such criticism of monotheism, and religion in general, as intrinsically intolerant and potentially violent; much more than its religious kin, Islam has come to embody the Otherness of monotheism and its incompatibility with modernity, democracy, the West, and so on. At some moments in the Enlightenment, notably in Montesquieu's *Lettres Persanes*, the figure of the Muslim served as a critical interlocutor who pointed out western follies and superstitions. By contrast, Hegel discusses Islam only briefly in his philosophy of history, claiming that it "disappeared from the stage of world history" a long time ago. Among contemporary authors, Alain Besançon discusses Islam *before* Christianity in his study of iconoclasm, suggesting the difficulty of situating Islam in history.[4] It comes as no surprise that in 2004 Besançon, a Catholic, contributed an article to a neoconservative US periodical in which he claimed that Islam is in fact not an Abrahamic religion, but a regression to idolatry.[5]

If "true" monotheism is used here as a yardstick, at other times Islam is criticized for being incapable of entering modernity and of being trapped in a "sealed time."[6] Enlightenment fundamentalists and Islamists alike have everything to gain from strengthening the conviction that Islam and modernity are mutually exclusive. Secularists are only too happy to take Islamist fundamentalists at their word: yes, what they say is all too true, they represent the true Islam, a religion of pure Otherness which has striven for world domination ever since it began, which knows no mercy, which has no culture to speak of, which oppresses women, and which legitimizes lies and deception in the name of faith. Hence, right-wing populists demand that the Qur'an, that original evil, be banned. Marxism and the Left in general are also often presented as belonging to the "other side" of anti-western "Occidentalists" who cannot cope with liberty.[7] There are, to be sure, points of contact: the Iranian thinker Ali Shariati incorporated Marxist jargon into his critique of capitalist modernity, even while criticizing external influences on Islam, and the disparaging remarks about superficial and unfulfilling American "fun" made in 1948 by Sayyid Qutb—leading light of the Muslim Brotherhood and one of the fathers of modern fundamentalism—which may at times recall Adorno's contemporaneous attacks on the American culture industry.[8] However, those who use such homologies to indict leftist thinking as a form of anti-modern crypto-fundamentalism obscure crucial differences between, say, Adorno and Qutb, in order to distract attention from their own complicity with their dear fundamentalist opponents. In modern thought and art, the questioning of received truths and dominant social practices inherent in religious iconoclasm is radicalized and turned against monotheism and monotheistic claims for absolute truth. For all the problems intrinsic to this secularized critique of idolatry, it still offers tools to intervene in the battle of the fundamentalisms. There is no escaping the looped time of iconoclasm, but there are differences in its reiterations, if one chooses to see and create them. Seeing them *is* creating them.

Modern theory and modern art alike are sometimes accused of iconophobia, of betraying a pathological fear of images.[9] There is, of course, evidence of this claim, but at its most relevant, theoretical and artistic critique seeks to *liberate* rather than annihilate images. If some iconoclasm does disenfranchise the image, the more interesting forms of modern and contemporary iconoclasm oppose the instrumentalization of the image. As Asger Jorn put it on one of the prints he designed in support of the May 1968 uprising in France, the aim is to "smash the frame that suffocates the image" (to be exact, what Jorn wrote in his idiosyncratic French shorthand was "BRISEZ LE CADRE QI ETOUF LIMAGE"—see fig. 1.1). Those accounts that cast the whole issue in terms of a radical opposition: texts versus image, iconoclasts versus idolaters, iconophobes versus iconophiles, cover up the complexity of the interaction between images and texts, as well as the cultural and political implications of iconoclasm (both visual and textual). As featured in various historical narratives and counter-narratives, iconoclasm is a linguistic fantasy that enables the articulation of different attitudes toward images and their inevitable shadow, language itself.

IMAGINING MYTH

While emphasizing the intolerance of monotheism, Jan Assmann paints a rather rosy picture of what he terms "cosmotheism"—the pantheistic, late antique religion that Christianity replaced.[10] Assmann downplays the status of ancient religion as the state religion, which, as such, was hardly as tolerant as his rhetoric often suggests: one had to comply and sacrifice to the official gods in order to be a subject or citizen. As the Roman author Varro noted, next to the "mythological theology" of the poets and the "natural theology" of the philosophers, there was the "civil theology" of the people.[11] Most prominently in the person of Socrates, Greek philosophy actively started to critique poetic fancy and popular faith—an exercise in iconoclastic mythbusting. However, the tendency to honor popular beliefs outwardly remained strong among Greek and Roman philosophers, and their critique remained an essentially elitist occupation, never amounting to a popular movement intended to actually suppress the use of images.[12]

Mythos denotes a mode of speech; as Varro's example shows, in antiquity the term had already come to be associated with mistaken beliefs, with fantastic stories associated with the social, cultural, and/or ethnic Other, whereas *logos* was the language of reason.[13] The early Christian church adopted and adapted the Greek critique of myths for its own ends, but ultimately it would be turned against Christian revelation, against the text of the Bible. By the eighteenth century, the existence of "mythical" or obviously fantastic stories in the Bible itself—in the Old Testament, but also in the Gospels—was increasingly used to question the monotheistic distinction between true religion and idolatry. Judaism and Christianity, the faiths that shattered the false gods, were shown to be riddled with falsehoods themselves.[14] While Christianity had always presented the Christ-event as a fundamentally historical occurrence, its historicity was now seen in terms of time-bound human beliefs and superstitions, not in terms of historical, divine revelation.

In 1835, the young theologian David Friedrich Strauss applied what he called "the mythical method" to the Gospels in his *The Life of Jesus Critically Examined.*[15] Strauss treated the Gospels as anything but gospel, finding them studded with mythic motifs. With his mythical method, Strauss exemplified the increasing dominance of the terms myth and mythology in the study of religions in the late eighteenth and early nineteenth centuries; authors on the subject increasingly tended to avoid the term "idolatry," associated as it was with monotheism. One might say that in modernity, "myth" came to function as its more acceptable, more neutral stand-in, both for Enlightenment mythbusters and for Romantic mythmakers. As idolatry that dare not speak its name, myth's *visual* character was often emphasized. Theorists such as Wagner and Nietzsche, who valued myth over abstract reason, characterized mythical language as concrete, sensuous, plastic, and visual. Nietzsche, who characterized Wagner as a mythopoetic "simplifier of the world," casually referred to "the images of myth."[16] The art of classical Greece always remained the highest point of culture for Nietzsche, who lamented that just when the Greek sculptors were giving the Greek gods their ultimate form, Socrates and Plato demolished traditional Greek religion by introducing dialectical reason, which would eventually find its way into Christianity.[17] In his *Twilight of the Idols*, Nietzsche attacked dialectical reason for being but an effect of language, "linguistic metaphysics," and as such nothing but a "grobes Fetischwesen" (coarse fetish being).[18] It is only consequential that, in the figure of Zarathustra, Nietzsche abandoned any pretense at philosophical rigor by proclaiming the Death of God in a quasi-mythical mode, using the garb of a prophet and a style that marks his discourse as (quasi) mythical. The passages on the Death of God are of course the culmination of Nietzsche's iconoclastic fight against Christianity in the name of his neo-Greek notion of a higher, post-Christian "man." It is crucial that Nietzsche does *not* declare God to be an illusion. He pronounces God to be dead, an ex-parrot, rather than non-existent. Only a new myth could replace the old.

For decades, until well into the 1990s, European intellectuals subscribed to a rather more straightforward, bluntly secularist myth: that modernization and progress would inevitably mean the continued decline of religion. Enlightenment fundamentalism is the bitter, defensive version of this myth in a radically changed situation. Under these present conditions, a new Nietzsche could conceivably write a myth about God's rebirth, or his return from exile. To be sure, there are many signs that religion is not returning in a straightforward way, that its resurgence is more a matter of image building than of lived reality, at least as that reality was once defined: in social, collective, and ritualistic terms. Should the return of God then be called a "myth" in the popular sense of the term, so that myth simply means an untruth or lie? This is the way in which secularist author Kenan Malik uses it.[19] Indeed, close inspection shows that if we apply traditional criteria, religion, including Islam, is still in decline. Theological debate is at a laughable level of sophistication and intensity if we take the great eras of Judaic, Christian, or Islamic theology as our standard. As Abdolkarim Soroush noted, even a fundamentalist regime such as Iran has no theory to speak of.[20] Organized religion is increasingly replaced by, or transformed into, personal and selective *religiosity* that can do without daily observance or a sophisticated theology; participation in religious rituals is down in favor of browsing web sites.[21] The digital *Übermedium* that is the Internet has increasingly made the experience of religion individual, leading many young Muslims, for instance, to construct an image of Islam that differs radically from that of their parents. By making their own myths of Islam they are, ironically, rather similar to those westerners who assemble their own personal form of "spirituality" outside the confines of organized religion.

Modern anthropology and theory of religion have emphasized the fundamental opposition of the sacred and the profane; if a social order can never be founded, recursively, on itself, there must always be some explicitly or implicitly sacred Other to the secular laws and rules that make up society—and to the discourse that seeks to challenge this order.[22] Monotheism exacerbated the instability of the sacred/profane dichotomy by historicizing it, by transforming it into a historical dialectic in which the sacred appears both as past and as future history, of ancient revelations and divine kingdoms to come, and of glimpses of both gleaned in our fallen world.[23] All this was always subject to interpretation, the nature of Divine Writ being such that it had to be interpreted in accordance with an accruing history of exegesis and in relation to real-world events. In contemporary fundamentalism, this process of mediation is largely abandoned, as one literal interpretation of the sacred text is imposed on profane matters, and as any distinction between religion and the secular is negated.

By robbing the sacred of its numinosity and using it as an instruction manual for everything under the sun, fundamentalism paradoxically *profanes the sacred* and *secularizes religion*; with characteristic hyperbole, Boris Groys has stated that its "violent politics of the letter" outs fundamentalism as "the most radical product of the Enlightenment and the materialist view of the world."[24] Then again, was monotheism not already an agent of secularization? Is fundamentalism a radical break with tradition, its logical consequence—or both?

MOSES AND ICONOCLASM

Rather than treat the apparent resurgence of religion as a myth in the popular sense—as mere urban legend, on par with crocodiles in the sewers—it might be more fruitful to argue that we are dealing with a historical myth that shapes social and cultural reality. Throughout the nineteenth and twentieth centuries, the notion of myth became increasingly generalized and abstracted from the tales of gods and heroes to which it was conventionally applied; increasingly, it was suspected that any kind of language could be infected by myth, that myth was in fact an innate disease of language. Jan Assmann argues that "History is transformed into myth as soon as it is remembered, narrated, and 'inhabited,' that is to say: as soon as it is woven into the fabric of the present."[25] In this sense, a historical event can come to function as a myth because of the role it plays in the present; the memory of an important battle, for instance, can be used to foster a sense of national unity. It is clear that the episode of the Golden Calf plays a comparable role in monotheism; this story is monotheism's founding myth, and although contemporary scholars would question its historicity, it functions as a founding myth precisely *because the believers see it as a historical event.*

In the case of the perceived return of religion—or, to put it in a more explicitly mythical mode, the return of God—things are somewhat more complex. It is, after all, *current events* such as 9/11, the rise of Creationism and the "cartoon wars" that come to function as the basis for the myth. However, these current events obviously point back in time, to biblical time. Current events are seen as the outcome of the intolerance programmed into the monotheistic tradition since Moses. While Jan Assmann's reconstruction of a tolerant, late-antique "cosmotheism" can be seen as a counter-myth aimed against the dominant Judeo-Christian tradition, in his take on the "Mosaic distinction" he finds himself in agreement with secularist ideologues who construct a grotesque myth that leads straight from Mount Sinai to the World Trade Center, or at least straight from the Prophet Muhammad to Muhammad Atta. It would appear that another counter-myth is needed, one that allows us to examine the status of contemporary religion, especially its dominant fundamentalist versions, more clearly. Are we witnessing a proper rebirth of God, or does God return as a specter, a sign, an invisible image haunting media events rather than inhabiting the lived reality of daily observance?

For Freud, the Jewish God already represented an uncanny return from the dead: in *Totem and Taboo,* he developed an iconoclastic myth in which all culture is haunted by the pre-historical killing of the father of the primeval horde by his sons.[26] In monotheistic religion the obscene and abusive father would resurface, sublimated, as the stern God. In his last book, *Moses and Monotheism*, Freud—who never fully acknowledged his debt to Nietzsche—developed the analysis of *Totem and Taboo* to shed light on the origins of monotheism, arguing that Moses was an Egyptian priest from the circle of the disgraced pharaoh Akhenaton, who attempted to impose a monotheistic cult of Aten, the Sun God, on Egypt. When Akhenaton died and Egypt reverted to polytheism, "Moses" imposed his own version of the Aten cult on the Israelites, only to be killed when his people rebelled against his stern regime.[27] This amounts to a reenactment of Freud's anthropological myth of the killing of the patriarch of the "primeval horde." Freud argues that collective traumas can have long-term effects similar to individual psychological traumas, and that the killing of Moses and the rejection of his God was such an event. Over a long period of time, the tribal deity Yahweh gradually took on characteristics of both Aten and Moses. At first, Israelite monotheism still fell short of the ontological monotheism at which Aten had arrived, the ban on the worship of foreign gods having the traits of a social contract rather than a philosophical stance; gradually, Yahweh would become a new Aten, albeit mixed with traits of Moses himself: the dead father returned as patriarchal deity.[28]

Assmann has shown that Freud is the last in a long line of thinkers who have theorized an *Egyptian* Moses—though Freud probably had no knowledge of this prior history, arriving at his construction on the basis of new archaeological insights. Assmann exhumes a tradition that started in the Renaissance and used antique sources to claim that Moses was an Egyptian blabbermouth who divulged secret Egyptian wisdom to the Jewish tribe. This is the Egyptian Moses, a heterodox doppelganger of the official *Jewish* Moses.[29] This neo-Egyptian tendency culminated in the Enlightenment, when authors argued that Mosaic monotheism was just a popularized, exoteric version of the true mysteries of Egyptian religion, which consisted of a cosmotheistic/pantheistic praise of creation. While Assmann takes cues from psychoanalysis for his own form of spectral *Gedächtnisgeschichte* (history of memory) his counter-myth is, in the end, very different from Freud's. Even while proposing a shocking de-sublimation of the biblical text, Freud considered monotheism a civilizing force.[30] Freud acknowledged that Moses had an irate trait, which was later transferred to Yahweh—but why not respond to the encroachment of past traumas on the present by reverse-haunting the past, by creating counter-myths that replace frenzy with civilized restraint?

This is what Freud did in his essay on Michelangelo's Moses sculpture, written long before his final Moses book. Like others before him, Freud felt challenged to address the vexing problem concerning the exact moment Michelangelo's sculpture depicts—taking it as a given that the piece indeed intends to depict one single moment from a narrative; which is not an unproblematical supposition (fig. 1.2). Finding symptomatic clues in the position of the right hand and the tablets, Freud posits that Michelangelo depicted a moment not represented in and, indeed, at odds with the biblical text: succumbing at first to his bad temper and preparing to shatter the tablets while witnessing the dance around the golden calf, Moses then controls himself and refrains from this destructive action. Thus, Michelangelo supposedly read the biblical story as much against the grain as Freud himself would; the irascible biblical figure was redefined as a hero of *Affektbeherrschung*, or emotional control, showing the greatest possible strength of spirit by controlling his emotional reaction.[31] Freud clearly does not regard Moses's radical step as a fall from cosmotheistic grace. Assmann's historical myth effectively seems to say that today's fundamentalists are correct in their interpretation of religion; after all, they are experts in intolerance and iconoclasm, seemingly embodying the spirit of violent image-smashing. Freud's appropriation—or series of appropriations—of Michelangelo's Moses is more radical. Freud pries the image from tradition, reading the biblical text either with an eye for symptomatic detail or going against it—liberating the image in an act of iconoclastic myth-making.

For Freud, Moses stands precisely for the civilizing and *secularizing* force of monotheism; there can be no mistake that Freud valued Moses's break with polytheism/idolatry as an act of liberation from oppressive superstition, even if Mosaic religion in turn created new dogmas and taboos. These, however, were at least partly the result of the "pollution" of Mosaic religion with traits of the Yahweh cult. Freud's Moses myth thus deconstructs the essential opposition between religion and the secular that is central to contemporary fundamentalisms. If the later *Moses and Monotheism* is effectively a tragedy, focusing on the discrepancy between zealous Moses and his regressive people, the earlier essay creates an alternative Moses who functions as an even more radical cultural hero than the biblical version. With this, Freud appears to suggest that iconoclasm should not be left to those who cannot handle it—that it takes great *control,* a suppression of the urge to smash things. Physical iconoclasm, then, would be a degraded reflection of this most fundamental form of iconoclasm: the spiritualized, conceptual iconoclasm that is the realm of great thinkers—and artists. Moses's real heir is not some image-smasher, but the divine Michelangelo.

But is not such a hymn to sublimation all too genteel and, in the end, profoundly conservative, as is Freud's social thinking in general? Is it not the *dialectic* of conceptual and physical iconoclasm that creates the revolutionary dynamic of iconoclasm's great historical moments? At certain junctures in history, the figurative iconoclasm transmitted through art and discourse over the centuries is actualized and politicized in iconoclastic events. Figurative iconoclasm may seem perfectly integrated, part of the symbolic order, yet it contains elements that can become explosive. Here, external factors play a crucial role. The "vandalism" of the French Revolution is not a direct consequence of a program dictated by the French Enlightenment, just as the iconoclasm of the Reformation existed in a complex relationship with the iconoclastic tendencies in the writings and preaching of the great reformers—even in the case of those advocating violent iconoclastic upheavals, and all the more so with those who, like Calvin, preferred to proceed in an orderly manner.

The monotheistic rejection of idols always had a social and collective aim that was missing from the Greek philosophical critique of images, which remained an elite activity. Clearly, the political and social circumstances must be right for monotheism's iconoclastic potential to become activated—as was the case in eighth-century Byzantium and sixteenth-century Germany. However, the long-term effects of iconoclastic episodes lie in their redefinition of the image itself; in this sense, both Luther and Calvin are greater iconoclasts than any statue-smasher.

REFORMING ART

Critics and historians have celebrated successive generations of modern artists as intransigent iconoclasts, creating a historical myth of permanent revolution in art. Some have sought to get beyond a loose application of "iconoclasm" by establishing historical genealogies between the Reformation and modern artistic iconoclasm. In his legendary 1983 exhibition *Luther und die Folgen für die Kunst*, Werner Hofmann not only argued that Luther's approach to the problem of images was more radical than Zwingli's or Calvin's, but also that it is at the origin of modern art.[32] Hofmann places great emphasis on Luther's insistence that art itself is neither good nor bad, and that art could also be shown in churches (including depictions of Christ, but not of God the Father); images are neutral and dependent on context and use, and thus Luther provides art with a "license" that inaugurates aesthetic modernity.[33] However, while Calvin *did* ban images from the church, he too allowed for the secular use of images and art—and the example of the Netherlands suggests that, under certain circumstances, Calvinism can have a highly stimulating influence on "profane" art. While they differ on the role of images in the church, just as they differ on many other points, Calvinism and Lutheranism both contributed to the destruction of the image's traditional status, its place in cosmic and social hierarchies, and thus opened it up to critique—at first stimulating a "realist" attention to the things of this world, which would in turn be questioned by modern art.[34]

Hofmann's historical construction may have the traits of an oversimplified founding myth, but it can indeed be argued that modern art re-opened the question of image—that problem or set of problems bequeathed by the Reformation. In this sense, modern art is a *repetition* of the Reformation, just as the Reformation was a repetition of the mythical Moses event: a repetition not in the sense of a return to sixteenth-century forms or concepts, but in the sense of yet another opening of the wounds inflicted on the rules of representation. As Slavoj Žižek put it in a different context, to repeat an event means to distinguish between what actually took place and "the field of possibilities [it] opened up."[35] This is how Freud's Mosaic counter-myth works: he revisits the hypothetical "Moses moment" to redefine iconoclasm. Freud uses the *inherently anachronistic* character of the concept of idolatry; like the Mosaic distinction itself, later repetitions such as Freud's effect *interruptions* in the discursive order of the day.[36] They were not "organic" parts of "the culture of the period"; they fractured time and opened up different futures, which always remained partly implicit, in a state of potentiality rather than actuality, thus occasioning new breaks.

Returning to Hofmann's construction, one may wonder if there is not a spiritualizing idealization of the Reformation at work here, and thus raise the question of whether the Reformation would have had significant effects had it failed to develop an intolerant rejection of images, which at times manifested in the destruction or alteration of images. Luther's opponent, Karlstadt, argued that it was every believer's duty to take matters into his or her own hands by smashing any idolatrous image encountered, for it would offend God if such practices were allowed to continue; thus we see in Karlstadt a "fully developed concept of revolutionary iconoclastic violence."[37] In a recent series of photographs, part of a more extensive series on historical turning points, Gert Jan Kocken reëxamines the remains of the Reformation's physical iconoclasm by showing scarred surfaces in great, almost unreal detail.[38] By allowing the viewers to see the images as highly complex amalgams, Kocken seems to suggest that even physical destruction is not a real argument against iconoclasm, for even physical destruction shows iconoclasm to be productive. What matters is the dialectic of physical and conceptual iconoclasm—a dialectic that creates a properly *visual iconoclasm,* redefining rather than negating the visual. Kocken's art is thus an art of repetition that reëxamines the iconoclasm of the Reformation in the context of contemporary image wars, seeking to make it meaningful and productive for contemporary practice.

As high-resolution photos made with a large-format camera, Kocken's photographs have a different scale than illustrations, even if some resemble pictures from art-historical publications. Rather than reducing these objects to disembodied representations, the photographs zoom in on their physical qualities (and are usually printed at the same size as the objects they depict). Kocken does not station his camera normally, directly in front of a motif, but slightly off to one side; this brings out shadows and results in an emphasis on texture and relief, while perspectival correction ensures that the motif still appears parallel to the picture plane. The enhanced materiality of the image helps to undermine the hierarchy between the "original" image and its modification, while the cropping sometimes emphasizes the surrounding context as much as the relief or painting in question. One picture shows part of a wall and a pillar in the Grote Kerk (or St. Michaelskerk) of the Dutch town, Zwolle (fig. 1.3). Part of the wall is occupied by a white stone relief that has been chipped off considerably by iconoclasts. While this was probably once an epitaph representing a deceased donor surrounded by his patron saints, with the Virgin Mary above, one now sees little more than a vague figure suspended in mid-air, in front of gothic church architecture.[39] Little more, that is, except for the irregular surface of the “modified” parts of the relief, which enter into a complex dialogue with what remains of the representation; the illusionist space of the relief interrupts the shallow space of the chipped parts, and vice versa. Furthermore, this relief is set in a whitewashed wall next to a column, creating a montage of surfaces held together (just barely) by some painted red lines.

Associations with abstract paintings and collages of the early twentieth century are unavoidable, and such associations were explicit in the 2006 collaboration between Kocken and Krijn de Koning, an installation combining three of Kocken’s iconoclast photographs with a mural that acted as their extended frame, and a meandering blue-and-white geometric pattern by de Koning—a sprawling modern ornament that spread over the walls and ceiling (fig. 1.4). But how are such similarities to be interpreted? If modern art can be characterized as a critique of the image, a perpetual reconsideration and reworking of its characteristics, it is not necessarily clear how such iconoclasm relates to earlier religious attacks on images, particularly those of the Reformation. As much as various modern artists have been influenced by their Protestant backgrounds, it is crucial to note that the survival or renascence of Protestant iconoclasm in modern art takes place in a radically different setting—a setting created in part by what Dario Gamboni has called the third major episode of iconoclasm, after the image wars of the Byzantine era and the Reformation.[40] This episode occurred around 1800, in the slipstream of the French Revolution.

During the Revolution, acts of vandalism against sculptures and other works of art associated with the Ancien Régime and the Church led to the creation of Alexandre Lenoir’s Musée des Monuments Français, which sought to salvage the discredited objects as works of art and historical documents. While the Musée des Monuments Français collected the national patrimony, the Musée Napoleon at the Louvre collected works plundered during Napoleon’s campaigns, even from the Vatican: in Hubert Robert’s view of the Salle des Saisons, painted just before or just after the museum at the Louvre was renamed Musée Napoléon, the antique *Diane chasseresse* from the former royal collection shares a space with the *Laocoön* (fig. 1.5). If this space contained only ancient works, the museum also received many unmoored works from the Renaissance and—crucial to the development of Romanticism—from the Middle Ages. In Germany, the Boisserée brothers also collected local, late Medieval art orphaned in the wake of the Napoleonic

Wars.[41] Arguably, the smashing of monuments by the mob was *not* in itself the definitive manifestation of physical iconoclasm during this period; much more significant in the long run was the physical de- and re-contextualization of artworks by the new museums, which was at the same time a *conceptual redefinition.*

Monotheism had already facilitated the transformation of idols into art objects. The culture of collecting statues—not unheard of among wealthy Christians in late antiquity and revived during the Renaissance—is as iconoclastic as the Reformation's simultaneous attacks on Catholic art: former idols were to be appreciated as art. For centuries there was a narrow canon of sculptures deemed Classical masterpieces, such as the *Apollo Belvedere* and the *Laocoön*, which were widely copied and distributed in plaster. From the late eighteenth century onward, the canon was progressively widened to include other forms of ancient and Medieval sculpture; the French Revolution did to Christian art what Christianity had done to pagan idols. In the process it stimulated a conceptual redefinition of the image, of art. In the long run, the most influential iconoclasts of the period were the young Romantic poets and Idealist thinkers including Friedrich Schlegel, Hegel, and Schelling—Schlegel studied paintings both in the Musée Napoleon and in the collection of the Boisserée brothers. Thus the literal destruction and physical relocations carried out during the French Revolution and the Empire existed in a dialogue with what can be termed the fundamental iconoclasm of modern art: its attempt to redefine the image as something other than a conventional, sentimental, or moralizing representation.

Jacques Rancière has conceptualized this shift around 1800 as the transition from the "regime of representation" to the "aesthetic regime." The regime of representation relied on codified meanings and rules of decorum to subordinate the visual to the textual, effectively grafting classicizing norms onto a Western visual tradition anchored in Christian incarnation theology, so as to curtail the *scandal* of the image; by contrast, the aesthetic regime conceived of works of art as "things of thought, insofar as they evince a thinking immanent to its Other and inhabited by its Other."[42] As *objets de pensée*, works of art question rather than implement the rules of representation. Around 1800 the work of art, which had lost many of its old political and religious functions in the upheavals of the 1790s, gained an unprecedented status: no longer a tableau depicting divine history or social hierarchy, the work of art came to be valued as a form of mute thought, as spirit playing with its Other in a dialectic of *logos* and *mythos*. The work of art became a persistent tussle between the concept and its non-identical Other—just as the "new mythology," craved by early Idealists and Romantics such as Schelling and Schlegel, was itself to be a "mythology of reason"; not an abstract negation of the Enlightenment, but its poetic completion.[43]

However, modern mythmaking rarely created identifiable new mythologies; in the case of artists like Barnett Newman and Mark Rothko, who strove to create a new mythic art in the mid-1940s, their symbols became ever more abstract, until only hieratic compositions, colors, and—in Newman's work—titles hinted at the old aspirations.[44] In 1961, *ArtNews* reproduced Barnett Newman's painting *Vir Heroicus Sublimis,* but the caption misspelled the last word "sublimus." The art historian and iconologist Erwin Panofsky sent a vicious letter, remarking that he found it "increasingly hard to keep up with contemporary art, particularly with titles," suggesting in so many words that Newman's apparent slip-up (which was, in fact, merely a typesetter's mistake; as Newman responded, if Panofsky had read the accompanying article, he would have stumbled onto the correct version) was symptomatic of a more fundamental malaise in modern art.[45]

For Panofsky, Newman's abstract planes and "zips" were *unreadable*: since they represented nothing and consequently signified nothing, pretentious Latin titles could only be an imposture. However, in recent decades art seems to have become more "readable" once again—is not modern art itself an art of the "painted word," as Tom Wolfe's populist myth has it, in which artists are the hapless stooges of aesthetic commands issued by critics? [46]

ICONOLOGY

The Protestant attitude toward art may have been a crucial first step in the liberation of art from its religious instrumentalization in the late-Medieval system, but actual Protestant art was often emblematic and legible—even literally, as in the case of the purely linguistic altarpieces erected in some Protestant churches during the sixteenth and seventeenth centuries, in which expelled Catholic images were replaced by language.[47] This word fetishism of radical Protestants has the effect of glossing over the complex status of Christ as the incarnated Son or *Logos*, who is, in turn, the *invisible image* of the Father.

Like Hellenistic Judaism, early Christianity eagerly absorbed Platonism and neo-Platonism. Plato distinguished between true and false images, between *eidos* and *eidolon*—the latter being a derivative, second-degree, or false image. In Plato, the *eide*—forms or ideas—are invisible to the physical eye, but the gods and sages can still *see* these incorporeal ideas in a kind of inner *Anschauung*. The ideas are thus *invisible images*; adopted by Christianity, this theory and theology of the image would prove to be thoroughly ambiguous, as both enemies and defenders of the image would use Platonism for their own ends.[48] The appropriation of Stoic notions was also of crucial importance; like Hellenistic Judaism, early Christianity adopted from the Stoics the concept of the *Logos* as an active (divine) principle of reason, which ruled and animated creation. The Jewish author Philo characterized the *Logos* as an image of God, and Christian theology adapted this by identifying the *Logos* with the Son: In contradistinction to the Judaic *Logos*, the Son is consubstantial with the Father, but he too is an *image* of the Father.[49] The notion that man was also created in God's image made the relation between Father, Son, and man a theological conundrum of the highest order. The Son, the second person of the Trinity, was the invisible image of God; through his incarnation in/as Jesus Christ, the Son assimilated himself to the imperfect visible image of God, the human being. Thus both Greek and Christian philosophy, for all their iconoclasm, often came to conceive of reason itself in visual terms—without resolving the issue of the relationship between these philosophical images and actual, physical representations.

In a reversal of the visualization of the concept of myth, Marx's forerunner Ludwig Feuerbach *textualized* the notion of idolatry. In his *The Essence of Christianity,* Feuerbach argued that there is progress in religious history insofar as one religion perceives the previous one to have been idolatry, and that God can, in the end, be revealed to have been a mere projection of human characteristics. Thus, in a move that was crucial for the young Hegelians and early socialists, Feuerbach appropriated the concept of the Incarnation from a materialist perspective. God had indeed become man, as God was shown to have been man all along: man, alienated from himself, worshiped his own essence in the image of God, the image that *is* God. Speaking of Christian (catholic) visual culture and using all his dialectical skills, Feuerbach argues that "The worship of the sacred in the image is the *worship of the image as something sacred*."[50] Christian iconophilia is simply a consequence of God's status as an image, a *conceptual* image that is present in language even when it is not concretized in actual visual representations. After all, "The word is an abstract image …"[51]

Feuerbach thus extends the notion of idolatry to include language as "an abstract image." Is not language, as used in the Conceptual art of the 1960s and 70s, just such an "abstract image"? Joseph Kosuth's blow-ups of dictionary definitions replaced objects and their representations by "ideas," evincing a Platonic belief in language as the proper medium of these ideas, radically breaking with previous theories of plastic, mythical language as being properly artistic—even while Kosuth ended up turning his logical statements into textual images.[52] If images in general are never "pure" and always in some sense infected with language, language itself is riddled with visual metaphors; Conceptual art, however, emphasized the visual aspects of the *presentation* of texts. More generally speaking, the rise of "theory" and of "artistic research" in recent decades can be said to have resulted in a market-oriented logocentrism in which artists summarize their work in "statements" that function like sales talk.[53] This would seem to be a perversion of the modern aesthetic project; the work of art is once more made *readable*, whereas modern art frustrated such readability. However, there are strands in modern art that oppose such reduction—not least those taking cues from psychoanalysis.

Freud's iconoclastic discipline is habitually portrayed as an iconophobic Jewish "talking cure," but it is important to go beyond this myth and to note that Freud's "readings" of images radically undercut any attempts to transition smoothly from identifying representations on a primary level to identifying conventional meanings.[54] With Freud, the relationship between the visual and the textual is highly complex and constantly questioned, and it is not surprising that psychoanalysis was swiftly appropriated by artists. Jacques Rancière has argued that the Freudian unconscious must itself be seen as a product of the aesthetic regime. The link between psychoanalysis and art is therefore a given from the start. Since in the modern conception the work of art as an object and subject of thought is the site of a confrontation with non-knowledge, it can be said to possess an "aesthetic unconscious," and

Freud accordingly theorized the human subconscious in art—in particular Sophocles's *Oedipus Tyrannos, or Oedipus Rex*. The play shows the very struggle between conscious and subconscious thought, between human self-determination and enslavement to mythic forces; in his appropriation of Sophocles, Freud puts the mythical logic of art, its dark and resistant reason, in the service of analyzing the human unconscious.[55] In developing his myth of the primeval horde and the killing of the father, Freud abstracted from Sophocles in order to reveal its anthropological foundations by both proving and explaining its alleged universality—its returns from Oedipus to Hamlet and Freud's own Moses myth.

Georges Didi-Huberman, who has long waged a war against the logocentrism of Panofskyan iconology, defends Freud against accusations of linguistic bias. Didi-Huberman fights what he terms the reduction of images to the visible, which is always in the process of being transformed into *le lisible*, the legible; what is rejected are those *visual* (rather than *visible*) remainders that cannot be subsumed into concepts. One way to characterize these visual qualities is to term them *symptomatic*, and for Didi-Huberman it is especially Freud's work on the symptom that differentiates his writings from iconological attempts to make the visual readable.[56] No doubt Freud's focus is often on language, but in some of his best moments Freud frees the image through the very medium of language. If we look at Freud's interpretation of Michelangelo's Moses or his equally famous decoding of Leonardo's Saint Anne with the *Virgin and Child,* it can be seen that he liberates unexpected qualities in the image, rather than subjecting the image to textual tyranny; this Freud seems to have an only partially tapped potential. In his analysis of Leonardo's painting, Freud encroaches on Panofsky's territory, but in a way that marks the differences. Freud zoomed in on a shape that is clearly not an intentional representation, nor a part of the composition that one would normally identify as representing an object or a figure: the shape of a vulture formed by limbs and drapes. Freud related this to a childhood memory of Leonardo's featuring (at least to a faulty translation used by Freud) a phallic vulture, and analyzed this in the context of Leonardo's homosexual inclinations. As evidence of this rather abstruse interpretation, Freud also lists the Egyptian goddess Mut, who was depicted as a vulture. A lifelong Egyptophile, Freud had already encountered line drawings of various Egyptian gods in the family Bible—the famous nineteenth-century illustrated

Hebrew Bible edited by Ludwig Philippson (fig. 1.6).[57] The rejected idols are resurrected in the Bible itself, now understood as symbols.

The term *symbol* is key here, but there are various conflicting concepts of the symbol in the nineteenth and twentieth centuries. Many theorists considered the symbol to be distinct from the concept, from language. Hegel saw Egyptian culture as marked by obscure symbols, symbols that are concepts trapped in grotesque form; the Sphinx was the symbol par excellence, and in Hegel's idealist take on the Oedipus myth, the hero's solving of the Sphinx's riddle was the triumph of Greek reason over the as yet unconscious Egyptian mind.[58] Writing after Champollion, Freud sees symbols as hieroglyphs that can be deciphered, but not with a simple dictionary in hand.[59] He emphasized the status of the symbol as a product of *work,* of psychological mechanisms such as displacement (*Verschiebung*).[60] There can be no handy universal iconology of psychic symbols—even if some are rather common. But the Freudian symbol also functions as a symptom, as reality experienced, rather than as a theoretical entity, and as such it is highly contingent. In one instance, Freud discussed the status of the hat as a symbol of the (male) genitalia in relation to neurotic, symptomatic behavior involving hats; the difference between the vortex opened up by such an analysis and Panofsky's linear interpretation of hat-lifting, in which the observation of a visual fact neatly leads to an interpretation of its established cultural significance, could not be more pronounced.[61]

Starting with Duchamp's iconoclastic appropriation of the Freudian take on Leonardo with his mustachioed Mona Lisa, *L.H.O.O.Q.* (1919), artists have latched onto Freud to wrench images from the normalizing effects of various iconologies by creating *symptomatological* practices.[62] A 2007 exhibition of Gert Jan Kocken's iconoclasm pictures included an enlarged microfilm of the front page of *The New York Times* for September 11, 2001—a front page featuring only news that would become rather irrelevant that very same day, when Islamist iconoclasm brought down the Twin Towers (fig. 1.7). By a curious coincidence, one article on the front page informed the readers that thirty years after he had hijacked a plane, a "black power revolutionary" had been tracked down through the Internet and arrested. This largely textual image is a subtle critique of the orchestration of forgetting—including the forgetting of the social and political background of the September 11 bombings, which is present in an article on

"Violence in Mideast." Even a piece on "School Dress Codes vs. a Sea of Bare Flesh" could be linked to fundamentalist rejections of the glorification of the body in the contemporary West. Kocken's photograph suggests that in dealing with the events of September 11, it is crucial to look behind images, to establish patterns and genealogies that may help us see beyond the terror that constitutes our horizon.

In a further case of uncanny synchronicity, the September 11 edition of *The New York Times* also contained an interview with another 1960s radical, former Weathermen member Bill Ayers, in which Ayers tells the reporter that he wished he had blown up *more* buildings.[63] During the 2008 presidential campaign, Barack Obama's contact with Ayers, who now teaches at the University of Illinois, led to attacks from right-wing media.

Donald Rumsfeld, the former United States Secretary of Defense, once made a famously rambling epistemological statement in which he mused about the "known knowns," "known unknowns," and "unknown unknowns" in the War on Terror, leaving out one final option—that of the "unknown knowns" of a society; its ideological unconscious, its repressed knowledge.[64] Kocken's visual-textual symptomatology is aimed precisely at these unknown knowns.

THE CULT OF ART

Such active symptomatology is in contradistinction to the theoretical tendency to read art's formal characteristics as symptoms of the conditions and contradictions of artistic production, revealing more about society than the artist may have realized. Symptomatological approaches in recent art depend on an actively critical role for the artist; however, it is important to remember that critical intentions have their own unconscious, their own unknown knowns.[65] Conservative and left-wing authors alike often present modern and contemporary art as being a "mere symptom," nothing but the pathological manifestation of a culture that is brandished for being overcommodified and decadent.

Currently, modern art is often presented as a crypto-religion created and maintained by mythical narratives that are complicit with the market—as a cult in dire need of iconoclastic critique. Hans Belting is not alone in characterizing modern art as a "myth," and as a "fetish" that is "idolized."[66]

Such a "debunking" discourse, which reads some aspects of modern and contemporary art as symptoms of insufficient modernization, seems to have become consensus. But as Fredric Jameson argues, "the idea of a symptom is often misunderstood as encouraging a vulgar-sociological or content approach to works of art.... It might be worth adding that as much or even more than content, form is itself the bearer of ideological messages and exists as a social fact." Jameson states that "Literary forms (and cultural forms in general) are the most concrete symptoms we have of what is at work in that absent thing called the social," and that "works of the past afford all kinds of uniquely aesthetic openings onto their own moment; while those of the present include all kinds of coded data on our own—that blind spot of the present from which we are in many ways the farthest. What we tend to neglect, however, are the utopian projections works of past and present alike offer onto a future otherwise sealed from us."[67]

If self-styled critics of art's continuing debt to religion attack art's anachronistic "mythic" characteristics, this can be seen as an attempt to not only neutralize the past, but also seal the future; what they argue for in the end is an impoverished time, a here and now of market-driven normality. This certainly seems to be the case with German art historian Wolfgang Ullrich, who has considerable success with writings that argue for a less "religious" and more down-to-earth approach to contemporary art, praising the rise of event culture in museums (think of the nocturnal openings, or "museum nights," which have become popular in Europe, or of the "spectacular" Turbine Hall commissions at the Tate Modern) as breaking with art's striving for transcendence and celebrating the "ephemeral and profane."[68] In support of Ullrich's thesis that museums have long held a sacred status they should now abandon, the cover of his book boasts an installation view of three of Mark Rothko's *Seagram Murals* from the Tate Gallery's collection. Rothko, of course, had a particularly charged, romantic, quasi-religious conception of art, and the installation view of the Seagram murals almost automatically conjures up that other Rothko space—the non-denominational Rothko Chapel in Houston, a shrine to an abstract spirituality.

Insofar as there is a cult of art, it is, of course, the product of Romanticism. In response to the conceptual and physical iconoclasm of the Enlightenment and the French Revolution, the Romantics tried to infuse the disenchanted modern world with a new spirituality, dreaming of either renewing Christianity or founding a new religion altogether—in one delightful moment of hubris, Friedrich Schlegel pictured himself as a new Muhammad.[69] And yet, for all its religious pretensions, Rüdiger Safranski rightly notes that, in the end, Romanticism amounts to a project of "transforming religion into aesthetics," rather than the other way around.[70] No matter how much some Romantics wanted to get art out of the museums and into churches and chapels again, Hegel coldly remarked that while it was still possible to admire a representation of Christ or the Madonna as a work of art, it was no longer possible—appropriate—to kneel in front of it.[71] Or, as a later author put it, while the museum may be a temple, a sacred precinct, it shows Heracles next to Christ, thus deëmphasizing them and reducing both to dead deities.[72] The "cult of art" was always both product and producer of iconoclasm; ideologizing art's profane status is as counterproductive as harping on its cult-like, sacred nature. In monotheism's historicization of the sacred/profane dichotomy, what is sacred and what is secular is forever open to iconoclastic reconsideration. In this respect, monotheism was the ideal preparation for the cult-like profanations of modern art. Removing "graven images" from their sacred context as questionable idols and frequently turning against its own visual productions, monotheism enabled the transformation of cult objects into art objects with a secularized aura.

This transformation is wonderfully encapsulated by Rosemarie Trockel's *Untitled (Double Cross)* (1990), which consists of two identical plaster casts of an old wooden sculpture of Christ, hanging directly on the wall, without a crucifix (fig. 1.8).[73] The piece literally decentralizes Christ and seemingly destroys the aesthetic cult value of the original artifact, replacing it with two casts in the cheapest of materials, plaster. From the seventeenth through the nineteenth century, plaster casts were an important part of European (and American) culture; although some classicists preferred the even plaster surface to that of marble, in general, the casts were viewed as passably neutral stand-ins for revered originals.[74] But as the work of a successful contemporary artist, *Untitled*'s casts gain a new aura, and the double Christ becomes a unique and valuable piece that reflects, and reflects on, the role of modern artistic iconoclasm in producing value—to put it bluntly, its complicity in the capitalist creation of surplus value, and ultimately with the violent imposition of Western interests on the global scene.

Like Greek philosophy, such works seem to exist in relative isolation from truly public affairs and are far removed from any form of social contestation. In most modern and contemporary art, iconoclasm reverts to the "Greek" status of elite critique. It is not surprising that, historically, attacks on the cultishness of art were a specialty of the Left: in the 1930s, Walter Benjamin famously argued that much modern art still depends on the aura of the unique object and its "cult value," a value rooted in the sacral status and limited accessibility and visibility of cult images. With the rise of photography and film, cult value gradually gave way to "exhibition value."[75] Adorno characterized Benjamin's *Kunstwerk* essay as analyzing the "dialectic self-dissolution of the myth, which is aimed at here as the disenchantment of art," but Benjamin's version of this dialectic hardly did justice to the complexity of the matter.[76] What is relevant, however, is that Benjamin—like the Situationists—criticized art for being fatally implicated in a mystifying and mythicizing economy, whereas the contemporary would-be Benjamins attacking the "cult" of art seem intent on eradicating all difference within contemporary capitalism.

In 1993 Mike Kelley suggested one avenue for analyzing the incomplete secularization and modernization of art by taking Freud's essay on the uncanny as the theoretical starting-point for an exhibition in which he pitted a neo-Surrealist collection of uncanny figurations against modernist abstraction. Kelley noted the emergence of new figurative and polychrome sculpture in the 1990s, and he interpreted this development in the light of Freud's classic essay on the uncanny, in which he discusses the uncanny sensation that something we know to be inanimate, such as a sculpture, is in fact alive as a symptomatic return of infantile narcissism and of what Freud considers to be its anthropological correlate, the animistic beliefs of "primitive" man. A few years before his essay on the uncanny, Freud had already invoked the uncanny power of Michelangelo's Moses, noting that it sometimes made him sneak out of the church "as if I belonged to the rabble *[Gesindel]* he is looking at, which can hold no conviction, has neither patience nor trust, and rejoices when it has regained the illusions of the idol."[77] Freud never made this much more explicit, but the suggestion here is that the monotheistic critique of idolatry was a defense against the uncanniness of graven images and thus an attack on the irreducible, pre-linguistic aspect of images, their presence, their physical appeal to the viewer, their status as potentially alive and animated—even though Freud would, in turn, use his own iconoclastic imagination to give new life to Michelangelo's Moses, to reanimate the art-historical idol. Kelley developed what Freud merely hinted at: referring to medieval attitudes toward sculpture, which Christianity always deemed a bit suspicious, he suggested that the ban on graven images stems from their uncanny effects, from the fear that these statues are really (inhabited by) gods or demons.[78]

A photo that is included both in the catalogue of the 1993 *Uncanny* show and in that of its 2004 restaging in Liverpool and Vienna depicts Muslim protesters hanging an effigy of Salman Rushdie whilst brandishing Khomeini portraits and placards in less than impeccably spelled English (fig. 1.9). Regrettably, the 2004 exhibition did not expand on this motif; while the show included some more recent work by British artists, these were rather minor modifications. The "Sunday curator's" show may not be an official Kelley artwork, but its second coming was accompanied by symptoms of reification that can only be explained by the fact that it was, after all, a show "by Mike Kelley, *Artist,*" as the new, swanky version of the catalogue announces on its cover.[79] Essays by other authors in this new version somewhat widen the scope of the project, but they also increase Kelley's prestige—an important, and perhaps the most important, function of any catalogue essay. Theory and criticism become highbrow sales talk; art becomes an idol of the market.

The museum is indeed an instrument of mystification, but Ulrich's "profane" museum, which is no longer distinct from the surrounding culture, would itself be as critical as Fox News. Perhaps the museum's insufficient secularization, its elitist and mystifying form of publicness, also enables critical practices that would not be possible otherwise. Granted, the art market is obscurantist and museums mystify, but one may wonder if this is really what disturbs those who attack the "idolization" of art. The discourse on art's cultish and mythical status is itself a historical myth, which has the effect of neutralizing the lingering alterity of art in today's culture. Art's myths can enable practices that would not otherwise be possible. Secularist myths that aim to "profane" art seem to target, completely and primarily, this enabling status. In a situation in which capitalism appears so triumphant that even symbolic alternatives and mythical exceptions are no longer needed (this, surely, is the rationale behind Wolfgang Ullrich's secularist attempt to do away with art's exceptional status), the blanket rejection of art must itself be rejected so that the reactionary becomes potentially progressive. It then makes sense to exploit whatever archaic remains of the nineteenth-century "ideology of the aesthetic" still survive to make alliances with other tentative spaces for critique and dissent—for iconoclastic interventions in the realm of the visible, which are aesthetic and theoretical, as well as, however tentatively, something else. Yes, art is also fetishized and idolized, but attacking art's exceptional status in the name of quasi-secular sameness is a conservative attempt to remove pockets of difference and critique. It is the *use* of this status that counts.

With its exhortation to "smash the frame that suffocates the image," scribbled around a scrawled drawing like a textual frame of a distinctly non-regimented kind, Asger Jorn's 1968 print protests against the disciplinary effects of discourse in more than one way. As an edition made for an art dealer, rather than a cheap poster intended for mass distribution, it is itself framed by the art world and its institutions. Jorn's former comrades of the Situationist International would not have approved. In the late 1950s and early 60s, the Situationist International increasingly demanded cessation of artistic activity in favor of revolutionary agitation, leading to Jorn's resignation; the artistic avant-garde had to become a full-fledged revolutionary avant-garde. Mirroring and disfiguring the framework that conditions and enables it, the print manages to sketch a practice that transcends its own limitations. Analyzing it no doubt dissolves it into theory to some extent, yet the image is also a solvent for theory: it is itself imaginative theory, a re-imagining of what an image is and what an image can be. Such re-imaginings—with an obtuse, mythical logic of their own—are urgently needed in our fundamentalist spectacle, in which the status of the image is ever more dubious.

NOTES

1 James Johnson Sweeney, "An Interview with Mondrian" [1943], in *The New Art—The New Life: The Collected Writings of Piet Mondrian*, ed. and trans. Harry Holtzman and Martin S. James (Boston: Macmillan, 1986), 357.

2 Joseph Leo Koerner, *The Reformation of the Image* (London: Reaktion Books, 2004), 99. A telling case of anti-idolaters having a more idolatrous imagination than their opponents, having to do with the response to a 1999 exhibition called *The Divine Comedy* in Fort Asperen, located in the Dutch Bible Belt. The curator found herself confronted by fundamentalist Protestants, who at first were offended by the use of the term "comedy" in combination with the divine. When Dante was explained to them (the stages of the Divine comedy were to be represented, indirectly, in artists' installations), this did not make things any better, for to represent heaven and hell—let alone purgatory, that Catholic fraud—was tantamount to popish idolatry. One of the Protestant elders screamed at the curator's three-week old infant son that his mother would burn in hell. One can speculate that he must have pictured the horrors of hell with far more idolatrous detail and splendor than any of the people involved in the show. In fact, among the often contradictory arguments against the show was the complaint that the evocation of Heaven was all too impoverished and did not give an adequate impression of the splendor of the Heavenly Jerusalem, where the streets are paved with gold. Personal communication from Brigitte van der Sande, curator of *De Goddelijke Komedie* (Fort Asperen, Acquoy, June 18–September 5, 1999).

3 Jan Assmann, *Moses der Ägypter: Entzifferung einer Gedächtnisspur* (Munich: Hanser, 1998), 17–23, 242. On the last page of the book, Assmann focuses on the hatred felt by those excluded by the Mosaic distinction, rather than that of those who do the excluding.

4 G. W. F. Hegel, "Vorlesungen über die Philosophie der Geschichte" [1822/31], in *Werke 12* (Frankfurt am Main: Suhrkamp, 1970), 434; Alain Besançon, *The Forbidden Image: An Intellectual History of Iconoclasm*, trans. Jane Marie Todd (Chicago: University of Chicago Press, 2000), 77–81.

5 Besançon's article "What Kind of Religion is Islam?" appeared in the May 2004 issue of *Commentary*. An abstract is at http://www.commentarymagazine.com/viewarticle.cfm/what-kind-of-religion-is-islam--9750; a critical response by Spengler, "Has Islam Become the Issue?," is at http://www.atimes.com/atimes/Front_Page/FE04Aa01.html.

6 Dan Diner, *Versiegelte Zeit: Über den Stillstand in der Islamischen Welt* (Berlin: Propyläen, 2005). Diner blames the sealed time or "stasis" of contemporary Islamic culture on the all-pervasive dominance of the sacred in Muslim societies.

7 In their book *Occidentalism: The West in the Eyes of Its Enemies* (New York: Penguin, 2004), Ian Buruma and Avishai Margalit distinguish between the critique of commodity fetishism by "that bitter grandson of a rabbi" and the renewed literal use of the concept of idolatry by Islamists; while they do suggest that Marx and his ilk are secular Occidentalists, they are presented as less threatening than the religious Occidentalists (102–103, 111). Others are less scrupulous when it comes to such fine distinctions.

8 Ibid., 31–32.

9 The notion of iconophobia figures prominently in Martin Jay's *Downcast Eyes* (Berkeley: University of California Press, 1993).

10 In *Die Mosaische Unterscheidung*, a volume in which Assmann responds to the debate about his thesis (which also includes some texts by other authors who were part of this debate), Assmann clarifies that he obviously does not believe that the ancient world was peaceful, but that a new form of hatred nonetheless came into being with monotheism. *Die Mosaische Unterscheidung, oder der Preis des Monotheismus* (Munich: Hanser, 2003), 28–29, 35. This book sees Assmann battling the rhetorical excesses of his earlier volume, which made many suspect that he subscribed to some neo-pagan and even anti-Semitic ideology, and that he longed for the peaceful days of cosmotheism (28–29).

11 For instance, Besançon, *Forbidden Image* (see note 4), 18.

12 Ibid., 52–53. For the debates among the later Epicurean and Stoic schools about popular beliefs and cult practices, particularly with regard to images, see Keimpe Algra, *Conceptions and Images: Hellenistic Philosophical Theology*

and Traditional Religion, Mededelingen van de Afdeling Letterkunde, Koninklijke Nederlandse Akademie van Wetenschappen, vol. 70.1, 2007.

13 For an account of this development, focusing on the socio-political and ideological aspects of the emerging *mythos-logos* distinction in antiquity, see Bruce Lincoln, *Theorizing Myth: Narrative, Ideology, and Scholarship* (Chicago: University of Chicago Press, 1999), 3–43.

14 Still the best synthetic analysis of eighteenth-century critical mythology, starting with Pierre Bayle and his early mythology of (Old Testament) scripture is Frank Manuel's *The Eighteenth Century Confronts the God* (Cambridge, MA: Harvard University Press, 1959).

15 Strauss also speaks of "the modern mythical view," stressing the modernity of his critical mythology. David Friedrich Strauss, *The Life of Jesus Critically Examined*, trans. George Eliot, from the 4th German ed. [1840] (Ramsey, NJ: Sigler Press, 2002), 43.

16 Friedrich Nietzsche, "Die Geburt der Tragödie aus dem Geiste der Musik" [1871], in *Kritische Studienausgabe* 1, ed. Giorgio Colli and Mazzino Montinari (Munich/Berlin: dtv/de Gruyter, 1999), 145, and "Richard Wagner in Bayreuth" [1876], in ibid., 447.

17 For an early account by Nietzsche of Socrates, dialectics, and the end of the great period of ancient art, see "Die Geburt der Tragödie," 83–102; for a later version of the same trope see "Götzendämmerung oder Wie man mit dem Hammer philosophiert" [1889] in *Kritische Studienausgabe* 6, ed. Giorgio Colli and Mazzino Montinari (Munich/Berlin: dtv/de Gruyter, 1999, 67–73, in particular the section titled "Das Problem des Sokrates."

18 Nietzsche, *Götzendämmerung*, 77.

19 Kenan Malik, "The Return of Religion—and other Myths" (2007), http://www.kenanmalik.com/lectures/religion_stmarys.html.

20 Abdolkarim Soroush, *Reason, Freedom, and Democracy in Islam* (Oxford: Oxford University Press, 2000), 23.

21 Kenan Malik uses this term, as defined by Olivier Roy, in the aforementioned lecture (see note 19).

22 In twentieth-century theory, the sacred/profane dichotomy played a central role in the work of Mircea Eliade.

23 Terry Eagleton makes this point in *The Body as Language: Outline of a 'New Left' Theology* (London: Sheed & Ward, 1970), 67.

24 Boris Groys, "Repetition vs. Progress," lecture given on January 15, 2009 in Amsterdam as part of the series *Now is the Time*.

25 "Geschichte verwandelt sich in Mythos, sobald sie erinnert, erzählt und 'bewohnt,' d.h. eingewoben wird in das Gewebe der Gegenwart." Assmann, *Moses der Ägypter* (see note 3), 33.

26 Sigmund Freud, *Totem und Tabu* [1923/13], (Frankfurt am Main: Fischer, 1991), 195–210.

27 Sigmund Freud, *Moses and Monotheism*, trans. Katharine Jones (New York: Random House, 1939), 35–44. Since the 1939 English edition is the original one, instigated by Freud, I use this rather than a German edition.

28 Ibid., 86–87, 101–117.

29 Assmann, *Moses der Ägypter* (see note 3), 73–72, 138–210.

30 Assmann depicts Freud as "the most decisive destroyer of the Mosaic distinction" (ibid., 22) without discussing the degree to which this destruction of the Mosaic distinction is indebted to it. He does, however, address this aspect of Freud's thinking in *Die Mosaische Unterscheidung* (see note 10, 119–143), without fundamentally addressing the question of how this relates to his own portrayal of Moses's original sin.

31 Sigmund Freud, "Der Moses des Michelangelo" [1914], in: *Der Moses des Michelangelo. Schriften über Kunst und Künstler*, (Frankfurt am Main: Fischer, 1993), 73–80.

32 *Luther und die Folgen für die Kunst*, exh. cat., ed. Werner Hofmann (Hamburg: Hamburger Kunsthalle, 1983).

33 "Mit diesem Freibrief beginnt die Moderne." Werner Hofmann, "Die Geburt der Moderne aus dem Geist der Religion," in ibid., 46.

34 For Hofmann on Dutch art, see ibid., 59–59. For Calvin on secular art, see Marta Grau, *Calvins Stellung zur Kunst*, PhD dissertation, Munich, Ludwig-Maximilians-Universität (Würzburg: Franz Staudenraus, 1917), 44–52.

35 Slavoj Žižek, "Afterword: Lenin's Choice," in *V.I. Lenin, Revolution at the Gates: A Selection of Writings from February to October 1917* (London/New York: Verso, 2002), 310.

36 Georges Didi Huberman, *Devant l'image: Questions posées aux fins d'une histoire d'art*

(Paris: Les Éditions de Minuit, 1990), 29. The most extensive discussion of anachronism by Didi-Huberman is found in *Devant le temps: Histoire d'art et anachronisme des images* (Paris: Les Éditions de Minuit, 2000).

37 Carlos M.N. Eire, *War Against the Idols: The Reformation of Worship from Erasmus to Calvin* (Cambridge: Cambridge University Press, 1986), 65.

38 I wrote an essay titled "Gert Jan Kocken: The Art of Iconoclasm" for the newsletter accompanying the exhibition *Gert Jan Kocken: Defacing* at Stedelijk Museum Bureau, Amsterdam; elements of which I am using here.

39 My thanks to Peter van Dael for his help in identifying this motif.

40 Dario Gamboni, *The Destruction of Art: Iconoclasm and Vandalism since the French Revolution* (London: Reaktion Books, 1997), 10.

41 In France, Quatremère de Quincy in his *Lettres à Miranda sur le déplacement des monuments de l'art de l'Italie* [1796] opposed Napoleon's relocation of objects from Italy, but he did so by acknowledging the reality of "museumification," arguing that Italy was a vast open air museum much superior to the Louvre.

42 See above, Jacques Rancière, *Le Partage du sensible: esthétique et politique* (Paris: La fabrique éditions, 2000), 26–45.

43 The term "mythology of reason" is from the so-called *Ältestes Systemprogramm des deutschen Idealismus* (probably from 1797), a text whose author(s) may be Hegel, Schelling, and/or Hölderlin. See also Sven Lütticken, "After the Gods," in *New Left Review* 30 (November/December 2004): 83, 87.

44 In 1947 Clement Greenberg noted that Adolph Gottlieb, Mark Rothko, Clyfford Still, and Barnett Newman constituted "a new indigenous school of symbolism," questioning "the importance that this school attributes to the symbolical or 'metaphysical' content of its art." Clement Greenberg, "Review of Exhibitions of Hedda Sterne and Adolph Gottlieb" [1947], in *The Collected Essays and Criticism,* vol. 2: *Arrogant Purpose, 1945–1949* (Chicago/London: University of Chicago Press, 1986), 188–189.

45 See Barnett Newman, "Letters to the Editor (Replies to Erwin Panofsky), ARTnews" in *Selected Writings and Interviews,* ed. John P. O'Neill (Berkeley: University of California Press, 1990), 216–220.

46 Tom Wolfe, *The Painted Word* (New York: Farrar, Straus and Giroux, 1975).

47 Koerner, *Reformation of the Image* (see note 2), 282–307.

48 As Alain Besançon has noted, "sooner or later, all enemies of the image will employ Platonic arguments," yet Plato's notion of a higher vision of the truth also made him the "father of iconophilia." Besançon, *Forbidden Image* (see note 4), 36.

49 Ibid., 82, 84.

50 "Die Verehrung des Heiligen im Bilde ist die *Verehrung des Bildes als des Heiligen.*" Ludwig Feuerbach, *Das Wesen des Christentums* [1841, 3rd ed. 1949] (Stuttgart: Reclam, 2005), 138.

51 "Das Wort ist ein abstraktes Bild..." Ibid., 140.

52 For a nuanced analysis of the visual aspects of the use of language in Conceptual art, see Margriet Schavemaker, *Lonely Images: Language in the Visual Arts of the 1960s*, PhD dissertation, Universiteit van Amsterdam, 2007.

53 See also my essay "Theory and the Sphinx: Art between Riddle and Research," in *Jong Holland,* 22:4 (2006): 54–59.

54 George Didi-Huberman has argued this forcefully in a number of books, including *Devant l'image* (see note 36).

55 Jacques Rancière, *L'Inconscient esthétique* (Paris: Galilée, 2001), 17–23, 43–50. For more on Freud and Oedipus, see also Richard H. Armstrong, *A Compulsion for Antiquity: Freud and the Ancient World* (Ithaca/London: Cornell University Press, 2005), 59.

56 Didi-Huberman, *Devant l'image* (see note 36), 9–17, 171–269.

57 Sigmund Freud, *Eine Kindheitserinnerung des Leonardo da Vinci* [1910/19] (Frankfurt am Main: Fischer, 1995), 62–63; Freud's family bible (a first edition of the Philippson Bible) is still kept at the Freud Museum, London (LD-FRD 2729), as well as a later edition (LDFRD 818–825).

58 For the symbol, see chapter 3; also Lütticken, "After the Gods" (see note 43).

59 Sigmund Freud, *Die Traumdeutung* [1900] (Frankfurt am Main: Fischer, 2003), 344.

60 Didi-Huberman, *Devant l'image* (see note 36), 184f.

61 Ibid., 215–217. Didi-Huberman here discusses Panofsky's indebtedness to yet another form of symbol theory: Cassirer's neo-Kantian philosophy of symbolic forms, which Didi-Huberman radically contrasts with the Freudian dialectic of symbol and symptom. See also his *L'image survivante: Histoire de l'art et temps des fantômes*

selon Aby Warburg (Paris: Les Éditions de Minuit, 2002), 303–305.

62 In a 1961 interview, Duchamp characterized Freud's conclusions as slightly exaggerated, but interesting nonetheless, only to go on to claim that his intervention reveals the masculine identity of the Mona Lisa; with the moustache and goatee, she looks like an actual man, not a woman in drag. Interview with Herbert Crehan [1961] in *Marcel Duchamp: Interviews und Statements*, ed. Serge Stauffer (Stuttgart: Cantz, 1992), 127–128.

63 The news about the former hijacker made it to the front page, and thus onto Kocken's photograph; the interview with Ayers did not. The online version of the interview is here: http://query.nytimes.com/gst/fullpage.html?res=9F02E1DE1438F932A2575AC0A9679C8B63&sec= &spon=&pagewanted=all (accessed July 20, 2008).

64 US Department of Defense news briefing, February 12, 2002, www.defenselink.mil/transcripts/2002/t02122002_t212sdv2.html.

65 See also Sven Lütticken, "Unknown Knowns: On Symptoms in Contemporary Art," in *On Knowledge Production: A Critical Reader in Contemporary Art*, ed. Binna Choi, Maria Hlavajova, and Jill Winder (Utrecht: BAK; Frankfurt am Main: Revolver, 2008), 84–107.

66 Hans Belting, *Das unsichtbare Meisterwerk. Die modernen Mythen der Kunst* (Munich: C. H. Beck, 1998), 9, 19, 25ff.

67 Fredric Jameson, "Symptoms of Theory or Symptoms for Theory?" *Critical Inquiry* 30, no. 2 (2004), http://criticalinquiry.uchicago.edu/issues/v30/30n2.Jameson.html.

68 Wolfgang Ullrich, *Tiefer Hängen. Über den Umgang mit der Kunst* (Berlin: Wagenbach, 2003), 56.

69 Rüdiger Safranski, *Romantik: Eine deutsche Affäre* (Munich: Hanser, 2007), 136.

70 Ibid., 135.

71 G. W. F. Hegel, "Vorlesungen über die Ästhetik I," in *Werke*, vol. 13 (Frankfurt am Main: Suhrkamp, 1970), 142.

72 Hans Sedlmayr, *Verlust der Mitte. Die bildende Kunst des 19. und 20. Jahrhunderts als Symptom und Symbol der Zeit* (Salzburg: Otto Müller, 1948), 31–32. The remark on Heracles and Christ is part of a quotation by Sedlmayr from a text by the architectural historian (and Nazi) Hubert Schrade.

73 The piece was originally shown in 1993 at the Kunst-Station Sankt Peter in Cologne, a church now used as an art center by the Jesuit priest Friedhelm Mennekes.

74 On the culture of the cast in Renaissance and the following centuries, see the classic study by Francis Haskell and Nicolas Penny, *Taste and the Antique* (New Haven, CT: Yale University Press, 1982).

75 Walter Benjamin, "Das Kunstwerk im Zeitalter seiner technischen Reproduzierbarkeit," in *Abhandlungen, Gesammelte Schriften*, vol. I.2., ed. Rolf Tiedemann and Hermann Schweppenhäuser (Frankfurt am Main: Suhrkamp, 1991), 482-485.

76 "...der dialektischen Selbstauflösung des Mythos, die hier als Entzauberung der Kunst visiert wird." Theodor W. Adorno, letter to Walter Benjamin, March 18, 1936, in Adorno/Benjamin, *Briefwechsel 1928–1940*, ed. Henri Lonitz (Frankfurt am Main: Suhrkamp, 1994), 168.

77 "...als gehörte ich selbst zu dem Gesindel, auf das sein Auge gerichtet ist, dass keine Überzeugung standhalten kann, das nicht warten und nicht vertrauen will, und jubelt, wenn es die Illusion des Götzenbildes wieder bekommen hat." Freud, "Moses des Michelangelo" (see note 27), 59.

78 Mike Kelley, "Playing with Dead Things," in *The Uncanny*, exh. cat. (Arnhem: Sonsbeek 93, 1993), 18.

79 *Mike Kelley: The Uncanny*, exh. cat., Tate Liverpool, 2004.

Chapter Two

FROM ONE SPECTACLE TO ANOTHER

Rome is no longer in Rome.
Racine, quoted by Guy Debord[1]

At the opening of the 2005 Venice Biennale, Francesco Vezzoli's *Trailer for a Remake of Gore Vidal's "Caligula"* seemed oddly site-specific. A fake trailer for a fictitious new version of a 1979 film written by Gore Vidal, who had his name removed when the production turned in an ever more pornographic direction, Vezzoli's short film is a concentrate of Roman decadence and excess, introduced by Gore Vidal himself and performed by many well-known actors; the climax features Courtney Love as a gender-bending incarnation of Caligula. Vezzoli's work invited parallels to be made between the dissipation of the late Roman Empire and the potlatch that is the contemporary art world, in which today's elites engage in another kind of conspicuous consumption. In this way, the ironic exercise in site-specificity actually signals the erosion of art's relative autonomy in the spectacle, of art's site.

In the 1960s, Guy Debord and the Situationist International had already attacked art's entanglement in a mystifying economy; even while art still claimed an exceptional role, it was in fact completely commodified and integrated into the society of the spectacle. In 1963, Debord painted a series of "directives"—one of them on a piece of "industrial painting" by Pinot Gallizio. Two others, on white canvases, proclaim or demand the "Dépassement de l'art" and the "Réalisation de la philosophie" (fig. 2.1).[2] The realization of Marxist philosophy through a revolution would thus have to go hand in hand with the end of art as we know it; for Debord, the latter even had to precede the former in an attempt to speed up the imminent overthrow of capitalism. This desperate gambit hardly holds up to scrutiny; what if the revolution does not take place? Does not even compromised art hold a potential—however stifled—that makes such a compromise preferable to no art? While Vezzoli's work may at first make a radical neo-Situationist rejection of such art appear attractive, there is more than monetary value in the outrageous way in which Vezzoli highlights the increasing integration of the "real" culture industry and its art-world double by paying campy homage to a curious entry in the list of American and European "sandal" films. In thus revisiting the modern culture industry's fascination with ancient Rome as the home of imperial spectacle. Vezzoli's piece may be an incentive for a more thorough historicization of the notion of the spectacle, which always seems to have one sandal-clad foot in the past.

Even though he takes cues from Marx's relatively mild characterization in *The Eighteenth Brumaire of Louis Bonaparte*, where the French Revolution's neo-Roman posturing is presented as a basically irrelevant disguise that nevertheless does not diminish the historic importance of revolutionary events, Debord is rather more stern with those who dressed themselves in antique garb: "The irreversible time of a bourgeoisie that had just seized power was called by its own name and assigned an absolute origin: Year One of the Republic. But the revolutionary ideology of generalized freedom that had served to overthrow the last relics of a myth-based ordering of values, along with all traditional forms of social organization, was already unable completely to conceal the real goal that it had thus draped in Roman costume—namely, generalized *freedom of trade*."[3] Here, antique forms take on a sinister role. They are not merely the result of an inability to accept the new without having recourse to the familiar; they are a disguise meant to conceal "the real goal." Given such a dismissal of anachronistic disguises, it is somewhat ironic that Debord's "modernization" of the notion of the spectacle is now sometimes criticized for itself being an anachronism. In reducing Debord's enterprise to "sources," which are seen as essentialist and iconophobic and can thus be used to discredit it, some theorists seem all too keen on burying whatever potential Debord's thinking may still hold.[4] The "anachronophobia" of such authors is as problematic as Debord's own impatience with historical recurrences.

The critique of the spectacle would be unthinkable without either Platonism and its dismissal of appearances or the monotheistic rejection of idolatry. While emphasis is usually placed on the former genealogy, here the focus will be on the latter. Although Egypt and Babylon were the idolatrous societies par excellence of the Old Testament, the Roman Empire was the paradigmatic idolatrous society for the early Christians. Tertullian, the most puritanical of the important early Christian authors, went furthest in denouncing idolatry as an all-encompassing system. In his *De Spectaculis,* he argued that something as seemingly "secular" as the Roman games was in fact suffused with *eidolatreia;* the games were dedicated to the false gods and thus part of the heathen cults.[5] In part because of Tertullian and his central place in the Christian tradition, the term *spectacle*—referring to all kinds of theatrical entertainments—was always ready to take on negative connotations and be used as a weapon. Protestant communities in particular inherited Tertullian's attitude, and in the eighteenth century the Protestant criticism of spectacles was secularized by Rousseau. In his *Letter to d'Alembert* (1758), Rousseau objected to the latter's suggestion that Calvinist Geneva might be ameliorated by building a theater and allowing actors to perform. Even while citing Calvin and referring to *notre religion*, Rousseau attempts to justify banning *les spectacles* on secular grounds: an important argument is that the theater is antisocial and stimulates the citizen to withdraw into a world of make-believe in which family, neighbors, and duties are forgotten.[6]

Rousseau's complaint conjures up the famous image from English-language editions of *The Society of the Spectacle,* an audience of passive zombies wearing 3-D goggles, and Martin Jay detected in Debord's stance "a touch of the stern Rousseauist injunction to force people to be free by compelling them to shut their eyes to illusion, whether they wanted to or not."[7] While such a remark disregards the fact that, in Debord's work, Enlightenment moralizing was replaced by an analysis of the political economy, just as *les spectacles* gave way to *le spectacle,* anachronisms are an integral part of the spectacle *and* of its critique. Neo-Roman posturing is met with contestations that derive strength far from contemporaneous sources. Of course, the ever-increasing speed of economical and technological transformation means that the critical tools of yesteryear are necessarily problematic and questionable, but it is precisely this questionable status that makes them suitable for problematizing and questioning the contemporary spectacle.

"Disguises" in cultural production should be taken as seriously as survivals and returns of theory—without neglecting crucial differences and transformations. Ironically, it is the religious thinkers who suspect that contemporary religion is rather too secular, a mere dressing-up of temporal concerns in religious garb. But to paraphrase the husband in Max Ophüls's film *Madame de…*, the appearance of superficiality may itself be superficial. Simplistic versions of materialism that regard the superstructure as a passive—albeit sluggish—reflection of the substructure are unproductive if the aim is indeed to smash the frame that suffocates the image, to create a critical event in the current empire of signs.

IMPERIAL NOW-TIME

Nineteenth- and twentieth-century capitalism often found guilty pleasure in an uneasy identification with Roman spectacles, from Salon painting, popular drama, and literature to cinema and television. At the time Debord started to analyze advanced capitalism as a society of the spectacle, Hollywood was busy invoking ancient Roman spectacles through the genre of wide-screen Technicolor epics, just as the late nineteenth- and early twentieth-century culture industry had mined Rome for titillation. Occasionally, Situationist publications provide glimpses of these and earlier returns to Rome. In the sixth issue of the journal published by the German SPUR group, which was affiliated with the Situationist International, an article by Dieter Kunzelmann was illustrated with a partial monochrome reproduction of Jean-Léon Gérôme's 1872 painting *Pollice Verso* (fig. 2.2). One of the most famous compositions by the academic painter, *Pollice Verso* depicts vestal virgins gesturing "thumbs down" to a gladiator at the circus, signaling to him to finish off his prostrate opponent.[8] The accompanying text by Kunzelmann mixes impressions of daily life with Jungian terminology and the author's late-pubescent brand of machismo and hysterical actionism, and is thus indicative of the divide between SPUR and the Parisian SI headquarters; nonetheless, the Gérôme painting in combination with a Jung quotation on the sense of play as the dynamic principle of the imagination is an interesting *détournement* of the conservatively used Roman-contemporary parallels. Robbed of its slick illusionism by having been printed in red on colored paper, *Pollice Verso* becomes a graphic surface that disrupts any lustful, guilty identification with the scene, suggesting a transformation of imperial games into Situationist play.

In the fourth issue of *Internationale situationniste,* an aerial view of what appears to be a Roman town was accompanied by a caption describing it as the set of Alexandria built for the film *Cleopatra,* which proved useless when Elizabeth Taylor fell ill, and was subsequently burned—a brief, yet scathing, indictment of the society of the spectacle's oneiric identification with the Roman Empire and a gleeful prediction of its demise (fig. 2.3).[9] In *détourning* this image, the Situationists implicitly acknowledged the power of such representations and the narratives associated with them, thus suggesting that Debord's summary dismissal of "clothing history in Roman dress" may underestimate the force that such identifications can develop. Not for nothing has identification with the spectacles of Imperial Rome been a mainstay of not only the colonial Empires of nineteenth-century capitalism, but also of the Cold-War United States and contemporary capitalism, theorized by Negri and Hardt as the global, post-national Empire.[10] In an account that is severely critical of Negri and Hardt, Ellen Meiksins Wood has sought to develop a more nuanced account of the relations and differences between the various phases of imperialism, for instance, in regard to slave labor and its abolition.[11] However, in this case, the focus is not on the nature of imperial-colonial exploitation, but on the varieties of identification running across historical divisions. Did not Debord himself analyze the way in which history relapsed into "pseudo-cyclical" time under the conditions of advanced capitalism? The "mythical" temporality associated with agricultural cycles returns through the regular alternation of work and "free time," thus folding history back into myth.[12] Cannot historical disguises be seen as the logical cultural manifestation of this pseudo-cyclical temporality?

Like Marx, Debord was not very keen to acknowledge his debt to the monotheistic tradition. Debord regarded monotheism as a compromise between myth and history, the cyclical time of traditional societies and the linear time first instigated by ruling dynasties. "The religions that evolved out of Judaism were the abstract universal recognition of an irreversible time, now democratized, open to all, yet still confined to the realm of illusion. Time remained entirely oriented toward a single, final event: 'The Kingdom of God is at hand.' These religions had germinated and taken root in the soil of history; even here, however, they maintained a radical opposition to history. Semi-historical religion established qualitative starting points in time—the birth of Christ, the flight of Muhammad—yet its irreversible time, introducing an effective accumulation, which would take the form of conquest in Islam and that of an increase in capital in the Christianity of the Reformation, was in fact inverted in religious thought, so as to become a sort of *countdown:* the wait, as time ran out, for the Last Judgment, for the moment of ascension to the other, true world. Eternity emerged from cyclical time; it was that time's beyond. Eternity was also what humbled time in its mere irreversible flow—suppressing history as history continued—by positioning itself *beyond irreversible time,* as a pure point, which cyclical time would enter, only to be abolished."[13]

In the 1930s, Walter Benjamin was likewise preoccupied by the tension between capitalist concepts of economic and industrial progress and an apparent return to a cyclical, "mythical" temporality—associated with preindustrial, agrarian communities—caused by the impact of commodity production and consumption. For Benjamin, the commodity is behind Blanqui's and Nietzsche's nineteenth-century theories of eternal recurrence, even though Nietzsche strongly distinguished his notion of eternal return from the stylistic versions in historicist culture.[14] The revolutionary mode of time that can shatter this temporality is now-time, which, as Benjamin theorized, is effectively a *détournement* of cyclical-mythical time. Now-time also shatters linear history, but not in order to reinstate a cycle, nor to fold history back into natural history. In now-time, the present is not an inevitable recurrence of the past: not sameness, but difference; an *explosion* of the past into the present as exemplified by the French Revolution's identification with Republican Rome. Benjamin read Marx's remarks in *The Eighteenth Brumaire* very differently than Debord, focusing on Marx's acknowledgement that neo-Roman elements had helped to fight and glorify contemporary conflicts: "History is subject to a construction, whose place is not homogenous, empty time, but time charged with now-time. Thus, for Robespierre, Ancient Rome was a past charged with now-time, which he blasted out of the historical continuum."[15] Debord's pithy remark about the French revolutionaries dressing up the real truth of the historical process in Roman attire suggests that the real effects of the revolution—the liberation of capitalism from feudal restrictions—had little to do with a return to Roman values. However, one could also state that later developments meant a betrayal of this moment of *Jetztzeit,* and that the apparent charade in fact represented the truth.

In Napoleon's and subsequent empires, a different Rome returned as a dream image and nightmare, as the dominant states of the nineteenth and twentieth centuries recognized themselves variously in the heyday or decadence of the Roman Empire—the former always in danger of morphing into the latter. *Detourning* Benjamin's notion, one might call this temporality "imperial now-time." Imperial now-time also breaks up the historical continuum, but not in the service of revolutionary action: imperial now-time consists of an uneasy, yet pleasurably complicit, identification with Imperial Rome and its hubris. Imperial now-time is the product of the complicity of Benjamin's two enemies: the *répétition du mythe* of neo-cyclical time, on the one hand, and the capitalist-bourgeois mythologizing of history as the ideology of progress, on the other.[16] Both conspire to create a regime of fashions and delirious innovations, repetitively plotted on the axis of progress, a pseudo-cyclical economy—to use Debord's term—in which change itself has a static quality. This is the doom-laden now-time of empire, which hopes that its dynamics will safeguard it against repeating Rome's fall, even while continuing to return to Rome, both to question and reassure itself. Painted two years after Louis Napoleon's Second Empire ended, and in the heyday of Victorian Britain, Gérôme's *Pollice Verso* is an important example of this morbid fascination with a visual culture that was both alien and familiar. But perhaps the nineteenth century's ultimate scene of late-Roman decadence is Lawrence Alma-Tadema's *The Roses of Heliogabalus* (1888), in which the Emperor Heliogabalus showers his favorites so abundantly with roses that many of them suffocate.

Imperial now-time was not limited to Victorian England or the France of Louis Napoleon; it returned to haunt later empires, particularly the United States. Thomas Cole's series of paintings "Course of Empire" (1834–1836), which depict a quasi-Roman, ancient society's rise and fall, could be seen as a prescient warning to the young United States, which, according to some, was already forgetting the values of its founding fathers. In the 1950s, the rise of television led Hollywood studios to emphasize "spectacular" values in widescreen Technicolor epics, including a series of sandal films suggesting a return to the heyday imperial now-time of both the Second Empire and Victorian England, at a time when the United States had fully grasped an imperial role—even if, as Negri and Hardt argue in *Empire*, this would result in a supranational empire of global capitalism.[17] In this context, Hollywood returned to Rome once more with Ridley Scott's *Gladiator* (2000), this time without any Christian moralizing or distancing. *Gladiator* shows the decadence of imperial Rome, and its addiction to cruel spectacles is depicted in lavish detail. That certain shots in the film visually resemble nineteenth-century salon paintings is not surprising, because producers and researchers collected such source material even before Ridley Scott signed on to direct: "That image spoke to me of the Roman Empire in all its glory and wickedness. I knew right then and there I was hooked," Scott said of Gérôme's *Pollice Verso*.[18] The story of *Gladiator* follows a loyal soldier of Marcus Aurelius, Maximus, who is persecuted by his general's perverse son and successor, Commodus. Maximus becomes a gladiator, and the film contains scenes of the Coliseum, in which the gladiator ends up fighting Commodus himself. The historical Commodus did, in fact, repeatedly step into the ring; Gibbon, in his *Decline and Fall of the Roman Empire*—that inexhaustible mine Roman fantasies for the nineteenth and twentieth centuries—regarded this participation in lowly spectacle as the most inexcusable symptom of his decadence.[19]

In imperial now-time, Christian motifs served either as a warning or a reassurance. In contrast to *Pollice Verso,* Gérôme's other Roman spectacle, *The Christian Martyrs' Last Prayer* (1883), introduces a set of figures with whom the viewer is supposed to identify, creating a distance from the heathen spectacle: the Christians about to be eaten by lions. In his 1880 novel *Ben-Hur: A Tale of the Christ,* Lew Wallace mitigated the unease of imperial now-time even more resolutely: his protagonist is a Jewish prince, persecuted by the Romans, whose life intersects at various points with that of Jesus. By choosing a rebel against Rome as his protagonist, and linking him to Christ, Wallace softened the potential analogies between Rome and the United States and their histories of slavery, stressing instead the differences—as a Christian society, the United States is heir to fighters against Roman slavery and tyranny. Christianity thus offered the promise of taking modern societies beyond cyclical time, safeguarding them against relapses into cyclical patterns of rise and fall. Ben-Hur becomes a chariot driver, and the famous chariot scene, which would become the highlight of the later film versions, again emphasizes modern culture's fascination with Roman spectacles. A lavish Broadway production of *Ben-Hur* was staged in 1899; the monumental silent film of 1925 was followed by several others, including the equally monumental 1958 color version.

While *Ben-Hur*'s incorporation of the quintessential Roman chariot race was legitimized by the narrative's Christian slant, representing Christ himself in the context of a commercial—albeit devout—spectacle went too far for Lew Wallace, who imposed a ban on directly representing Jesus in dramatic versions of his novel.[20] In order to effect a Christian distanciation from Roman spectacles, *Ben-Hur* paradoxically goes out of its way to avoid representing Christ, while nevertheless representing the spectacles. Thus in the 1925 film version, we see a Last Supper scene directly inspired by Renaissance painting (Leonardo's *Last Supper* mural in particular) excepting that the centrally seated Christ is obstructed by a lone apostle positioned in front of him. All the viewer sees of Jesus is a halo and some hands (fig. 2.4). Possibly the apostle figure is Judas, who was often set apart from the others in medieval and Renaissance painting, though never placed in front of Christ. The absent Christ in *Ben-Hur* is an apt testament to Christian ambivalence—in particular that of American Protestants—toward the new media of mechanical reproduction, which might pose a threat to salvation history by causing a relapse into Roman idolatry.[21]

One can criticize Debord for clinging to an overly neat opposition between myth and history, but in contrast to the Enlightenment fundamentalists and their cherished battle between Enlightenment and religion (Islam), Debord refused to identify myth with the Other; always a lingering presence in the compromise that was monotheism, it reasserted itself even more in the capitalist spectacle. In this spectacle, monotheism became its own simulation, a farcical repetition dissimulating the true historical process. Do not *Ben-Hur* and its dramatizations gloss over the historical antinomies at work in modern society, by replacing issues of class struggle with a quasi-cyclical return to monotheistic time, just as today's religious fundamentalisms distract attention from real problems? When Islam is identified as a backward religion stuck in the Middle Ages, trapped in a "sealed time" without progress, then there is no need to investigate the social and political conditions of Islamism.

When Islamist ideologues say that they want to return to the beginnings of Islam because the intervening time has been spurious non-history, a fall from the true nature of Islam, this explains a great deal about the attraction that Islamism exudes. But that the impression of superficiality may only be superficial is true of religious discourse, as well as of the spectacle—and are not the two all but indistinguishable by now? As we have already seen, the apparent revival of religion shows all the hallmarks of secularization, and in a sense, this is only consequential: wasn't the critique of monotheistic idolatry an agent of secularization, turning idols into images?

MEDIA MONOTHEISM AND BESTIALIZING SPECTACLES

The imperial spectacle has increasingly become a fundamentalist spectacle, its images framed in fundamentalist-religious terms that frustrate the articulation of political projects. As we have noted, religion has become more and more a matter of media controversy rather than daily observance or sophisticated theology. Controversies surrounding images propel the integration of religion and spectacle forward; the political challenge is to articulate what is repressed in the image wars, which means that today's spectacular religion must be read against the grain rather than rejected outright. Religion, that medium of secularization, always articulates social issues, even while displacing them, and manifest religious content must not be summarily dismissed in favor of "real" issues.

It would be a mistake to assume that attacks on specific images indicate a radical rejection of the image as such. If anything, contemporary religion seems intent on exhibiting its iconophilia. Even its seeming iconoclasm is purely instrumental; like theorists and historians, contemporary iconoclasts have understood that iconoclasm always produces new images, and they exploit this mechanism to the fullest. The erstwhile Calvinist opposition to the "dictatorship of visibility" in advanced capitalism is commemorated in a 2003 video by Arnoud Holleman, which shows girls in the Dutch Calvinist enclave of Staphorst ducking away and hiding their faces when they realize they are being filmed (fig. 2.5).[22] In this appropriation and editing of film footage from the 1950s, Holleman elegantly reminds us that the radical rejection of being portrayed, of being subjected to the dictatorship of visibility, is not a strange nor a recent exotic import from the East—as European Enlightenment fundamentalists like to claim. However, fundamentalist Christian *and* Islamic opposition to mass media now seems to be largely a thing of the past. Instead of boycotting mass media in principle, various organizations try to police their content. The Catholic church has long regarded mass media as a potential force for good, even going so far as to name St. Clare the official patron saint of television—a position for which she apparently qualified on the basis of a vision she saw on the wall of her cell. By now, Protestant and Muslim fundamentalists have followed suit. The iconoclasts have stormed the reality studio in order to use it, rather than smash it.

For Islamist fundamentalists, western media culture shows the deep complicity and compatibility of Christianity and the spectacle. If the spectacle is the result of Christianity's Trinitarian relapse into polytheist idolatry, Christians should not be surprised at the creation of more and more idols. For Islamists, the model of idolatry is not ancient Rome, but the "state of ignorance" in Arabia before the advent of Islam, and the "new jahiliyya" that the modern West has brought about is its return.[23] Many Salafists, in particular, idealize the early years of Islam, trying to break through the current state of ignorance by returning to original, pure Islam—which would mean, paradoxically, going both backward and forward in time. But even the most fanatical of purists nowadays do not seem to reject media technology as such. An out-and-out rejection of media technology is as rare among contemporary Muslims as it is among today's Protestants. One should remember that outside the sacred context of the mosque, Muslim societies often had a thriving visual culture. When the Taliban disfigured traffic signs or publically "executed" televisions, video equipment and computers, the iconophobic clampdown on visual media was a revolutionary innovation rather than a return to the "essence" of Islam; such symbolic acts are irrelevant when one recalls the Taliban's careful documentation of the destruction of the giant Bamiyan Buddha sculptures.[24] Meanwhile, the cult of terrorist leaders and "martyrs" contributes to a use of images that may give rise to feelings of reverence and hero worship, which was the grounds for the prohibition of *Tasweer*. Regarding the complicity of media and terror, Boris Groys observed that "video art" has become the "medium of choice" for contemporary warriors.[25] In Groys's words, the contemporary terrorist "wants to reinforce the belief in the image, to reinforce the iconophilic seduction, the iconophilic desire. And he takes exceptional, radical measures to end the history of iconoclasm, to end the critique of representation."[26] In its own way exacerbating the secularizing tendencies of monotheism, contemporary fundamentalism seems to break decisively with the iconoclastic impulse.

By the early twentieth century, photography had a significant impact in countries ranging from Algeria to Iran. Members of the elite went to studios to have their pictures taken, changing the (self) image of men, and particularly of women. As the camera became more prominent, the veil receded—sometimes through legal measures, as in Algeria.[27] In recent years, there has been greater examination of the rich photographic culture of the twentieth-century Arab world and its neighboring regions—exemplified, for instance, in publications and exhibitions realized by the Beirut-based Arab Image Foundation. With her archival work, photographer Parisa Damandan has restored part of the lost photographic culture of Iran, which was at its peak around the mid-twentieth century. One salvaged photograph shows three calligraphers sitting on and in front of Persian carpets (fig. 2.6). A sign before the men features a sample of their skills, the calligraphic sentence "*Alahoma sale ala Mohammad va aale Mohammad*," a *salavaat,* or blessing, spoken by believers when the name of the Prophet is mentioned. Thus, the spoken word is integrated into the suspicious new medium. For the time being, in the space delineated by the quasi-abstract carpet patterns and elegant writing, the calligraphers can (re)present themselves as faithful Muslims. However, as Damandan notes, photography's status remained open to religious opposition. At the time of the Iranian Revolution, "Some photographers' studios were burnt down and it was forbidden to take photographs of women who were not wearing full Islamic attire."[28]

Even today, *fatawa* such as one by Sheikh Ahmad Kutty from 2003, reflect the history of Muslim anguish over photography: "Photography as a medium of communication or for the simple, innocent retention of memories without the taint of reverence/*shirk* does not fall under the category of forbidden *Tasweer.* One finds a number of traditions from the Prophet, peace and blessings be upon him, condemning people who make *Tasweer,* which denotes painting or carving images or statues. It was closely associated with paganism or *shirk*.... In other words, *Tasweer* was forbidden precisely for the reason that it might lead to *shirk*. The function of photography today does not fall under the above category. Even some of the scholars who had been once vehemently opposed to photography under the pretext that it was a form of forbidden *Tasweer* have later changed their position on it—as they allow even for their own pictures to be taken and published in newspapers, for videotaping lectures and for presentations; whereas in the past, they would only allow it in exceptional cases such as passports, drivers' licenses, etc. The change in their view of photography is based on their assessment of the role of photography."[29] As Silvia Naef emphasizes, the Muslim interpretation of the ban on idolatry placed great emphasis on the perceived blasphemy of the image-maker, who appears to compete with Allah by making a copy of the Creation; mechanical reproduction, on the other hand, seems to take the responsibility away from the maker, as the indexical image seems to be a product of nature rather than made by human hands.[30] Curiously, this focus on the indexical aspect of the photographic image recalls the important role played by quasi-photographic images such as the Veronica Veil and the Turin Shroud in the Christian tradition; the latter really only became visible after a photographic negative of the shroud was produced in 1898.[31]

Today there are photo-based Muslim equivalents of Christian "true images" in the form of putative photographic portraits of Muhammad that are circulating in Shi'ite Iran, but such photographic representations have no "official" status.[32] Attempts to turn the story of Muhammad into a film have proven highly contentious; in 1926, a planned film version of Muhammad's life, in which the prophet was to be played by Egyptian actor Jûsuf Wahbi, was cancelled after a massive press campaign and government action. When director Mustapha Akkad planned his film about the origins of Islam in the 1970s, there were controversies in the Islamic world about the script, the director (Muslim, but American citizen) and, horror of horrors, the Jewish screenwriter.[33] The resulting 1976 film, *The Message,* scrupulously adheres to the ban on representing the prophet, choosing a rather risqué method of integrating Muhammad into the narrative: at certain moments the "subjective camera" point of view makes the viewer see things *through Muhammad's eyes*. The current DVD release of *The Message* is splashed with review quotes praising the film as "Spectacularly Done!" and "A Breathtaking Spectacle!"

By using a modern mass medium to spread the message, *The Message* is characteristic of contemporary Islamic, as well as Protestant, approaches to media. Rejection has been replaced by instrumentalization. Protestant groups in the United States in particular have become more vocal, effectively blackmailing large media corporations into being "family friendly." Reverse-engineering Clare's vision, Protestants now take control of heathen media to produce technological versions of the *vera icon* amid spurious images that are modern *eidolons*. Television evangelism is case in point; a more curious instance of contemporary fundamentalist Protestant media politics is the Disneyland-style Creation Museum in Ohio, which includes displays of Adam and Eve coexisting with dinosaurs. This Creationist museum is based on a literalist reading of the biblical creation story, which must be reconciled with the existence of dinosaur fossils and those of other extinct species. The success of the Creationist assertion that evolution theory is incompatible with Christianity is perhaps the saddest symptom of the intellectual decline of (especially Protestant) Christianity in the last couple of decades. Turning the literal text into fetish creates unprecedented and paradoxical images: animatronic dinosaurs are clearly a product of modern science, whose legitimacy is, all the same, denied. One museum plaque explains that the creatures were originally vegetarians, like all other animals, for this was a perfect creation.

While the former iconoclasts became fanatical image-makers, Peter Sloterdijk launched an attack on contemporary visual media in the late 1990s, presenting the contemporary spectacle once more as Rome returned—the decadent Rome of gladiatorial fights, Tertullian's old enemy. But Sloterdijk would not wish to present himself as a latter-day Tertullian, having since espoused Jan Assmann's rather bleak diagnosis of monotheism, with its focus on the intolerance that can spring from worshiping "the one true God."[34] Instead, Sloterdijk posits the humanism of antiquity as true counterpart to the "bestializing" spectacles of the Roman world, which created an unprecedented triumph of the "homo inhumanus."[35] Reducing history to an oneiric media conflict, a fight to the death between civilizing word and bestializing image, Sloterdijk presents today's "media culture" as the recurrence of these bestializing spectacles. Whereas traditional *Bildung* represented a humanizing, civilizing impulse with its emphasis on text, Sloterdijk assumes that image-saturated mass media loosen inhibitions—even if, as the aforementioned cover of *The Society of the Spectacle* suggests, the mass media may reduce spectators to passivity, or Rousseau's abhorred state of "unsocial" absorption.

Sloterdijk interprets the decline of ancient Rome—that favorite trope of cultural pessimism—in terms of a clash between the spectacular medium of gladiatorial fights and the medium of writing. "As the book lost the fight against theater in antiquity, so the school could now lose the fight against indirect forms of violence, in television, in the cinema and other disinhibiting media."[36] In ancient Rome, theater (i.e., gladiatorial combat and similar brutal entertainments) triumphed over the culture of the classical orators, with well-known consequences. In the present, humanist *Schriftkultur,* or written culture, is once more threatened by Dionysian mass media that threaten to destroy civilization by appealing to the beast in man.[37] Modern culture is thus seen as neo-Roman spectacle, insofar as it is a culture of the image, of image-media. Any consideration of historical difference is absent. History is reduced to the eternal return of a Manichaean fight among media devoid of sociopolitical specifics: all that matters is the battle of visual spectacle against the word, and vice versa.

Sloterdijk would seem to exhibit the symptoms of a pathological distrust of the visual—*iconophobia*.[38] However, his blunt media Manichaeanism is tailor-made for the media he professes to abhor—perfect for a media landscape in which fights over images shore up the status quo. In a way, the manifest content of the image wars *is* their latent content. These affairs *really are* about representation, in the sense that the religious (or sacrilegious) images, which are the manifest content of these image wars, can be read as ciphers for an absent representation, for the repression of political representation—which, in turn, is the flipside of the frozen representation of social relationships in and as spectacle.

AGAINST REPRESENTATION(S)

"All that once was directly lived has become mere representation"; this famous phrase of Debord's is not, however, simply an attack on "the media."[39] While Debord is among the authors most often accused of iconophobia, his target is not images or media, but an economic regime that turns all of life into a reified representation of human relationships: "The spectacle is not a collection of images, but a social relation among people, mediated by images."[40] In defining the spectacle as a consequence of the capitalist mode of production, in which capital finally accumulates to such a degree that it becomes an image, Debord countered essentialist and ahistorical moralizations about the bestializing effects of visual media. To be sure, Debord's writings are marked by a struggle with phobic elements handed down by tradition. Their quasi-Hegelian valorization of the conceptual over the representational and their concomitant refusal to acknowledge that this is anything but a stable opposition ultimately have their roots in both Judeo-Christian religious and Greco-Roman philosophical aniconism, but their position in relation to these traditions is highly complex—a dialectic of influence and appropriation, of continuity and *détournement*. Those who neglect the latter seem intent on burying whatever critical potential Situationist theory may still hold.

It is not only in Debord's writings that representation is attacked and deconstructed with the fervor of a secularized iconoclasm. In her novel *Empire of the Senseless,* Kathy Acker explicitly renders the status of representation one of modern theory's stand-ins for idolatry, when her narrator proclaims: "We should use force to fight representations which are idols, idolized images"; that is to say, "all the representations which exist for purposes other than enjoyment."[41] The notion of representation may refer both to visual and mental—as well as political—representation. Furthermore, it is sometimes attacked as a theoretical fallacy, and at other times as a social and cultural reality. Whereas Debord exemplifies the latter approach, Deleuze attackes the concept of representation itself as an imposition on *Becoming*, a mental straightjacket that restrains *Being*, resulting in a "culture of the cliché."[42] Thus, representation as a theoretical fallacy creates a reality as grim as Debord's. To oppose these cliché-representations, Deleuze glorifies the kind of image Plato decried as false—the *eidolon* or, in Latin, the *simulacrum*—for having no "original" and no model, thus resisting essentialist notions of representation.[43] "Reverse Platonism" is thus pitted against the idolatrous spectacle.

Sylvère Lotringer, who did much to import Deleuze and other leading figures of "French theory" into the United States, defined it as being engaged in a permanent suspension of representation: "Most often, to represent means to settle, answer, resolve, and control the represented—the experiences of the world put in the "right" place. Instead, representation as conceived by French theory was turned to entirely critical and productive purposes—to make thought experiments."[44] Acker's work is part of this genealogy, rather than the Situationists'. Like most of her writings, *Empire of the Senseless*—in which the Algerian war has taken over France, colonizing the colonizer—uses quotations, cut-ups, or *détournements* to enact a polymorphously perverse deconstruction of identity; sexual and otherwise. Acker's works are, in turn, appropriated by visual artists. Natascha Sadr Haghighian quotes a passage that includes the sentence on "representations which are idols" in her piece *Empire of the Senseless Part 1* (2006). The Acker text is painted on a wall in phosphorescent letters that become visible when a series of lights—including one UV light—are switched on by the viewer's movements, and remain so once the lights turn themselves off again. In the darkened space, the writing on the wall appears as spectral letters that gradually fade away (fig. 2.7).

In the passage used by Sadr, a "young whore" tells the narrator to "whip my cunt." The narrator replies that it is wrong to hurt or kill another human being, that we must not act like corporate executives in order to fight them, and that "[w]e should use force to fight" these neo-idols. But while force is needed to "annihilate erase eradicate terminate destroy slaughter slay nullify neutralize break down get rid of obliterate move out destruct end fight" idols, the whore should remember that "Julien's sarcasms did more damage than Nero's tortures." As the viewer/reader makes his or her way down the lines of text, the letters fade until the tantalizing non sequitur that ends the quote—"'Decomposing flesh moves me the most,' the young whore said. 'Give me hell'"—is hardly discernible.[45] The changing visibility of the text underscores the act, the work of reading. Being in Sadr's space is a performance in itself, a self-reflexive exercise in the contingent production of sense rather than the reception of some transcendent Word of God or Platonic idea—as in Joseph Kosuth's Conceptual art.

Although Acker's *Empire* is as far removed from Debord's analysis of the spectacle as Sadr's *Empire* is from Debord's "directives," all drive home the point that critique of the spectacle or of representation should not be reduced to a phobic rejection of images—which would mean that an oneiric fight against "the image" takes the place of a sustained analysis of—and action against—a specific economy governing the use, or abuse, of the visual. Rather than focusing exclusively on those moments in modern thought when the critique of representation reverts to full-on iconophobia, one should revisit far more productive strands of theory and practice that put iconoclasm to the service of *liberating* rather than disenfranchising the image. But doesn't the Situationist International clearly belong to the former tendency? Aspiring to leave behind its background in artistic bohemia and become a fully-fledged, revolutionary, avant-garde movement, did the SI not indeed become rabidly anti-aesthetic and anti-visual?[46]

As much as Debord's *Directives* suggest otherwise, the SI was an aesthetic project precisely because of its unremitting attacks on representation—or rather, it was a project situated at the point of indifference, where the potential complicity of art and radical politics seems to become an actuality. For aren't both engaged in questioning representations seen as fraudulent, and in attacking a regime that creates invisibility—the invisibility of neo-colonial exploitation, of creeping ecological disaster—*through images?* Other and more performative modes of visuality have existed and must exist again in the future, Baroque festivals being one example of the future life of constructed situations.[47] To be sure, just as the commodity, that riddled representation of labor, can be seen as a grim parody of the work of art—a point to which we shall return in the next chapter—so the spectacle that results from the aggregation of commodities can be seen as an anticipatory parody of the Situationist utopia of a revolutionary, living art of "constructed situations." As the utopian ideal of a different form of enacted, experienced aesthetic practice, these constructed situations would finally realize the lived art whose prophetic parody is the commodity.

Overlaying appropriated or *detourned* film clips with his monologue on the spectacle can be seen as a symptom of Debord's "iconophobia," as evidence of a desire to subject unruly images to the order of language. Debord was indeed suspicious of images, but in his view, the problem of the spectacle was that its commodity images were artificially impoverished. For Debord, the cinema's moving images barely dissimulated the notion that capitalism was a regime of deadly stasis. Cannot the seemingly deadening, didactic monologue of his films be understood as an attempt to restore some sense of meaning and movement to these images? Going beyond this *détournement* of the spectacle's misleading images, Debord developed a more positive use of personal counter-images in works such as his last film, *In girum imus nocte et consumimur igni* (1978), and in the posthumously published second volume of his autobiographical *Panégyrique*. In the introduction to this volume, Debord states his intention was to use pictures as "iconographic proof" to illuminate a "true discourse." While this could still be seen as betraying a secularized version of the Christian desire to prevent images from becoming too autonomous, Debord also notes that he appreciated images that had not been "artificially separated from their meaning."[48] This, in turn, may be ambiguous: is "true meaning" laid down in words, in captions? Perhaps such captions—like the filmic voiceovers—are makeshift measures taken under the conditions of the spectacle, momentarily restoring life and meaning to images.

It is a problematical aspect of Debord's critique of representation that he summarily dismissed media studies that emerged in the 1960s and 70s. To him, all the media talk distracted from what really mattered.[49] A cider advertisement reproduced—with an obligatory, didactic, new caption—in *Internationale situationniste* shows the completion of the commodity's transformation into image; as it were, the cider transmuted into second-degree spectacle: an image of people enjoying a relaxed evening of carefree sociability and romance, courtesy of cider. Here, photography is merely handmaiden to capital's attractive image; it is not itself a historical agent. Debord thus can be accused of neglecting interconnections between the emergence of modern media and the development of industrial capitalism, as well as their *effects,* their role in shaping and transforming the spectacle. Compared to McLuhan's—albeit overly deterministic—attention to the effect of specific media, Debord can come across as an unreconstructed idealist. For Debord, the specific characteristics of photography or film could be safely ignored, as more or less neutral media for the real enemy, representation; by contrast, in his recent work artist Sean Snyder suggests that a materialist analysis of representation cannot ignore the details of contemporary image production. Snyder focuses on the use of digital photography and video in the current "War on Terror"—by the Pentagon as well as al Qaeda and related groups.

Snyder quotes from Department of Defense Manuals that instruct photographers to identify the "Primary Interest Component" of a scene; in one work based on an official US photograph, Snyder does not zooms in on Donald Rumsfeld (during a visit to Iraq), but rather on the Coke and Fanta cans sitting atop the "Iraq Reference Map" in front of him (fig. 2.8). It is interesting to note, here and elsewhere, that Snyder focuses on objects—on commodities—as well as on the cameras that record pictures of these commodities. Frequently using successive enlargements of an image, Snyder questions the issue of resolution (and its manipulation) in digital photography; strategically sensitive details may be artificially pixelated. In engaging with such practices, Snyder draws attention to the coded nature of the digital image, to its coded matrix. Thus the images produced and reproduced by contemporary fundamentalists are themselves rooted in an aniconic code. Boris Groys has compared the digital image to the Byzantine icon, since both are "a visible representation of invisible digital data."[50] But in the "video art" of fundamentalists, like the images distributed by the Pentagon, reflection on this status remains implicit; it is left to artists like Snyder to read the symptoms.

At its most insightful and urgent, modern critique of the visual in art and theory is not aimed against images as such, but against the instrumentalization or imprisonment of the visual in regimented representations. (Although the notion of representation itself should be saved from identification with the alienating implementation of schematic models; why not consider aesthetic and/or political practices that challenge the status quo as amounting to a different form of representation, one that celebrates representation as active and productive, as producing difference, as "smashing the frame that suffocates the image"?) As Natascha Sadr Haghighian put it, in discussion with artist Ashley Hunt: "How [does one] erase the images that create invisibilities?"[51] How indeed? If anything is obvious after decades of confusion and retreat, it is that there is no single, royal road; no guarantee that an all-encompassing revolution will arise out of historical necessity. In this situation, successful religious revolutions such as the advent of Christianity or of Islam—both of which rapidly transformed entire societies—take on a newly alluring aura. If the imperial now-time of the fundamentalist spectacle is to be countered with other pasts and different futures, religion must be reappropriated.

JESUS AND MUHAMMAD AGAINST THE EMPIRE

In his two-channel video *Godville* (2005), Omer Fast painstakingly reassembles, word for word, monologues by the staff members of a "living history" museum, creating a hallucinatory form of speech in which repressed elements in the speakers' normal discourse come to the surface. The speakers work at Colonial Williamsburg, where visitors can experience life around or just before the time of the American Revolution, complete with "interpreters" in period dress (fig. 2.9). Fast filmed these interpreters, and their re-edited monologues became an orgy of slippages. Characteristic of *Godville* are the all but imperceptible transitions between different modes of speech and ideologies: it is hard to establish whether the speaker is talking about the late eighteenth century or the present, about colonial or imperial America. The speakers are seen on one side of the double projection that is *Godville*; the other side shows images from Colonial Williamsburg, and at times images from other locations such as contemporary gated communities and shopping malls. The monologue of a black man, Will, whose role is—unsurprisingly—that of a slave, ends in an extended rant about God: "God is the performance, without someone to present it. God is not knowing the facts. God is perhaps a lack of knowledge. ... God is something. That four-letter word! God is white. God is working class. God is American. God is taking over. God get beaten all the time."[52] God thus appears to infiltrate and take over everything, in a kind of perpetual incarnation, while he at the same time continues to resist positive knowledge.[53]

Insofar as the slippages in *Godville* suggest a symptomatic reading, the obvious option would be to view them as symptoms of Evangelical fundamentalism and neoconservative paranoia. Here it may be worthwhile to take cues from Eric Santner and Slavoj Žižek, who have both developed a reading of symptoms as "defense formations[s] covering up the void to intervene effectively in the social crisis."[54] In other words, both individual neurotic symptoms and outbursts like Kristallnacht can be seen as indices of "past failures to respond to calls for action," to intervene in an oppressive order. For Žižek—who, like Santner, adopted and adapted Alain Badiou's notion of the truth-event—these failed attempts are not so much small-scale and individual, as they are for Santner, but past revolutions (or attempts at revolution). The symptom is a temporal trace of lost liberatory moments that may yet be reactivated. In this vein, are not *Godville*'s slips symptomatic of the unfinished and—in this sense—failed character of the American Revolution, its curtailment and ideological abuse as a pretext for fundamentalist imperialism? Since Evangelical Christians are intent on transforming the United States into one big Godville, Will's discourse comes across as rather chilling. But progressive politics in the United States, whether in the guise of reformism or of radical dissent, has likewise drawn strength from Christianity. If the divine infiltrates and overwhelms all aspects of life, this can take the form of theocracy (there is little doubt that the ideal society for many Evangelicals would be a Christian version of Iran), but even—or especially—in a theocracy, religion becomes secularized to an absurd degree, entangled as it is in all aspects of life. It is this implicit and disavowed secularization that left-wing thinkers seek to exacerbate.

Capitalism seems to be the parodic fulfillment of Trotsky's edict of "permanent revolution": which social system has ever achieved a similar pace of innovation? Debord and other leftist theorists have argued that this means the dynamics of capitalism are more show than substance and that history is, in the end, reduced to the same repetitive innovation. Nonetheless, this version of history has marched on apace, and here one might again say that Debord was not anachronistic enough—clinging, for instance, to classic Marxist notions of the proletariat as the revolutionary class at a time when the economy was undergoing fundamental transformation.[55] In the 1990s, the emergence of a shaky assemblage of groups that constituted the anti-globalist "movement of movements" seemed to be a possible answer to the erosion of the old revolutionary subject. Antonio Negri, who, as a leading figure of Italian Operaismo, was highly attuned to the decline of the traditional proletariat and the rise of immaterial labor, provided philosophical branding for this movement, with its concept of the multitude. Negri, with Michael Hardt, created an updated, post-Fordist version of the revolutionary subject, while also considering the early Christians a prefiguration of the "multitude" that opposed the new Empire.[56] More and more, the revolutionary potential of religious movements is reconsidered by leftists in search of a revolutionary subject.

The Left has a long and complex relationship with religion. Under Feuerbach's influence, the young Marx speculated on the relation between the Reformation and modern revolutions; noting that "historically, theoretical emancipation has had specific practical significance for Germany," that "Germany's *revolutionary* past is theoretical" and that its name is the Reformation, which started "in the brain of the *monk,*" just as now the revolution "begins in the brain of the *philosopher.*" Thus there is a genealogical link between the Reformation and (Socialist) Revolution, in the sense that "the criticism of religion is the prerequisite of all criticism," for it can morph into "the *criticism of the valley of tears* whose *halo* is religion."[57] This already indicates that religion is something to be overcome, a thing of the past. In *Capital,* religion would be presented as a "mystical veil" that has to be removed in order for a true view of material production to emerge.[58] But is capitalism itself not quasi-religious, as the notion of the commodity fetish suggests? In a recent lecture, Paul Chan refers to a note by Walter Benjamin on "Capitalism as Religion," and argues that secularization "has not separated and freed us from divine authority, but has instead retooled it," resulting in a society in which "every exchange is an unwitting prayer for the continuance of the economic miracle."[59]

If capitalism is anything but completely secular, can monotheism—critique in the guise of religion—function as an oppositional and revolutionary force? Some on the Left now dream of an alliance "with Hamas and Hezbollah against the Empire" or else seek alliances with Muslim groups on the basis of the supposition that the *umma*—the community of believers—is proto-socialist.[60] Such delusional coalitions play into the hands of those who want to discredit any possible alternative to the current order by stressing similarities between Islamist terrorists and the Left or the avant-garde. After September 11, Jean Clair accused the Surrealists of having been consistently pro-totalitarian and proto-terrorist. Claiming to trace a "genealogy of violence," Clair quoted Louis Aragon, who rhapsodized in 1925 about drug traffickers attacking the West, and America's "white buildings" collapsing.[61] A clear foreshadowing of September 11, if ever there was one! The Situationists, too, are attacked for advocating terrorism. On the other hand, Debord's concept of the spectacle is also criticized for being "too total" and discouraging of more limited political actions. In this way, the notion of the spectacle is said to be depoliticizing, breeding passivity rather than inciting terrorism. For Debord, it was a question of all or nothing, and therein lay his scandal, his *Unzeitgemässheit*. But as for instilling passivity, a systemic analysis would seem to be a prerequisite for any political opposition going beyond meek reformism without necessarily discouraging more immediate forms of political or social engagement. On the contrary, such engagement may be the only possible way to prepare the ground for more fundamental change, as remote as this possibility seems at the moment.

Continuing the good work of casting doubt on any moment in history that might inspire radical contestation in the present, authors like John Gray tell us that bin Laden has a lot in common with Robespierre, and that Islamist radicalism can be seen as a continuation of "radical Western ideologies."[62] Robespierre and other revolutionaries thus function as inner aliens, as enemies of western democracy and liberalism, and hence, as strange bedfellows of al Qaeda. In 2007, commentators harped on the "Marxist" jargon in bin Laden's video message, released on the anniversary of September 11. Bin Laden (whose beard had mysteriously changed from gray to black, fuelling speculation about whether this was western-style vanity or some kind of coded message), exhorted the "[p]oor and exploited Americans" to "unite against your capitalist laws that make the rich richer and the poor poorer."[63] However, comparisons of bin Laden and Marx, which "reveal" Islamism's affinity to another ideological bogeyman, neglect to mention that bin Laden's jargon is, at best, a generic brand of romantic anti-capitalism. While the hybridization of leftist and Islamic jargon was pioneered decades ago by authors such as Ali Shariati, the resulting language sits comfortably with the Right. A website run by German neo-Nazis offered a convert to Islam a forum to rail against American "cultural imperialism" and "stone-age capitalism," with its mentality of egotism, addictive behavior, and "sexual obsessions."[64] Nonetheless, the notion of the *umma* can be fruitful—if its potential is set free by turning the concept against the readings and practices that frame it, thus retranslating religious time and its eschatological destiny into human history. This is not the same as seeing religion as an illusion which must be stripped away; rather, it is a matter of activating religion's materialist potential to intervene in the secular idolatry of the spectacle.

Traditionally, as the predominant religion in the West, Christianity has dominated leftist attempts to activate the progressive potential inherent in religion. Early utopian socialists such as Saint-Simon sought to appropriate the dominant religion by presenting their politics as a return to an early, radically egalitarian Christianity.[65] Terry Eagleton was active in the Catholic Left of the 1960s and wrote a book proposing a "New Left theology"; more recently, he introduced the text of the Gospels in a Verso series of revolutionary writings.[66] In the same series, Slavoj Žižek presents Trotsky—the same Žižek who has argued that the "Christian legacy is worth fighting for."[67] In a period of rabid neo-conservative instrumentalization of secularism, the time has clearly come for the Left to reëxamine its relationship to monotheism, to acknowledge the latter's role in the emergence and continuing force of attacks on the capitalist market as latter-day idolatry, and to address the problems contemporary media monotheism poses for political analysis and action. It is obvious that various religious movements and leaders respond to and shape political issues, while the manner in which they are articulated prevents true politicization. In this sense, contemporary religion often remains proto-political. Can the dormant political potential of today's fundamentalist spectacle be actualized?

An oddity of the contemporary political scene is that the self-proclaimed defender of the Enlightenment and of secularization, Ayaan Hirsi Ali, is happily rubbing shoulders with Newt Gingrich at the neoconservative American Enterprise Institute—the same Gingrich who reassured us that Jerry Falwell's death does not mean that "the opportunity to convert all of America has gone" and who claimed that Franklin D. Roosevelt foresaw that the "fight against pagans" would be the big task of the future.[68] As a Christian fundamentalist movement grows in strength in the United States without much opposition from those who claim to uphold the Enlightenment against Islamic barbarians, one cannot help but wonder if the two positions are two different yet compatible legitimizations of imperial politics in the service of the spectacle, and vice versa. Imperial policy is still largely drawn up in Washington, something Negri and Hardt acknowledge in their conceptualization of the post-national empire, in which they also invoke the specter of early Christianity as a revolutionary force.[69] Thus, Negri and Hardt suggest that religion may be wrenched from those who claim to be its guardians and that anachronisms can be productive forces in the dynamic archaism of today's imperial spectacle.

An earlier anti-imperial *détournement* of Christianity can be found in the novel *Valis* and other late writings by Philip K. Dick. In these works Dick developed a paranoid mythology, according to which 1970s America was an illusion, underneath which fictitious present the Roman Empire still existed. During a psychotic breakdown in 1974, which *might* also have been a divine revelation (he struggled with this question until his death), Dick saw a girl wearing a fish, an old Christian symbol now popular among Protestants, which occasioned a shattering insight: "The girl was a secret Christian and so was I. We lived in fear of detection by the Romans. We had to communicate with cryptic signs. She had just told me this, and it was all true."[70] The year is not actually 1974, Dick surmised, but 70 A.D. Christians are being persecuted by the empire, which has created an artificial reality to hide its continuing existence. Dick's paranoid fiction, encapsulated by the mantra-like repetition of the phrase "the Empire never ended," may be arcane, abstruse, and far removed from anything resembling real politics, yet as a *fiction* of political activism, his revolution of Christians against the Empire, or the "Black Iron Prison," in *Valis* and related works constitutes a cunning reversal of imperial now-time into a Christian-revolutionary now-time. What is problematic is the Gnostic character of Dick's semi-fictitious cosmology: reality is a false appearance in which we are trapped; it is a "hologramatic universe," created from the interaction of two cosmic twins, yin and yang, one of which has become sick and defective and is infecting the hologramatic universe with his madness.[71] Christ—whom Dick equates with other deities, such as Zeus-Zagreus or Dionysus—is a "micro-form" sent by the healthy twin to heal the hologramatic universe, but he is killed off by the forces of evil. The possible birth of a new "micro-form," a new prophet or Messiah, consequently becomes an important motif in Dick's work.[72]

While such alternative mythologies may seem like progressive alternatives to dominant orthodox Christianity, Slavoj Žižek has a point in arguing that "against today's onslaught of New Age neo-paganism, it... seems both theoretically productive and politically salient to stick to Judeo-Christian logic."[73] For Žižek, Christianity is the religion of history, a religion based on a historical event that shattered paganism and its cosmology of cosmic harmony and "mythic" cyclicality. What matters is less the specific Christ event—let alone the return to a supposedly "pure" early stage of religion, in the manner of Islamists' thoroughly modern construction of "original Islam"—than the notion of the event as such. Žižek follows the lead of Alain Badiou, who has analyzed Saint Paul's take on the death and resurrection of Christ and the revolutionary universalism Paul derived from it, as an example of how the symbolic order can be shattered by a truth-event.[74] Badiou mentions his "incorporation" into the events of May 1968 as a decisive factor in propelling him to elaborate his theory of the truth-event that shatters a situation, a status quo ruled by a certain order of knowledge. Such events cannot be predicted or brought about intentionally; one may find oneself in an event, or more likely after said event, but in both cases one has to decide that the event is taking place or has taken place. As an event that upset the symbolic order of the period, May 1968 continues to demand loyalty—fidelity to the event—from those who choose to accept it as an event, and in this way constitute themselves as subjects. But May 1968, which was in many respects a glorious failure, is perhaps an event of all too limited proportions; the Christ-event as defined by Saint Paul may have greater potential. In the revolutionary now-time of Badiou and Žižek, Saint Paul and the early Christians appear as contemporaries, not because of their dogmas, but because of their intransigent oppositional stance. Ironically, while Badiou and Žižek abide Paul's neglect of the life of Jesus, the far-from-Marxist film director Paul Verhoeven wrote a study lambasting Paul for covering up Christ's Che Guevara-like career as a revolutionary in Judea. The president of the conservative Catholic League in the United States, Bill Donohue, told Verhoeven to "go back to Sharon Stone's legs."[75]

It is intriguing that the contemporary theorization of the revolutionary event places it in the past; if there is a future, in a sense, it has already happened. It is potential waiting to be activated. This is partly a response to the increasingly discredited, confident and overly linear left-wing forecasts of the inevitability of revolution. In swapping eternity for the goal of a truly human society, Marx and the thinkers in his wake inverted what Debord regarded as the religious inversion of historical time, even if Marxist thought still derives strength from the narratives and eschatological imagery it negates.[76] But in some forms of Marxism, including Debord's writing, history again becomes a "countdown" to a revolution that is imagined to be inevitable, and insufficient analytical attention is given to the factors which prevented it. Thus, Debord's own analysis of the spectacle can be accused of being crypto-religious, attempting to create a secular Heavenly Jerusalem on earth. As much as the utopian imagination must be defended against secularists who see any symptom of religious roots as shameful, it is dangerous to act as if a New Jerusalem is just around the corner.

"Event theory" attempts to take this into account by pledging allegiance to a past event whose full potential remains, for the time being, dormant. However, if theoretical critique becomes active dissent, this leads to new events of often problematical status. If we look at the anti-globalist movement, that neo-Christian contestation of the Empire, its potency as a proto-revolutionary force was marred by an overdependence on hackneyed forms of public protest easily neutralized by the dominant media: in essence, these ended up becoming overly-familiar *representations* of political activism. In this sense, anti-globalist street theater was as commodified as the gallery-based art that theorists associated with the movement liked to attack. Though the distribution mechanisms are different, in both cases the results are commodified images. The images themselves are, in turn, new commodities. But to what extent are they still *images*?

We have already noted that Sean Snyder's work examines the dialectic of aniconic code and visual surface, a dialectic that puts the image in the position of surface effect—a temporary incarnation of the digital *logos*. By giving center stage to branded goods such as Coke cans, Mars bars and Sony video cameras in his work relating to the War in Iraq and the "War on Terror" in general, Snyder suggests that such commodities are really at the heart of the conflict—rather than what the Pentagon considers the "Primary Interest Component." Is the manifest religious content of the contemporary image wars thus once more "unveiled" as illusion, in the time-honored Marxist fashion? The religious rhetoric of fundamentalism, deluded as it is about its own secularizing tendencies, may indeed distract from pressing social, political, and ecological issues; this makes it all the more important to argue for an understanding of religion that is not above Coke cans and camcorders. If "secularism means attachment to and concern for the material world, which is the time-bound world," then monotheism has always contained a strong, secularizing impulse.[77] This is the truth that both religious fundamentalists and secularists seek to suppress. The current tendency to associate religion purely with *Weltflucht* and fanatical otherworldliness must be rejected. Staging spectacular protests does not amount to a revolutionary contestation; at most, such media events serve as focal points for a process that must involve reorganizing the production, distribution and consumption of things.

"The life process of society, which is based on the process of material production, does not strip off its mystical veil, until it is treated as production by freely assembled men and women, and is consciously regulated by them in accordance with a settled plan."[78] This quotation from Karl Marx's *Capital,* written in capitals and without any punctuation, was arranged by Carl Andre in a square grid (fig. 2.10). Even though he uses Marx's indictment of religion here as a mystical veil, Andre is apparently more willing than Marx to recognize positive impulses in some forms of religion, once ascribing to himself a "dissatisfaction deriving from the history of Protestant dissent in Europe."[79] Andre's use of Marx's text is markedly different from the reverential Protestant approach to the biblical text: printed on the cover of the 1970s art magazine *Art-Rite,* Andre's text is not easy to read. Deciphering it takes some effort—as does Sadr Haghighian's *Empire of the Senseless*—turning the act of reading and the production of meaning into more conscious processes. Andre always lambasted the idealism of conceptual art à la Joseph Kosuth: quasi-platonic dictionary definitions disavow that art is part of material production, which, as yet, is far from being "treated as production by freely assembled men and women." However, Andre's Marxism is characterized by an all too non-dialectic rejection of anything that smacks of idealism. What does "materialism" mean when the economy itself seems to follow a spiritualizing narrative?

Sean Snyder's focus on objects such as the Sony video camera suggests that the material world itself is changing fundamentally; both in photograph and in video, Snyder shows this camera—with its Carl Zeiss lens—in a disassembled state, its inner circuits visible. A crucial tool for terrorists, the camera is itself a programmed, "informed" object. Like the images it produces, it is generated in a digital matrix: it is the materialization of information. The critique of commodity fetishism has sometimes been interpreted as a symptom of crypto-idealist suspicion of (dependency on) objects. Materialism, then, so adept at debunking culture's spiritual pretensions, would itself be idealism in disguise. But what is the status of the commodity-as-object, of material production, in a spectacle that increasingly seems to abandon objecthood as it makes the transition from industrial Fordism to immaterial labor and the information economy?

NOTES

1 "Rome n'est plus dans Rome, et la Mafia n'est plus la pègre." Guy Debord, *Commentaires sur la société du spectacle* [1988] (Paris: Gallimard, 1992), 104. An annotated English translation is available at http://www.notbored.org/commentaires.html.

2 The five paintings, three of which still survive, were executed by Debord in Denmark and exhibited that same year in Odense in J. V. Martin's exhibition *The Destruction of the RSG-6*. See Guy Debord, "Directives," in *Œuvres,* ed. Jean-Louis Rançon (Paris: Gallimard, 2006), 654–655.

3 "Le temps irréversible de la bourgeoisie maîtresse du pouvoir s'est d'abord présenté sous son propre nom, comme une origine absolue, l'an I de la République. Mais l'idéologie révolutionnaire de la liberté générale qui avait abattu les derniers restes d'organisation mythique des valeurs, et toute réglementation traditionnelle de la société, laissait déjà voir la volonté réelle qu'elle avait habillée à la romaine: la *liberté du commerce* généralisée." Guy Debord, *La Société du Spectacle* [1967] (Paris: Gallimard, 1992), 134. English translation by Donald Nicholson-Smith, http://www.cddc.vt.edu/sionline/si/tsots05.html. Karl Marx, "Der achtzehnte Brumaire des Louis Bonaparte," in *Marx/Engels Gesamtausgabe* (MEGA), part 1, vol. 11.1 (Berlin: Dietz, 1985), 96–98.

4 A case in point is Juliane Rebentisch, "Spectacle," in *Texte zur Kunst* 17, no. 66 (June 2007): 122–123.

5 Tertullian also wrote a treatise *De Idolatria. De Spectaculis* focuses on the games as one instance of *idolatria.*

6 Jean-Jacques Rousseau, *Lettre à Mr. d'Alembert sur les spectacles* [1758/1782], ed. M. Fuchs (Lille: Giard, Geneva: Droz, 1948), 15.

7 Martin Jay, *Downcast Eyes: The Denigration of Vision in Twentieth-Century French Thought* (Berkeley: University of California Press, 1993), 430.

8 D. Kunzelmann, "Hommage à C. G. Jung," *SPUR*, no. 6 (August 1961): n.p. Gérôme's interpretation of the phrase "police verso" as meaning "thumbs down" is historically incorrect, the latter being in fact the gesture used to signify that a gladiator's life should be *spared.* The impact of Gérôme's painting on modern culture has been such that his misinterpretation is still the norm.

9 *Internationale situationniste*, no. 6 (August 1961): 11.

10 Michael Hardt and Antonio Negri, *Empire* (Cambridge, MA: Harvard University Press, 1999).

11 Ellen Meiksins Wood, *Empire of Capital* (London/New York: Verso, 2003).

12 See parts V (*temps et histoire*) and VI (*le temps spectaculaire*) of *La Société du Spectacle.*

13 "Les religions monothéistes ont été un compromis entre le mythe et l'histoire, entre le temps cyclique dominant encore la production et le temps irréversible où s'affrontent et se recomposent les peuples. Les religions issues du judaïsme sont la reconnaissance universelle abstraite du temps irréversible qui se trouve démocratisé, ouvert à tous, mais dans l'illusoire. Le temps est orienté tout entier vers un seul événement final: 'Le royaume de Dieu est proche.' Ces religions sont nées sur le sol de l'histoire, et s'y sont établies. Mais là encore elles se maintiennent en opposition radicale à l'histoire. La religion semi-historique établit un point de départ qualitatif dans le temps, la naissance du Christ, la fuite de Mahomet, mais son temps irréversible—introduisant une accumulation effective qui pourra dans l'Islam prendre la figure d'une conquête, ou dans le Christianisme de la Réforme celle d'un accroissement du capital—est en fait inversé dans la pensée religieuse comme un *compte à rebours:* l'attente, dans le temps qui diminue, de l'accès à l'autre monde véritable, l'attente du Jugement dernier. L'éternité est sortie du temps cyclique. Elle est son au-delà. Elle est l'élément qui rabaisse l'irréversibilité du temps, qui supprime l'histoire dans l'histoire même, en se plaçant, comme un pur élément ponctuel où le temps cyclique est rentré et s'est aboli, *de l'autre côté du temps irréversible.*" Debord, *Société du Spectacle* (see note 3), 134–135; emphasis in original. English translation by Donald Nicholson-Smith, http://www.cddc.vt.edu/sionline/si/tsots05.html.

14 Walter Benjamin, "Das Passagen-Werk," in *Gesammelte Schriften,* vol. V.1, ed. Rolf Tiedemann and Hermann Schweppenhäuser (Frankfurt am Main: Suhrkamp, 1991), 169–178.

15 "Die Geschichte ist Gegenstand einer Konstruktion, deren Ort nicht die homogene und leere Zeit sondern die von Jetztzeit erfüllte bildet. So war für Robespierre das antike Rom eine mit Jetztzeit geladene Vergangenheit, die er aus dem Kontinuum der Geschichte heraussprengte." Walter Benjamin, "Über den Begriff der Geschichte" [1941], in *Abhandlungen, Gesammelte Schriften,* vol. I.2, ed. Rolf Tiedemann and Hermann Schweppenhäuser (Frankfurt am Main: Suhrkamp, 1991), 701.

16 Benjamin, "Passagen-Werk" (see note 14), 177.

17 Negri and Hardt, *Empire* (see note 10), 160–182. Negri and Hardt argue that the imperial tendencies in the US constitution have given the United States a crucial role in the emergence of the global empire.

18 Quotation formerly on a *Pollice Verso* page of the Phoenix Art Museum web site, http://www.phxart.org/collection/verso.asp, now no longer available. For Gérôme's impact on earlier film productions, particularly the 1913 film *Quo vadis?* see Ivo Blom, "Gérôme en Quo vadis? Picturale invloeden in de film," in *Jong Holland* 17, no. 4 (2001): 19–28.

19 Edward Gibbon, *The Decline and Fall of the Roman Empire,* part 1 (London: J.M. Dent/E.P. Dutton, 1910), 93.

20 Gordon Thomas, "Getting It Right the Second Time: Adapting Ben-Hur for the Screen," in *Bright Lights Film Journal*, no. 52 (2006), http://www.brightlightsfilm.com/52/benhur.htm.

21 For more on this subject, see David Morgan, *The Lure of Images: A History of Religion and Visual Media in America* (New York: Routledge, 2007), 173–183.

22 Jorinde Seijdel, "Staphorst Revisited," *SMBA Newsletter,* no. 76 (September 2003), http://www.smba.nl/en/newsletters/n-76-being-there.

23 On the historical context of the Islamic notion of *jahiliyya*, see G. R. Hawting, *The Idea of Idolatry and the Emergence of Islam: From Polemic to History* (Cambridge: Cambridge University Press, 1999). For an influential portrayal and analysis of Islamism's attacks on the West as "the new *jahiliyya*," see Ian Buruma and Avishai Margalit, *Occidentalism: The West in the Eyes of Its Enemies* (New York: Penguin, 2004).

24 Silvia Naef made the comparison between Muslim societies and Calvinist Holland in a talk that was part of the project *The Return of Religion and Other Myths* at BAK, basis voor actuele kunst, February 1, 2009.

25 Boris Groys, "The Fate of Art in the Age of Terror," in *Making Things Public: Atmospheres of Democracy,* ed. Bruno Latour and Peter Weibel (Karlsruhe: ZKM; Cambridge, MA: MIT Press, 2005), 970.

26 Ibid., 972.

27 For more on the camera and the veil, see Christina von Braun and Bettina Mathes, *Verschleierte Wirklichkeit: Die Frau, der Islam und der Westen* (Berlin: Aufbau Verlag, 2007), 24–31.

28 Parisa Damandan, "Foreword," in Portrait *Photographs from Isfahan: Faces in Transition, 1920–1950* (London: Saqi Books, 2004), 8.

29 Sheikh Ahmad Kutty, "Fatwa on Photography," September 16, 2003, http://www.islamonline.net/servlet/Satellite?pagename=IslamOnline-English-Ask_Scholar/FatwaE/FatwaE&cid=1119503545144.

30 Silvia Naef, *Bilder und Bilderverbot im Islam: Vom Koran bis zum Karikaturenstreit*, trans. Christiane Seiler (Munich: C. H. Beck, 2007), 103–105.

31 Hans Belting, *Das echte Bild: Bildfragen als Glaubensfragen* (Munich: C. H. Beck, 2005), 63–67.

32 Naef, Utrecht lecture (see note 24).

33 Naef, *Bilder und Bilderverbot* (see note 30), 107–108.

34 Peter Sloterdijk, *Gottes Eifer: Vom Kampf der drei Weltreligionen* (Frankfurt am Main: Verlag der Weltreligionen, 2007).

35 Peter Sloterdijk, *Regeln für den Menschenpark: Ein Antwortschreiben zu Heideggers Brief über den Humanismus* (Frankfurt am Main: Suhrkamp, 1999), 18.

36 Ibid., 46.

37 Ibid.

38 Jay, *Downcast Eyes* (see note 7), 13–14.

39 "Tout ce qui était directement vécu s'est éloigné dans une représentation." Debord, *Société du Spectacle* (see note 3), 15. English translation by Donald Nicholson-Smith, http://www.cddc.vt.edu/sionline/si/tsots01.html.

40 "Le spectacle n'est pas un ensemble d'images, mais un rapport social entre des personnes, médiatisé par des images." Ibid., 16.

41 Kathy Acker, *Empire of the Senseless* (New York: Grove Press, 1988), 94–95.

42 Gilles Deleuze, *Cinéma 2: L'image-temps* (Paris: Les Éditions de Minuit, 1985), 33.

43 Gilles Deleuze, *Différence et répétition* (Paris, Presses Universitaires de France, 1968).

44 Sylvère Lotringer and Sande Cohen, "Introduction," in *French Theory in America,* ed. Lotringer and Cohen (New York/London: Routledge, 2001), 4.

45 Acker, *Empire of the Senseless* (see note 41), 95.

46 See two 1963 attempts by Debord to come to terms with the status of the SI as an artistic and/or revolutionary avant-garde: "L'avant-garde de la présence" from *Internationale situationniste*, no. 8. English translation at http://www.cddc.vt.edu/sionline/si/avantgarde.html (this text is presumably collective, but Debord is clearly the sole author, or at least one of the authors), and "Situationnistes et les nouvelles formes d'action dans la politique ou l'art," English translation at http://www.cddc.vt.edu/SIOnline/si/newforms.html.

47 Debord, *Société du Spectacle* (see note 3), 182–183.

48 Guy Debord, *Panégyrique: tome second* (Paris: Librairie Arthème Fayard, 1997), n.p.

49 Debord, *Commentaires* (see note 1), 51–52.

50 Boris Groys, "Repetition vs. Progress," lecture given on January 15, 2009, in Amsterdam as part of the series "Now is the Time."

51 Natascha Sadr Haghighian and Ashley Hunt, "Representations of the Erased," in *On Knowledge Production: A Critical Reader in Contemporary Art,* ed. Binna Choi, Maria Hlavajova, and Jill Winder (Utrecht: BAK; Frankfurt am Main: Revolver, 2008), 172.

52 *Omer Fast: Godville* (Minneapolis: Midway Contemporary Art; Frankfurt am Main: Revolver, 2005), 58–59.

53 See also Hito Steyerl's interpretation of *Godville* in *Die Farbe der Wahrheit: Dokumentarismen im Kunstfeld* (Vienna: Turia + Kant, 2008), 68–69.

54 Slavoj Žižek, *Welcome to the Desert of the Real* (London/New York: Verso, 2002), 23, quoted by Santner in "Miracles Happen: Benjamin, Rosenzweig, Freud, and the Matter of the Neighbor," http://www.cjs.ucla.edu/Mellon/Santner_Miracles_Happen.pdf (p. 14).

55 In recent years, using Walter Benjamin as a model, Georges Didi-Huberman has accorded a central role to the anachronism in historical writing; see in particular his *Devant le temps: histoire de l'art et anachronisme des images* (Paris: Les Éditions de Minuit, 2000).

56 At an early point in their argument in *Empire* (see note 10; p. 18), Negri and Hardt ask if "we are in a situation very close to the traditional definition of Empire, the one promulgated in the ancient Roman-Christian imaginary?" Three pages later (21), the rise of early Christianity in and against the Roman Empire is explicitly used as an analogy for the present.

57 "Für Deutschland ist die *Kritik der Religion* im Wesen beendigt und die Kritik der Religion ist die Voraussetzung aller Kritik." (170) "Die Kritik der Religion ist also im *Keim* die *Kritik des Jammerthales*, dessen *Heiligenschein* die Religion ist." (171) "Selbst historisch hat die theoretische Emanzipation eine specifisch praktische Bedeutung für Deutschland. Deutschlands *revolutionaire* Vergangenheit ist nämlich theoretisch, es ist die *Reformation*. Wie damals der *Mönch*, so ist es jetzt der *Philosoph*, in dessen Hirn die Revolution beginnt." (175) Karl Marx, "Zur Kritik der Hegel'schen Rechts-Philosophie. Einleitung" [1844], in *Marx/Engels Gesamtausgabe (MEGA)*, part 1, vol. 2 (Berlin: Dietz, 1982). The German *Kritik* can be translated either as "criticism" or as "critique"; the former seems to do more justice to Marx's belligerent stance.

58 In German this phrase, usually rendered in English as "mystical veil," is "mystische[r] Nebelschleier," literally, "mystical veil of fog." Karl Marx, "Das Kapital: Kritik der politischen Ökonomie" [1872 edition], in *Marx/Engels Gesamtausgabe (MEGA)*, part 2, vol. 6.1 (Berlin: Dietz, 1987), 110.

59 Paul Chan, "The Spirit of Recession," lecture delivered on April 30, 2008, in New York as part of the Public Art Fund Talks.

60 Richard Gebhardt, "Links, Inch'Allah!," *Jungle World*, no. 38 (September 20, 2007), http://www.jungle-world.com/seiten/2007/38/10632.php.

61 Jean Clair, *Du surréalisme considéré dans ses rapports au totalitarisme et aux tables tournantes* (Paris: Mille et Une Nuits, 2003), 118. While seemingly offended by Surrealism's antidemocratic and occult leanings, Clair seems especially upset by Surrealism's success since the 1960s, accusing the 1968 "rioters" of turning Bataille and Artaud into "idols" and using Breton's plea for free love to stage "Fourierist orgies" such as Woodstock and, later, raves and Love Parades (19). Clair, who is keen to read

Surrealism as a symptom, must live with the suspicion that, here, he symptomatically betrays his true opponent: western art and culture since the 1960s, which is the object of his conservative revulsion. The enemy is not so much terrorism; terrorism is a stick to beat all artistic tendencies that are opposed to French values, to order and clarity, and to a clear separation of the blessed *vita contemplativa* of art and the *vita activa* led by "the men of action who govern us" (65).

62 John Gray, "Radicale Moslims hebben meer op met Robespierre en Lenin dan met Allah," in *NRC Handelsblad,* September 1, 2007, 15.

63 Fawaz A. Gerges, "Bin Laden's New Image: Younger, More Marxist," *Christian Science Monitor,* September 13, 2007, http://www.cs-monitor.com/2007/0913/p09s01-coop.html.

64 Udo Wolter, "Man denkt deutsch: Die Welt deutscher Islam-Konvertiten und der Drang zum Unbedingten," Jungle World, no. 38 (September 20, 2007): 4, http://www.jungle-world.com/seiten/2007/38/10633.php. For a right-wing take on the Left, Islam and anti-Semitism, see www.hetvrijevolk.com/?pagina=6095.

65 When Saint-Simon went so far as to call his philosophy "*Nouveau Christianisme*," the reasons for this move were no doubt largely tactical.

66 Terry Eagleton, *The Body as Language: Outline of a 'New Left' Theology* (London: Sheed & Ward, 1970); Jesus Christ [sic], *The Gospels*, introduction by Terry Eagleton (London/New York: Verso, 2007).

67 Leon Trotsky, *Terrorism and Communism: A Reply to Karl Kautsky,* foreword by Slavoj Žižek (London/New York: Verso, 2007). On their covers, the books from this series are billed as "[Contemporary Theorist] presents [Historical Figure]."

68 Newt Gingrich, "Liberty University Commencement Address," May 19, 2007, http://newt.org/EditNewt/NewtNewsandOpinionDB/tabid/102/ArticleType/ArticleView/ArticleID/2621/PageID/2696/Default.aspx.

69 Negri and Hardt, *Empire* (see note 10), 21, 182.

70 Philip K. Dick. "How to Build a Universe That Doesn't Fall Apart Two Days Later," [1978/1985], in *The Shifting Realities of Philip K. Dick: Selected Literary and Philosophical Writings,* ed. Lawrence Sutin (New York: Vintage Books, 1995), 271.

71 See Philip K. Dick, "Two-Source Cosmogony," in *Valis* (1981; London: Gollancz, 2001), 266–268. The section is from Dick's "Exegesis" of his experience.

72 Ibid., 267.

73 Slavoj Žižek, *The Fragile Absolute, or, Why Is the Christian Legacy Worth Fighting For?* (London/New York: Verso, 2000), 107.

74 Alain Badiou, *Saint Paul: La fondation de l'universalisme* (Paris: Presses Universitaires de France, 1997).

75 Paul Verhoeven (with Rob van Scheers), *Jezus van Nazaret* (Amsterdam: Meulenhoff, 2008). Verhoeven's approach is nineteenth-century in spirit; he wants to strip accounts of Christ's life of all myth. While Badiou and Žižek are interested in the historicity of Christ, in the sense of his historical effect, and thus end up primarily studying, Paul Verhoeven is only interested in the historicity of Christ's life. Verhoeven studies the failed revolution of Jesus in Palestine, which ended with his crucifixion; Badiou and Žižek, the revolution that was only *enabled* by his crucifixion. Immediately, Verhoeven's discussion of the ancient rumors about Jesus being the offspring of Mary and a Roman legionary, Pantera, and indeed of her rape by Pantera, was decontextualized and sensationalized by right-wing media, which also reported the Donohue quote about Sharon Stone's legs, invoking a famous scene from *Basic Instinct* that obviously had a profound impact on the Catholic League's president. Even more oddly, Donohue lampooned Verhoeven for having studied his subject for twenty years, only to come up with probabilities rather than hard facts—as if carefully argued probabilities are not the best one can hope for in this case. See http://www.foxnews.com/story/0,2933,352277,00.html.

76 The historical connection preserved in this small but decisive shift was perceived by many leftists—and by some of their opponents—as a skeleton in the closet. Debord himself seems to protest a tad too much in the passage quoted above. But here, as so often, one should say *vive la petite différence*.

77 Abdolkarim Soroush, "Militant Secularism," http://www.drsoroush.com/English/On_DrSoroush/E-CMO-2007-Militant%20Secularism.html.

78 Carl Andre, untitled ("The Life Process of Society...") on the cover of *Art-Rite,* no. 14 (Winter 1976/77), reprinted in *Cuts: Texts 1959–2004* (Cambridge, MA: MIT Press, 2005), 72.

79 Carl Andre, "Letter to Sol LeWitt" [1970], in ibid., 37. See also Marx, "Kapital" (see note 58), 37.

Chapter Three

ATTENDING TO THINGS (SOME MORE MATERIAL THAN OTHERS)

Capitalist alchemy
Makes the visible invisible
Makes the material immaterial
Makes the sensual sterile
Makes the real virtual
Makes the physical conceptual
Carl Andre[1]

In the 1870s the Liebig Company, makers of a famous meat extract, started publishing series of collectible chromolithographs that illustrated every subject under the sun. One 1928 series dealt with the life of Muhammad; not bothered by Muslim sensitivities, Liebig portrayed Muhammad in the full.[2] One scene depicts the destruction of the idols in the Ka'aba: Muhammad is shown in the process of striking down a bird-shaped idol while idolaters flee or plead for mercy in vain. In the right foreground lies the rather realistic head of another idol, apparently already taken care of. Intriguingly, this head is mirrored by a jar of Liebig's in the lower left corner of the image (fig. 3.1). The idol in the lower right corner is more or less part of the tableau, although its position and use as *repoussoir* set it somewhat apart, in an intermediary zone; by contrast, the jar of Liebig's occupies a separate space—that of the market—delineated by a golden border with a pseudo-Islamic ornamental frame. It is as if the artist wanted to create an emblem signifying that although Muhammad may have ended idolatry in the Ka'aba, idolatry would have its revenge by integrating the story of Islam into an iconoclastic spectacle serving to sell Liebig's.

It has long been a mainstay of monotheistic idolatry discourse to accuse idolaters of worshiping dead matter, and Enlightenment theory constructed its own purely material version of idolatry in the guise of fetishism. Are idolatry critique and iconoclasm just symptoms of a transcendentalist aversion to matter, to the world of material objects? There is certainly plenty of evidence to back up such an assertion; one might quote Thomas a Kempis's Christian exhortation to "wean your heart from the love of visible things, and attend rather to things invisible," or any number of Muslim criticisms of the West's atheism and materialism, which even turns women into commodities.[3] In the 1970s, Ali Shariati characterized polytheism as a "faith based on worldly matters," a "system based on materialism," and in his view there was a logical progression from this materialism—which is also that of Christianity, with its crypto-polytheist trinity—to capitalism.[4] On the other hand, the Dutch right-wing populist Geert Wilders contends that Islam is not "really" a religion because it is fatally of this world—i.e., a project of unremitting political and military conquest, starting with the act of intolerance immortalized on the Liebig card.[5]

But the supposition that religion should be exclusively focused on "spiritual" matters is absurd. If the seeds of secularism lie in *abandoning abandoning the world,* to use Abdolkarim Soroush's phrase, then they are part and parcel of monotheism.[6] Time and again, believers came to realize that "attending to things invisible" brought with it an increased obligation to mundane matters. With Calvin and other Reformers, a radically transcendent conception of God led to a focus on work as a way of honoring His creation—contributing, in Max Weber's famous thesis, to the triumph of capitalism.[7] More recently, in the context of fully fledged global capitalism, a Muslim economist argued that "those who live in the vision of the 'right' ... must descend into the real world to turn the oppressive 'facts' of life into just forms."[8] It is primarily here that modern thought continued and radicalized religious thinking.

Bruno Latour had argued that modern thought as a whole, including Marx and his commodity fetish, evinced a crypto-idealist aversion to objecthood. Latour claims that the quintessential modern project is to liberate the subject from objects and from material constraints; Marx's commodity fetish is one example of the tyranny of the object over the (alienated) subject, which modern thinking seeks to overcome.[9] However, dialectical materialism regards the commodity as being *insufficiently material*, as too "theological," prone to idealist pretenses. In Terry Eagleton's words, "As pure exchange-value, the commodity erases from itself every particle of matter; as alluring auratic object, it parades its own unique sensual being in a kind of spurious show of materiality."[10] But this inherent duality of the commodity is not static; over time, the auratic object itself becomes increasingly dematerialized; its spurious materiality becomes more so as time goes on. Debord theorized that the spectacle is capital accumulated to such a degree that it has become image. This ambiguous "image" is not necessarily dependent on visual representations, such as photos; the objects themselves become image-objects, representations of social relations, forming a spectacle.[11] The Liebig company recognized and embraced the becoming-image of the commodity at an early stage, even if Liebig's approach was different from American companies such as Coca-Cola and Campbell's, which created recognizable logos for their brands, while Liebig focused on the exotic spectacles featured on the collectible cards. In the face of such images, critique often bemoans a lack of reality, but such pseudo-Situationist complaints are only apparently materialist. When capitalism takes on the guise of a quasi-theological narrative of dematerialization, materialism itself is in need of redefinition.

As a concrete symptom of complex social formations, the eccentric yet exemplary commodity that is the work of art can be highly illuminating. Even if Marx did not regard the work of art as a crucial commodity for modern capitalism, his "commodity fetish" is a caricature of the artwork, brimming as it is with "theological whims."[12] Is not the work of art the most theological of all commodities, an anachronistic repository of cult value? It is precisely art's insufficient modernization that makes it exemplary in economic terms.[13] This is not to depoliticize Marxian theory, but rather to emphasize that aesthetic thinking—seen, along with Jacques Rancière—as a contentious conceptualization and division of the sensible realm—is always political, implicitly or explicitly.[14] Works of art are themselves a mute form of political economy, offering insight into the changing nature of the schizoid entity that is the commodity, which now seems to be dematerializing into thin air.

THE ABSOLUTE COMMODITY, READY-MADE

In 1937, Meyer Schapiro noted: "The highest praise of [modern artists'] work is to describe it in terms of magic and fetishism."[15] Some fifteen years later, Robert Rauschenberg hung sundry little arbitrary-looking objects from trees in a Roman park, under the title *Personal Fetishes,* their unspectacular and random character evoking the concept of African fetishism as introduced by Charles de Brosses. The word fetish is based on the Portuguese *feitiço*, derived from the Latin *factitius*, which often referred to "magical" objects; later it was also used to describe objects encountered by traders and missionaries in West Africa. Based on reports about African *feitiços*, de Brosses constructed a theory of a primitive phase of religion, a prequel to idolatry proper, in which people revered randomly chosen objects. De Brosses wrote: "These divine fetishes are nothing else but the first material object it pleases each nation or each individual to select and to have ceremonially consecrated by priests, be it a tree, a mountain, the sea, a piece of wood, a lion's tail, a pebble, a shell, salt, a fish, a flower, an animal such as a cow, goat, elephant, or sheep; in effect, anything imaginable of this kind."[16] This was a misconception, since the materials used in Minkisi, the Central-African objects presumably at the origin of western notions of African fetishism, contain materials laden with meaning—being part of a "complex system of cosmological references."[17] With a fine disregard for the facts, Enlightenment theory thus appropriated and exacerbated the monotheistic accusation of idolatrous materialism; these objects indeed seemed to be nothing but base matter. Whereas idols at least represent some deity, however illusory, African fetishes were seen as arbitrary objects without any redeeming qualities: crude, primitive proto-idols.

Objects viewed through the lens of this theory were eagerly collected, not least in avant-garde circles. The 1935 exhibition *African Negro Art* at New York's Museum of Modern Art contained a "fetish with calabash and shells" from the collection of Tristan Tzara—a Congolese object consisting of a small anthropomorphic figure mounted on a gourd with a garland of shells (fig. 3.2).[18] Exhibited and publicized by a major museum, such an object is anything but base matter. Promoted by specialized dealers, the "African fetish" became a brand among connoisseurs—its own commodified doppelganger. When Adorno noted that "[o]f the work of art's autonomy… nothing remains but the fetishism of the commodity—a regression to the archaic fetishism from which art originated," he too implicitly posited "African" fetishism as the truth of modern art, but with the crucial difference that "archaism" resides in the value form of the commodity itself, not in any surface primitivism.[19] The Marxian commodity fetish is no arbitrary object, nor is it necessarily, or even purely, material. It is the economically progressive object that produces a neo-archaic state.

The 1936 exhibition of Surrealist objects at Galerie Charles Ratton included both ethnographica—the gallery's specialty—and Marcel Duchamp's bottle rack, signaling the exemplary status of both types of object, and implying that "archaic fetishes" and Duchampian readymades were equally important models for the surrealist object.[20] At the anti-colonial exhibition staged by the Surrealists in 1931, a group of objects labeled "European fetishes" was displayed: an anthropomorphic collection box for African missionaries, flanked on one side by a statuette of an erotic/exotic African woman and on the other by a Madonna with the Christ child.[21] But in general the notion of the fetish-object was not a negative one for the Surrealists; the Surrealist object, as theorized especially in the late 1920s and 30s, vindicated fetishism—sexual and otherwise. In a text from the 1930s, Bataille wrote that no connoisseur can love a work of art with the intensity with which a fetishist loves a shoe.[22] The Surrealist object was meant to be more akin to the fetishist's shoe than to the conventional work of art, more sexual fetish than ordinary commodity fetish—or rather, a commodity fetish revved up by allusions to sexual fetishism. The Freudian fetish, of course, is an object that stands in for the mother's absent phallus, in which the child wanted to believe; the fetish allows the infantile belief in the mother's phallus to survive, even against the subject's better judgment. A shoe, for instance, may serve as a stand-in for the phallus because of the lowly position from which the child looked up at the mother.

For the Surrealists, the sexual fetish was the perfect model for objects that allowed for more complex relationships between the subjective and the material—these were either produced by the Surrealists themselves or else they were *objets trouvés* found through objective chance at flea markets. The use of quaint, outmoded found objects—rather than new ones, as in the case of Duchamp's readymades—is crucial to Surrealism. Surrealism redeemed outdated commodities that had lost their original use value, recognizing in them a *promesse de bonheur* betrayed by history. Adorno appears to provide a theory for such a practice in a 1935 letter to Walter Benjamin (who was much closer to Surrealism than Adorno himself): "Since the use value of things gradually dies, the estranged things are hollowed out and become ciphers that attract new meanings. The subject appropriates them by projecting intentions of desire and fear onto them."[23] While this could be considered a theory of the objects found and made by the Surrealists at the time, these "useless" objects did regain a new use value in the end—as artistic commodities.

In Marx's analysis, art—visual art and otherwise—constituted a marginal category that could safely be discounted. In many respects, it remained artisanal and not fully integrated in capitalist surplus production. For Marx, capitalism is based on the difference between labor power purchased by the capitalist and the actual labor performed by the worker. Labor power, or "human labor in the abstract," is a standardized quantity expressed in wages.[24] A craftsman working independently does not create surplus value, and hence he does not generate capital. Only if he were employed in some company would this be the case; only then would he sell his labor power to an employer, who then pockets the difference between the price paid for this labor power and the labor actually performed. While Marx realized that publishers or gallery owners functioned as capitalist entrepreneurs, by and large, he considered art to be in the rearguard of the economy.[25] Nonetheless, as a quasi-autonomous entity ruled by obscure logic, Marx's commodity can be read as a macabre parody of the work of art. With the rise of the culture industry, art would become the ultimate commodity: the rearguard became the vanguard.

Until recently, works of visual art were unique rather than mass-produced; this made economic analysis, in terms of statistical averages such as labor power, extremely difficult. However, as mass (re)production increasingly penetrated art, and as the capitalist economy became increasingly "culturalized," the work of art attained a status that can be called exemplary. For Giorgio Agamben, the example is a singularity that transcends the opposition of universal and particular.[26] As a singularity, an example is always also an exception; the work of art is an exemplary commodity precisely *insofar as it is exceptional*. As the exemplary exception, the modern *and* the contemporary work of art can serve to focus on the changing status and even the changing nature of the object. If Modernist artists exacerbated their works' exceptional status through the formal purification of their idioms and by creating unique, hand-made pieces, artists in the Duchampian lineage created artistic commodities that are exceptional not as hermetic forms of Modernist withdrawal but as reflexive meta-commodities.[27] Their exception lies not in any claim to transcend the system, but in their mode of operating within it.

With the readymade—and its delayed reception in post-war art—the artistic commodity became, on the surface, all but indistinguishable from "regular" commodities, as artists became consumers who bought their works ready-made. However, as John Roberts has argued, this should not blind us to the fact that these artists also *produce* value: by recontextualizing pre-existing commodities, the artist performs an act of immaterial labor which not only, as Duchamp put it, "creates[s] a new thought for that object," but in doing so, also creates new value.[28] According to Marx, the exchange value of a commodity *actually* reflects the amount of labor invested in them—with the capitalist pocketing the surplus value that comes from purchasing the worker's labor power, rather than paying for specific amounts of labor done. Since the kind of labor performed by Duchamp is hardly quantifiable, his practice is perfectly attuned to an economy in which the "corporeal form" becomes valuable, not because of the work invested in it, but because it is seen to incarnate a "pure idea." In Marx's political economy, the commodity is defined as an object whose status as a *social* thing, as a product of labor, is obscured. Thus it appears as quasi-autonomous, endowed with a life of its own, measuring itself against other commodities on the market; in fact, however, the exchange value is determined by the labor invested in the commodity. The appearance of "autonomous" prices, determined by the interplay of various commodities on the market, is an illusion. But if an act of consumption—a mere choice—can produce value as Duchamp's example suggests, then the limits of the Marxian labor theory of value become all too apparent.

When—decades after they were "chosen"—Duchamp's readymades began fetching high prices, tabloid newspapers had a field day attacking the "absurd" prices paid by snobbish collectors for what were, after all, just urinals and bottle racks that one could buy for minimal cost at a hardware store. The work of art thus appears as supremely irrational, while the "behavior" of other goods on the market is experienced as natural; the work of art is then more irrational, more purely fetishistic, more regressive than the average commodity. What makes the exchange value of artworks particularly volatile is that they are speculative commodities akin to stocks: buyers gamble on their future value.[29] This would seem to set them apart from consumer goods, but the rise of "limited editions" of sneakers and other products reveals that certain brands seek to emulate art by producing scarce collectibles. While this is a somewhat marginal phenomenon, there is a much more fundamental way in which the artistic commodity has become a model for other commodities. As the work of art exposes itself as the absolute commodity, appearance and truth switch sides and the "archaic" proves to be economically progressive. Value is indeed increasingly determined by the "social relations" between the object and other commodities; the fetishist illusion becomes a reality.

When Duchamp stated that by turning a urinal into the readymade *Fountain,* he created "a new thought for that object," he might have been giving a definition for what Operaists such as Virno and Lazzarato later came to define as immaterial labor. However, this creation of "new thoughts" also raises questions about one of the central tenets of Operaismo, its glorification of the concrete labor performed by work as the *only* productive force, regarding the capitalist system itself as a mere parasite—and leaves unanswered the question of how capitalism was able to unleash productive forces in such an unprecedented way.[30] In the case of the readymade, Duchamp (or any other artist) does not actually create this value single-handedly, like a latter-day Romantic genius: critics, gallery owners, and indeed collectors all have a hand in it. The creation of value is an effect of the overall system. While one could still attempt to analyze this in traditional Marxian terms, as the sum of the labor-power invested in it by various parties, plus the surplus value, it is clear that the price of works of art develops a dynamic of its own that throws not only Operaism's labor fundamentalism into question but also its own footing: the Marxian labor theory of value itself.

Marx based all value on labor value, as an exemplary and eccentric commodity that enables the creation of value in the first place. However, the prices of a significant number of commodities have increasingly become unmoored from this fundamental form of exchange value; they have abstracted themselves from labor value to become a spectacle of quasi-autonomous prices. Such contemporary brands take cues from art—the exemplary commodity—by making fetishism a reality and a motor for growth.

CORPORATE TRANSCENDENCE

In Terry Eagleton's words, the commodity is "a schizoid, self-contradictory phenomenon, a mere symbol of itself, an entity whose meaning and being are entirely at odds and whose sensuous body exists only as the contingent bearer of an extrinsic form." If the commodity is "a mere symbol of itself," it is so because it is not identical to its material nature, which is merely the *pseudo-concrete* manifestation of its exchange-value.[31] Thus, the schizoid fetish becomes its own dematerialized double. Effectively, the Marxian notion of the commodity fetish is a montage of Enlightenment notions of the fetish and Romantic and Idealist theories of the *symbol*—another conceptual bastard son of the idol, but one seeking to rid the idol of its foundation in base matter, transmuting it alchemically into a dematerialized image. Thus the symbol prefigures the trajectory of the commodity as an increasingly "pure" image, as in the second-degree spectacle of cider advertisements and Liebig cards. During the 1840s, Marx studied both de Brosses's and Hegel's writings on the fetish, but the latter seem to have been less relevant for their conception of the commodity than for their take on the phase which, in Hegel's system, follows after that of fetishism: the culture of the symbol.[32] Hegel considered African fetishes characteristic of the lowest, sub-symbolic phase of religion. As an arbitrary object worshiped for irrational reasons, the fetish does not represent anything. In the evolution of Spirit it was followed by the symbol, which marked Egyptian religion and art.[33] As defined around 1800, the term *symbol* usually denoted the instantaneous visual manifestations of the absolute or of an idea, a perfect equilibrium of the real and the ideal in the form of an image. Schelling considered the gods of Greek mythology to be exemplary symbols; Goethe followed suit.[34]

While Hegel also saw Classical Greek art as a happy moment of perfection, he refused to characterize it as symbolic. By contrast, Hegel's pre-Greek, "oriental" symbol is the *failure* of an idea to fully manifest itself in an adequate form.[35] Hegel explains that the symbol is a "sensuous object," which is at the same time something more than that: for instance, the representation of a lion can symbolize "magnanimousness."[36] The site of conflict between content and form, the symbol is the bizarre or grotesque shotgun wedding between an idea that is still abstract and insufficiently determinate, and a sensuous form that cannot fully encapsulate this idea.[37]

This disconnect foreshadows Marx's take on the commodity—to employ Eagleton's words again—as "the site of some curious disturbance of the relations between spirit and sense, form and content, universal and particular: it is at once an object and not an object, 'perceptible and imperceptible by the senses' as he comments in *Capital*, a false concretizing but also a false abstracting of social relations."[38] Like Hegel's symbol, the Marxian commodity is a failed encounter between form and content, but the commodity's status as a representation (of social relations) is *obscured*. If the Hegelian symbol is a mythical connotation grafted onto a primary representation, in the case of the commodity, its magical, quasi-autonomous appearance is owed to the fact that this primary representation is disavowed, and the commodity appears to be autonomous.

In his *Symbolik und Mythologie der alten Völker*, the monumental Romantic mythology that saw several editions in the decades after its debut in 1810, Friedrich Creuzer also notes the symbol's "incongruence of essence and form," with its highly charged content and comparatively simple expression.[39] However, Creuzer did *not* see this as a reason to disparage the symbol; on the contrary, he used it as the basis for a romantic glorification of the symbol. Aren't dark intimations of profundity much more intriguing than clear statements or narratives? Creuzer contrasts the obscure and mysterious symbol with the banality of allegory, and in his view, *myth* is fatally allegorical. The original symbols, which were very crude signs for the cosmic or tellurian powers early humans worshiped, were later transformed into anthropomorphic gods. As these gods accrued elaborate myths, the instantaneous symbol was replaced by successive allegory.[40] Creuzer thus valorizes the "instantaneous" image over successive language; for him, the disparaged idol becomes an alluring symbol.

Creuzer exploits a fundamental ambiguity in the notion of the image. On the one hand, there are images executed in material media (the more physical the medium, the more easily it is suspect of idolatry), and on the other, there are mental images and visions devoid of such materiality. Like other Romantics and idealists, Creuzer rather slyly assimilates the former with the latter. When he mentions statues, these objects are only the material reflection of symbols, as it were, and they have value in so far as they are symbolic. Symbolic forms are only incidentally "corporeal." There are various types of symbols; through their obscurity and mysterious nature, many *mystic symbols* evince the problematic nature of any contraction and visual manifestation of the absolute, while in the *plastic symbols* of Greek art, the gods become beautiful.[41] The early Artemis (or Diana) of Ephesus, a fertility idol with large breasts and other symbolic attributes, over time became the beautiful goddess of the hunt known in classical Greek sculpture. This transition can be studied in Creuzer's illustrations, which show both the Artemis of Ephesus and her classical opposite, the Diana of Versailles (figs. 3.3 and 3.4). Creuzer's work is copiously illustrated with engravings belonging to the type of austere line drawing of which John Flaxman's Homer illustrations are significant early examples—and of which the Egyptian gods in Freud's Philippson Bible are later instances. The allure of this style of contour drawing was in its purifying effect; it abstracts from the concrete until only disembodied forms remain, subtly spiritualizing and dematerializing historical artifacts. In the realm of visual art, the contour drawing seemed as close to the sphere of pure ideas as one could get. Whether primitive, oriental, or classical, the images of the gods are cleansed in Creuzer's illustrations; it is not that they lack details, but rather all details shown are *necessary* details. This visual cleansing prepares the gods, both in their early and in their late incarnations, for Creuzer's symbolic reading.

Historically, one line of attack against idolatry was to argue that idols are mere material objects and worshiping them is foolish. By contrast, Creuzer stresses that they are matter stamped with symbolic meaning, and thus purified. The Hegelian symbol is spirit trapped in matter; the symbol's sensuous, material form is not adequate enough for its idea. This inadequacy is what makes symbols potentially sublime. They transcend the sensuous body, and in properly sublime symbolism this rift is emphasized.[42] Fundamentally, Creuzer agrees with this; we have seen that he, too, remarks on the "incongruence of essence and form" and he notes that symbols reflect the "world of ideas" through a medium that dims their light.[43] However, in practice, he does not focus on this medium's materiality, nor does he dwell much on the discrepancy between idea and form. It is therefore not surprising that the French translation of Creuzer's *Symbolik* boils down his notion of the symbol to this neat formula: "Pure ideas, dressed by corporeal forms, such are properly speaking symbols."[44] Here the whole question of inadequacy is dropped, and the "sensuous object" becomes an unquestioned manifestation of the transcendent idea. In any case, matter doesn't really matter: a divine symbol can be executed in any number of physical media; what matters is the image as a sensuous form hovering between matter and idea.

Creuzer's symbol can be seen as prefiguring the branded commodity. The brand is visualized in a logo, a quasi-symbol which, in turn, is stamped on a variety of objects. Naomi Klein notes that such commodities have become "empty carriers for the brand they represent. The metaphorical alligator, in other words, has risen up and swallowed the literal shirt."[45] Thus, the commodity is imprinted with a suitably Egyptian representation that symbolizes Lacoste-ness. The Lacoste crocodile relates to the shirt—or indeed to the archetypal fetish that is the shoe—as a Creuzerian divinity relates to its stone or wood medium. This becoming-symbol of the commodity is a logical outcome of commodity fetishism; the (commodity) fetish is always already a symbol of itself, its own spectral double. The "symbolic" value of the commodity—which at first was the systemic effect of productive relations and then later consciously masterminded by logo-design and branding—develops a dynamic of its own that turns illusion into reality. In the age of branded and expensive "designer water," symbolic value indeed becomes exchange value. Becoming-crocodile is the name of the game. At the same time, it must be noted that the commodity symbol radically exposes the differential and arbitrary character of Creuzer's symbols; whereas Creuzer's symbols laid claim to a platonic essence, the commodity is a semiological desublimation of such idealist symbol theory.

One can see this desublimation at work in Surrealist pieces such as Dalí's *objets à fonctionnement symbolique,* in eye-catching semiotic permutations and recombinations—telephone meets lobster. The object became a focus of Surrealist activity at the time of the groups' uneasy affiliation with the French Communist Party, which also resulted in the anti-colonial exhibition of 1931; the production of tangible objects seemed one way of countering the accusation of idealism and dreamy escapism.[46] After all, subjective desires are objectified, made tangible, in the object. Breton quoted Hegel to the effect that the art object lies "between the sensible and the rational. It is something spiritual that appears as material."[47] Hence, Breton anticipated the rhetoric of contemporary capitalism, according to which commodities are almost accidental materializations of a transcendent brand identity. Freud had stripped the symbol of its idealist trappings by redefining it as a contingent sign that must be decoded by reconstructing processes of censorship and displacement. It is these differential symbols that Dalí imprinted on his objects, abstracting them from the complex interplay of symbol and symptom, turning them into trademarks. One of Dalí's objects takes the archetypal sexual fetish, the shoe, as its point of departure. In the shoe is a glass of milk, above which dangles a sugar lump with an image of a shoe; other sugar cubes are stored by the heel of the shoe. For Dalí, the dipping of the shoe sign into milk evoked an Oedipal return to the mother, a loss of self by lacteal baptism (fig. 3.5).[48]

While Dalí's shoe seems to metonymically anchor his symbolism in the body, its sugar-based reproductions seem to signal that shoes and everything else become uprooted signs in a perpetual game of recombination. In the end, such objects would become logos for the Dalí brand—the birth of the branded commodity from the spirit of Surrealism, with special thanks to Marcel Duchamp. At the 1938 Charles Ratton exhibition of surrealist objects, Duchamp's *Bottlerack* (alternatively titled *Hedgehog*) entered into a dialogue with Dalí's even more explicitly phallic *Aphrodisiac Jacket*—a dinner jacket covered with glasses of crème de menthe with straws in them. Such a work, which essentially reverts to the most obvious form of phallic symbolism, makes the play of signifiers in Duchamp's readymades more explicit. Duchamp already turned his chosen objects into doubles of themselves through the act of selection, which makes one look for "family resemblances" between them (as well as between them and non-readymade work by Duchamp), and by using titular puns and other textual supplements. In this way, Duchamp turned his consumption into a form of "immaterial" production.

In 1970, Marcel Broodthaers had gold bars stamped with an eagle as part of the "Section financière" of his *Musée d'Art Moderne, département des aigles* (fig. 3.6). The eagle, a symbol of power and Empire which Broodthaers traced from ancient art to modern advertising, here becomes a logo for Broodthaers's own practice and for what Rosalind Krauss termed the "eagle principle" of Conceptual art, which signals the general—the concept—taking precedence over material or visual specifics.[49] Broodthaers determined that his gold ingots should be sold for twice the market price of gold, the surplus representing the value added by its status as art. With his eagle logo, Broodthaers announced a situation in which the material commodity becomes the reproduction of a brand logo, a symbol scattered into history—a history of repetitive innovation—commanding prices that are barely related to the labor invested in the object..

ABSOLUTE SIGNS

For a long time, Romantic/Idealist conceptions of the symbol as instantaneous apparition of an idea in a sensuous form reigned supreme in modern culture and modern art. In the end, however, all genealogies of the symbol seem to end in practices of radical de-symbolization. In the twentieth century the symbol became not only increasingly formalized, but also freed from tradition and convention; with Kandinsky, its meaning came to lie exclusively in its formal and chromatic characteristics. This formal symbol was picked up in the 1940s by American artists, including Newman and Rothko, whose work Greenberg described as a "new indigenous school of symbolism."[50] Newman argued that the pre-war European Modernists had still been too naturalistic by circumscribing the absolute in "measureable" forms; real symbols needed to break out of such geometrics, to be both abstract and sublime, and hence expansive. This symbolic aesthetic was threatened by practices that seemed to collapse art into the spectacle; Newman argued that Duchamp's readymades had helped to create a situation in which museums "show screwdrivers and automobiles and paintings" without making a fundamental distinction between them. Duchamp's readymades and the designs of "Bauhaus screwdriver designers" both claimed to be art, and thus were two manifestations of the same fundamental problem.[51] Against all attempts to blur boundaries, Newman maintained, in a thoroughly Creuzerian way, that "[the] God image, not pottery, was the first manual act."[52] One can characterize the tradition that culminates in Newman as that of the symbolic anti-spectacle; its entanglement with the commodity denied, the symbol is seen as the true domain of art and of "man"; opposed to a capitalist culture decried as materialistic and positivistic.

Newman pits the symbol against the fetish, Creuzer against de Brosses. But in spite of efforts by various Symbolist and abstract artists, the twentieth century saw the definitive demise of the dream of the symbol as an anti-idol, an instantaneous form of sensuous knowledge. As Adorno put it, "Art absorbs symbols by no longer having them symbolize anything... Modernity's ciphers and characters are signs that have forgotten themselves and become absolute."[53] This development can already be seen in Newman's work, in which the relation between titles and Newman's idiom of color planes and "zips" is opaque; by emphasizing the rift between content and form, which would later so upset Panofsky in the case of *Vir Heroicus Sublimis*, Newman may be said to have created properly *sublime* symbols à la Hegel. However, by the 1960s, younger artists such as Frank Stella would distance themselves from all symbolic pretentions. Stella permutated forms in a more systematic manner than Newman ever did, methodically working through formal options in one series after another. One critic noted the collusion of such art with the rigidity of corporate innovation when he observed "how often recent American painting is defined and described almost exclusively in terms of internal problem-solving.... The dominant formalist critics today tend to treat modern painting as an evolving technology wherein at any moment specific tasks require solution—tasks set for the artists as tasks are set for researchers in the big corporations."[54]

The results also *looked* corporate—serially executed in industrial paint, with compositions that recalled post-war logos, which are equally centralized and geometric. Caroline Jones, who compared Stella's *Sidney Guberman* (1963) to the 1960 logo for Chase Manhattan Bank, noted that in the post-war years corporate logos were increasingly simplified, moving "away from narrative and toward iconicity," so as to "form a visual imprint, as if *branded* on the retina."[55] Here, Jones is paraphrasing Stella himself—both artist and corporation aim to create signs that speak of innovation, and hence always refer to older and competing signs; in this sense, they are resolutely post-symbolic. In the "Protractor" series of the late 1960s and early 70s, Stella's quasi-logos would become more expansive and centrifugal, the paintings' interlocked and overlapping arcs suggesting that the more centralized and contained "retinal stamps" Stella produced earlier in the decade still had too many traces of quasi-symbolic autonomy (fig. 3.7).

If Creuzer's symbolic gods prefigured the branded commodity, Stella's work drives home the point that the commodity's realization of Creuzer's idea can only take place if the radical contingency of Creuzer's beloved symbols is acknowledged and exploited through the calculated permutation of arbitrary signs. Such a desublimation had already been performed in the mid-nineteenth century by Gustave Flaubert, who read Creuzer against the grain in his *La Tentation de Saint Antoine*. Since Walter Benjamin diagnosed an "empathy with the commodity" in the work of Gustave Flaubert, it is perhaps not surprising that Flaubert had already engaged in a thorough deconstruction of the prelapsarian visual plenitude Creuzer ascribed to his symbols.[56] The "episode of the gods" in *The Temptation of Saint Anthony* is studded with information culled from J. P. Guigniaut's French translation and reworking of the *Symbolik*. In his youth, this book had been something of a talisman to Flaubert and his friend Alfred Le Poittevin, but *The Temptation of Saint Anthony* thoroughly undermines Creuzer's aesthetic theology of the symbol.[57] Flaubert does, however, share an anti-narrative bias with the German author. *The Temptation* is a novel masquerading as a play, consisting mainly of a series of monologues and dialogues that alternate with descriptive passages. The result reads like a series of staged tableaux; it is a parade, a succession of temptations. Among them are pagan gods. For Anthony, temptation lies not so much in an inclination to worship them, but on the contrary, in the realization that these absurd and pathetic false gods were once actually worshiped. Now they are dead; might not the one true God meet with a similar fate in the future? While Creuzer aimed to reconstruct the original symbols before they degenerated into myth, before they fell from timelessness into history and anecdote, the fall of the symbol is the raison d'être of his book, and its effect cannot be undone; what else is his book, other than an inventory of dead symbols? Hence in *The Temptation,* deities appear in front of the early Christian hermit as dead gods. If they can die and lose the meaning they once had, then this meaning is historical and must have accrued in a more haphazard fashion than Creuzer allows for. It is as decontextualized, yet persistent, signs that the dead gods continue haunting the present, or Anthony's mind. No wonder that Freud owned several copies of *The Temptation*, although he misremembered a crucial detail: in *Moses and Monotheism,* Freud remarks that if the new Israelite religion had not succeeded, Jahve would have "taken his place in the procession of erstwhile gods which Flaubert visualized," apparently forgetting that Jahve *is* in fact part of Flaubert's parade.[58]

In the original 1849 version of *The Temptation of Saint Anthony,* the temptation of Anthony is still presented more or less as a "real" temptation by the devil and his minions. In the final version of 1874 it is clear that Anthony is hallucinating.[59] Himself a compiler, the delirious saint conjures up the gods, beliefs, and monsters known to antiquity, specifically to late Alexandrian antiquity. After all, the recluse's abode is not too far from Alexandria, the great capital of syncretistic scholarship, where he spent part of his life and where he was trained by Tertullian—who has a brief cameo as an iconoclastic fanatic. Historians had long presented the influx of "oriental" cults in the late Roman Empire as an important symptom or even cause of its decadence, and most of the deities that visit the hermit are Eastern. To a nineteenth-century European Orientalist sensibility, they appeared absurd and grotesque, yet also mysterious and alluring—a far cry from the plastic symbols of Greek art.[60] As a historical subject, Flaubert was part and parcel of a culture of colonial projection on the Orient, yet *The Temptation of Saint Anthony* goes well beyond standard Orientalism in suggesting that all ex-idols (and, implicitly, those still in service) are equally absurd.[61] In the first version of the "episode of the gods," the "classical" gods were part of the same parade as the others, but in the final version Jupiter and his associates enjoy the separate stage of Mount Olympus, where they dwell as plastic symbols, as beautiful forms.[62] Early in Flaubert's parade, among the "oriental" deities, we meet "the great Diana of Ephesus"; she is described exactly as she appears in Creuzer's text and image: "black, with enamel eyes, elbows against her sides, outstretched forearms, open hands."[63] This quintessential moon and fertility goddess is later followed by a "classical" Diana, goddess of the hunt, in the Olympus scene. In treating these Dianas as different beings, rather than the latter as a transformation of the former, Flaubert emphasizes the differential nature of signs; the two Dianas are equally conventional, equally absurd, and both are ex-parrots.

Given this predilection for juxtaposing incompatibilities, it is not surprising that Flaubert introduces a competing genealogy of divine images that clashes with Creuzer's narrative of aboriginal symbols. Before the walking and talking (un)dead gods, a procession of mute and merely material idols passes by Anthony: "Before them, idols of all nations and ages pass—made of wood, metal, granite, feathers, sewn skins."[64] By focusing on these idols' materiality and on cruel practices—human sacrifices—associated with them, Flaubert presents an alternate (and, to be sure, equally oneiric) picture of religion as originating from crude human practices rather than from aboriginal, symbolical wisdom. It is telling that Flaubert has no qualms about using the term "idol" in this context: while it was scarcely applied to classical sculpture (except perhaps by fire-and-brimstone Protestants), the term remained in wide use for objects belonging to "primitive" cultures, both ancient and contemporary. But before the procession of idols, there is an even more curious parade of objects: "and over the ground he sees passing by some leaves, stones, shells, tree branches, vague representations of animals; then some kinds of dropsical dwarfs; these are gods."[65] The first items mentioned are highly orthodox Brossean fetishes; in a move that is as iconoclastic as his portrayal of Jahve, Flaubert introduces fetishism as the repressed truth of the symbol. This could be brushed aside as a form of primitivism; have we not already argued that, on the contrary, the symbol is the truth of the fetish? What is crucial here is that Flaubert hones in on the arbitrary nature of the Brossean shells and twigs, and reveals the Creuzerian symbols to be just as arbitrary. Isn't this precisely the characteristic of the "African" fetish that returns with Marx's commodity fetish—if only to be unmasked as an illusion?

In *The Temptation*—and, more spectacularly, in *Salammbô*—the past is seen as a series of tableaux which are so precise as to be almost inorganic: shop-windows of the past. While Creuzer created a narrative of the gods' fall into allegory, Flaubert's paradoxical literature enacts the symbol's fall into a history that is oddly enumerative, like a sales catalogue. History becomes a dissecting table on which an umbrella meets a sewing machine. Flaubert's history is an abstract plane, blank space rather than historical process, a surface upon which various ruined symbols can be set side by side. Both shells and gods, fetishes and symbols, are ghosts of their former selves. They mourn not only their death, but also their uncanny resurrection as textual commodity-images. Flaubert thus prefigured the break of twentieth-century semiology as well as that of Freudian psychoanalysis with the Romantic/Idealist conception of the symbol by emphasizing the conventional and differential nature of signs—of language, but also, in one way or another, of various types of images. Flaubert's writing is an exercise in desymbolization.[66] He announced a time in which the "corporeal forms" in which "pure ideas" manifest themselves are revealed to be "empty carriers for the brand they represent."

In art, the lure of exclusive materials and unique objects is still strong, but even in the most extreme cases of conspicuous consumption, materials are primarily used for their sign-value. In August 2007, at the height of the art market boom, Damien Hirst's *For the Love of God,* a diamond-encrusted metal skull which garnered huge publicity as "the most expensive work of art ever created," sold for $100 million, some five to ten times the value of materials and labor invested in it. The creation of a unique diamond skull is an exercise in producing an auratic work shrouded in a carefully manufactured myth, an object whose exhibition value—to use Walter Benjamin's terminology—depends on cult value.[67] No wonder that in 2008 Hirst could not resist making *The Golden Calf* for the auction of his work held at Sotheby's, just as the financial markets were collapsing. The work consists of a pickled bull with a gold disk above its head—a reference to the Egyptian bull deity Apis, who was worshiped through the veneration of real bulls, and who is often regarded as the model for the biblical golden calf.[68]

Such practices are illuminating in their obscenity: they reveal the illusion of commodity fetishism in the process of creating its own reality. The artist told the press that by using the skull, he wanted to "celebrate life by saying to hell with death," by taking "the ultimate symbol of death and covering it in the ultimate symbol of luxury, desire and decadence."[69] Rather than instilling awe, the reduction of historical *vanitas* symbolism to a set of highly obvious and logo-like signs seems intended to induce a Warholesque emptiness, a fetishistic enjoyment of the pure surface of the commodity.[70] The success of the oeuvre is not so much due to the profundity of Hirst's "ultimate symbols," but to their *desymbolized* status. His artistic strategies barely dissimulate the conventional and coded character of the process of signification; rather than aboriginal and essential symbols, we are dealing with a semiotic industry of repetition and difference.

ALWAYS AESTHETICIZE!

In the post-colonial empire of global capitalism, farming out production to low-wage countries allows labor-power to be purchased for prices unrelated to wages in the countries where most of the products will be sold. For branded goods, expensive advertising and branding campaigns are, of course, necessary. But if successful, the result is that their exchange value is actually partially determined by their relation to other brands, for instance, the crocodile's relationship to the swoosh, or the eagle. One could say, with Jean Baudrillard, that we have moved from production to reproduction, that material goods now reproduce their own image. In his early work *Pour une critique de l'économie politique du signe,* Baudrillard insisted that fetishism must be defined not as some archaic magical force, but as "a generalized code of signs, a completely arbitrary (*faictice*, "fétiche") code of différences..."[71]

Like Deleuze, Baudrillard appropriated the term simulacrum to refer to "bad" signs, to untrustworthy eidolons, but whereas Deleuze celebrated these bad copies, Baudrillard indicted them with the fervor of a secular Tertullian.[72] In the spurious code whose theoretician he became—the desymbolized symbol of corporate idealism—the alleged arbitrariness of de Brosses's fetishes reasserts itself as the guiding principle of the commodity's symbolic value. Around 1970, Baudrillard supplemented the categories of use value and exchange value with his concept of *sign value*.[73] While exchange value is based on "equivalence," sign value is based on "difference." The difference between Brand A and Brand B is expressed in prices that are subject to the law of exchange and hence of equivalence.[74] However, sign value is not in a merely passive relation to exchange value; everything about Baudrillard's analysis suggests that sign value came to play such an important role because the circulation of sign value can *create* exchange value. Baudrillard thus broke with what he regarded as a Marxian fetishization of use value, which is just a case of nostalgia for a lost referent.[75]

Taking cues from Baudrillard's exploration of sign value, 1980s theories of postmodernism often diagnosed and criticized the "aestheticization" of capitalism, the "cultural turn" of the economy which completed the commodification of art. But what appears to be aestheticization can also be seen as an *impoverishment* of the aesthetic. There is a chance in proper aestheticization, if one refuses to limit the notion of the aesthetic to the play of commodified pseudo-symbols, and instead subjects the aesthetic to a wide set of questions pertaining to the sensible—including the (in)visibility of labor conditions and ecological costs. It is not that sign value must be iconoclastically smashed in order to resurrect some state of normality; rather, one needs to intervene in the signs' complexity and contradictions, to question the conditions under which their programmed surfaces came into being. If we reverse the perspective suggested by quasi-idealist narratives, that of a capitalism abstracting itself from the constraints of matter to such a degree that commodities become the practically indifferent bearers of transcendental corporate ideas, the commodity may be seen as doubly concrete, as the convergence of two trajectories of the incarnation of abstraction. Thus, "platonic" contemporary commodities contain potential for materialist practice.

To what state of affairs does a crocodile-adorned label stating that shirt or shoe was "Made in Peru" actually refer? Various organizations have already tried to raise consumer awareness of their banks' investments; if one bank invests heavily in destructive industries, why not switch to a bank that is demonstrably "cleaner"? Obviously, the danger is that this remains a merely cosmetic operation, while business goes on as usual. We are only very tentatively beginning to experience such a politics of visibility, which is constantly sidetracked and diverted by discussions of "product pirating" and intellectual copyright, or moralizing reports about child labor that seem designed to evade structural issues. Yet here, in the political aesthetics of things, lies the greatest chance to arrive at a revolutionary contestation of (and in) its circulation of commodities. After all, if the project of "rerouting the trajectory of things," to use David Joselit's phrase, entails more than a bit of feng shui to keep contemporary capitalism healthy, it will eventually have to amount to change radical enough to merit the term "revolution."[76] The rearrangement of the furniture would have to be radical indeed.

To reroute the trajectories of things, one first has to transform objects into things. As W. J. T. Michell puts it, objects are things that circulate within a total system. "Things" themselves "play the role of a raw material, an amorphous, shapeless, brute materiality awaiting organization into a system of objects."[77] In our society, this system of objects comprises the various forms of the commodity—in particular its most visible form: branded consumer goods. Transforming such pseudo-aesthetic fetishes might be called a transition from *objecthood* to *thingness*, but not in the sense of some primitivist return to "shapeless materiality". Rather, the aim should be to make the system visible in order to effect change in (and, ultimately, beyond) it. As Mitchell says, things "have a habit of breaking out of the circuit," of subverting the order of objects.[78] Latour calls this the transformation of seemingly self-evident objects into things that amount to "matters of concern" which are therefore open to questioning.[79] Here, Latour is at his most apposite, and his project is all the more urgent for echoing a long tradition; the Marxian tradition itself focused attention on human-thing interfaces, studying existing relationships in order to sketch possible alternatives—alternatives that would not result in some auto-da-fé of objects, but in a *different* production and use of things.

While the original notion of fetishism presupposed that Africans live in quasi-pathological dependency upon arbitrary objects, and while at times Marxian critiques of alienation and reification seem to betray an idealist horror of any form of dependency on objects, at their most cogent, Marxian thinking and practice sought to *liberate* rather than destroy the object along with the subject. Writing to his wife from capitalist Paris in 1925, Aleksandr Rodchenko proclaimed: "Our things in our hands must be equals, comrades."[80] The object was supposed to become a thing that was free to develop a "life" of its own, beyond its instrumentalization; the intent was to turn the object into a quasi-subject. Here we have a positive *détournement* of the notion of fetishism: is not the object as "comrade" the *real* fetish, a quasi-subject engaging in actual social relations with people, rather than staging a pseudo-social spectacle? The aim of the revolution would thus not be the suppression of the commodity, but its *liberation*. However, the socialist thing of which Rodchenko dreamt has remained elusive, indeed symbolical, taking the form of sparse and transparently constructed objects. But the articulation of a new politics of thing-ness needs utopian gestures as much as concrete actions. Transforming commodity-objects into matters of concern would involve, for instance, the realization that production and distribution do not obey quasi-natural laws, that they are open to contestation.

We have already suggested that capitalism has created an apparent dynamism that serves as a parodic fulfillment of Trotsky's famous slogan of permanent revolution. Gerald Raunig's gloss on anti-globalist activities as a series of events that would ultimately constitute a perpetual revolution fails to take this context fully into account: we already live in an anticipatory parody of the aesthetic revolution.[81] The crucial question is how this continually "re-territorialized" pseudo-revolution can be hijacked and reverse-engineered. In the late 1990s, anti-brand activism began by opposing the pseudo-aesthetic economy, in which value has become decoupled from labor, in which the fetishist illusion has become programmed reality. The broader anti-globalist movement, of which such activities were one aspect, could at least be seen as beginning to contest the empire of global capitalism. The carefully orchestrated "clash of civilizations," which has been ongoing since September 11, has successfully displaced questions of political economy with oneiric discussions about western versus non-western "values"; for some years, the impact of continuing activism was markedly less significant. In effect, "the West" and "Islam" have been transformed into super brands that enthrall the consumers of the fundamentalist spectacle. However, in an age of escalating ecological problems and a growing global food and resources crisis, the time is ripe to once more contest the current system of objects and "turn the oppressive 'facts' of life into just forms." Those who attend to this project can, if they are so inclined, fully claim to be true representatives of idolatry critique, and hence of monotheism. Everything else is everything else.

THE REALITY OF ABSTRACTION

The creation of things out of objects must not be seen as some move toward a more "real," less abstract society. If things to come strip off the commodity's pseudo-concrete appearance, it will be in order to *set abstraction free* from its current constraints. Rather than trying to smash Baudrillardian sign value in order to resurrect some state of normality, one must intervene in this semiotic regime to bring out the complexity and contradictions of signs: to read them as symptoms of repressed social content. In this sense, the quasi-platonic airs of contemporary branded commodities actually contain a potential for materialist practice. While it is imperative that the limits of today's pseudo-concrete commodities be left behind, future thing-ness cannot be a return to some dreamed-of state of pure concretion. A politics/aesthetics of things does not aim to fight abstraction as such, but to fight the creation of value through branding and intellectual property laws, which are tailor-made to propagate economic inequality and create ecological disasters whose consequences are unevenly felt. If there is any future at all, it will be abstract.

The exacerbation and exploitation of surplus value in art, à la Hirst or Koons, is by now only of limited analytical interest. What matters is the development of commodities that point beyond self-congratulatory capitalism—inverted readymades that are no longer content to create artistic surplus value, but rather investigate conditions for other objects, things that might indeed be "comrades." This should not be seen as a political instrumentalization of art; the stakes are indeed aesthetic, in that the modern aesthetic project was never about what the debased sense of the term "aesthetic" supposedly refers to—good design and the profane transcendence of "pure beauty." In the current political and economic situation, it is more crucial than ever to counter reductive aestheticism and stimulate the development of a political aesthetic. This, however, should not be conceived as a neo-Situationist erasure of all difference: in today's "culturalized" capitalism, such erasure is a problematic fact rather than an ideal to be realized. This is why further demonstration of surplus value production in the vein of Duchamp is now irrelevant: what matters is the development of (approaches to) things that point beyond the current destruction of entire continents and populations—and, in artistic terms, beyond the surplus value production of readymades and Surrealist objects.

Allan Sekula's photo series, writings, and films from his *Fish Story* project onwards chart the abstract structure of global capitalism. Sekula seeks to counter two interrelated manifestations of fetishism: the disavowal of the material conditions of commodity production and distribution, and the "spiritualizing" discourse on the post-industrial condition and "informatization" of the economy. A lecture diagram by Sekula—a thoroughly non-Creuzerian line drawing—depicts a hierarchy of commodities: the top layer of "consumer goods" is most visible to the eye, particularly branded goods such as the Disneyfied Winnie-the-Pooh dolls whose journey from manufacturer to consumers was traced by Sekula and Noël Burch in a film script (fig. 3.8).[82] The two layers below, including "raw materials" at the bottom, are all but invisible, and it is this invisibility as well as the complementary overvaluation of hyper-visible branded goods—of quasi-symbols like Pooh—that Sekula seeks to counteract. But one or more layers should perhaps be added to Sekula's diagram, *above* the eye, above the "classic" commodity-image. All these levels interact. The current financial crisis has also thrown the market for Sekula's "raw materials"—the commodity market—into turmoil; while these commodities are apparently pure material concretion, they are simultaneously their own digital monetary doubles, changing value and ownership according to transactions in a global data network.

Proper materialism cannot be content to privilege more pseudo-concrete industrial products over more purely abstract informational commodities, let alone dream of a return to gift economies. It is crucial to go beyond such nostalgia. On the other hand, theories of immaterial labor, post-Fordism, and other accounts of the progressive dematerialization of capitalism can unwittingly become complicit with triumphal accounts of a "new," post-industrial, quasi-platonic digital economy such as the one that accompanied the "New Economy" some years ago—accounts that are oneiric, in that they promise economic growth without accepting the material conditions and consequences. Flaubert wonderfully encapsulated his snarling rejection of idealist pretension in the Olympus scene of *The Temptation*, in which an "idealist" Apollo exclaims: "No! Enough forms! Further still! Toward the top! Into the pure idea!" even as he plunged into the abyss with his chariot.[83] This tableau can be regarded as an emblematic prefiguration of the looming ecological collapse—matter comes back to haunt "transcendental" capitalism, which claims to abstract itself beyond matter. But was not the commodity always pseudo-concrete, abstract to the core? Is there any basis at all for positing a narrative of increasing abstraction?

In the *Grundrisse,* Marx criticized Hegel's fallacy of "conceiving the real as the product of thought concentrating itself"; after all, "the method of rising from the abstract to the concrete [moving from abstract concepts to concrete analysis – SL] is only the way in which thought appropriates the concrete, reproduces it as the concrete in the mind. But this is by no means the process by which the concrete itself comes into being."[84] On the basis of Marx's remarks on abstraction in the *Grundrisse*, various Marxists have argued that abstraction is no longer purely "ideal" or conceptual under capitalism, but a social reality; it is "real abstraction" of labor-power and, by extension, of all exchange.[85] If the seemingly completely physical commodity is really abstract to the core, abstraction itself is a concrete reality. Guy Debord noted that "the abstract nature of all individual work, as of production in general, finds perfect expression in the spectacle, whose very *manner of being concrete* is, precisely, abstraction."[86] It is thus *exchange* —of labor as a commodity—that creates the real abstraction of relations between pseudo-concrete commodities. In a process that is as liberating as it is destructive, capitalism extracts people and goods from feudal social bonds, replacing them with the abstract bond of exchange value; as Adorno emphasized, the "universal implementation" of exchange in capitalism abstracts from qualitative aspects of the relation between producer and consumer, reducing all relationships to abstract links of exchange.[87]

As Vilém Flusser noted, to abstract means to subtract, and specifically to subtract data from matter; throughout history, abstraction has been a movement toward information.[88] The reduction to pure exchange value is part of this process of abstraction, but it is not the final word. While the idealist turn of capitalism in the age of the brand dissimulates the reality of abstract exchange by giving it a platonic face, camouflaging the rule of equivalence with the play of different brand ideas, it would be a mistake to assume that identifying exchange as "real" abstraction is sufficient reason to dismiss all consideration of the transformations of capitalism in the twentieth and twenty-first centuries. When the logo desublimates the symbol by revealing it to be a contingent sign that creates value through exchangeability, this can be seen as a further step toward the abstraction and hence the "spiritualization" of the object; however, while the quasi-platonic logo may pretend to exist in Creuzerian independence from the lowly shoe, its "incarnation" in the shoe changed exchange itself by turning fetishism into operative reality. But what if the shoe is a computer-designed contemporary sneaker, manufactured from advanced synthetic fibers? In the digital age, it is not so much that objects are transformed into signs, into their own quasi-symbolic doubles; rather, producing them is a matter of programming from the start. The brand logos and their interplay are only the visual manifestation of a binary *logos*. The abstract reality of the contemporary spectacle springs from the fusion of exchange and technology. This is what Baudrillard's notion of "sign value" announced, even if it was still predicated, to some extent, on older industrial models

Materialism can never mean nostalgia for Brossean shells, for some primitive "real." One may rejoice in the fact that "value-added brands" such as Starbucks have to close branches as consumers become more reluctant to pay more for a brand's sign value, but in their mystificatory platonic register, the quasi-symbols of branded capitalism have shown the reality of abstraction as the proper subject for analysis. In September 2008, when the "credit crunch" morphed into a full-blown financial and economic crisis, the *Guardian* quoted Pulp singer Jarvis Cocker's gleeful remark: "It's really nice seeing capitalism getting its come-uppance," since capitalism had progressed beyond the understandable level of "companies that make real products" to that of "organisations that just make money … that's abstract capitalism, it's beyond most ordinary—people—and I include myself among them. I mean, you see the FTSE index, or whatever, running along the bottom of the TV screen and generally it just doesn't impinge at all on the way you live your life, and then suddenly you're told your life is going to take a nosedive. Who understands that?"[89]

Who, indeed? Attacking the "abstract" nature of hyper-capitalism certainly does nothing to further anyone's understanding. Sub-prime mortgages and various arcane types of investment may be complex "financial products" that are difficult to understand, but they—like all financial transactions—undergo a qualitative change by becoming digitized and going online: even while they seem to reach the peak of abstraction, in this very abstraction their entanglement in the concrete affairs of daily life becomes ever more pervasive, ever more apparent. Every increase in abstraction is a step in the increasing *concretion of abstraction itself.*

"Attending to things invisible" takes on a new meaning when "immaterial" reason penetrates and transforms matter to an unprecedented degree, as increasing abstraction results precisely in the becoming-real of abstraction and in a *materialization* of the conceptual, of the immaterial. In an age in which objects are digitally designed and tested in simulations, does not the real indeed become "the product of thought, concentrating itself"?

NOTES

1 Carl Andre, "Capitalist Alchemy" [undated], in *Cuts: Texts 1959–2004,* ed. James Meyer (Cambridge, MA: MIT Press, 2005), 71.

2 As has been argued in the previous chapter, images of the Prophet are not unheard of in Islam—although, as a rule, his likeness is not used to sell meat extracts.

3 Thomas a Kempis, *The Imitation of Christ,* quoted in Carlos M. N. Eire, *War Against the Idols: The Reformation of Worship from Erasmus to Calvin* (Cambridge: Cambridge University Press, 1986), 33.

4 Ali Shariati, *Hajj* (*The Pilgrimage*), http://www.al-islam.org/hajj/shariati/25.htm.

5 Geert Wilders and Martin Bosma, "Het probleem is de Islam, niet de moslims," in *de Volkskrant,* March 22, 2008, http://www.volkskrant.nl/binnenland/article518395.ece/Islam_is_het_probleem,_niet_de_moslims?service=Print. Wilders and Bosma claim that Islam is "more of a political ideology than a religion," and as a political ideology it is similar to fascism (which itself was "the new Islam").

6 Abdolkarim Soroush, "Militant Secularism" (August 2007), http://www.drsoroush.com/English/On_DrSoroush/E-CMO-2007-Militant%20Secularism.html.

7 For all the criticisms that have been made of Weber's thesis in *Die protestantische Ethik und der Geist des Kapitalismus* (first published as a two-part article in 1904/05, then as a book in 1920), his argument that the strongly transcendental God of radical Protestantism led to a *Weltzugewandtheit,* rather than to withdrawal from the world, remains important. See Max Weber, *Die protestantische Ethik,* vol. I, ed. Johannes Winkkelmann (Hamburg: Siebenstern, 1973), 73–76f.

8 Syed Nawab Haider Naqvi, *Islam, Economics, and Society* (London/New York: Kegan Paul International, 1996), 163.

9 Latour's analysis, developed in *We Have Never Been Modern,* trans. Catherine Porter (Cambridge, MA: Harvard University Press, 1993), has been repeated and developed in a number of writings since then. Part of Latour's project is also an attempt to rehabilitate the fetish; see *Petite réflexion sur le culte moderne des dieux faitiches* (Paris: Éditions Synthélabo, 1996).

10 Terry Eagleton, *The Ideology of the Aesthetic* (Oxford: Blackwell Publishing, 1990), 209.

11 "Le spectacle est le *capital* à un tel degré d'accumulation qu'il devient image." Guy Debord, *La Société du Spectacle* [1967] (Paris: Gallimard, 1992), 32. English translation by Donald Nicholson-Smith, http://www.cddc.vt.edu/sionline/si/tsots01.html.

12 "Ihre Analyse ergibt, daß sie ein sehr vertracktes Ding ist, voll metaphysischer Spitzfindigkeiten und theologischer Mucken." Karl Marx, "Das Kapital" [1872 edition], in *Marx/Engels Gesamtausgabe (MEGA)*, part 2, vol. 6 (text) (Berlin: Dietz, 1987), 102.

13 The Situationists contrasted the perversion of art that is spectacle with their utopia of a non-alienated life of play and "constructed situations," which itself is clearly an aesthetic one. The spectacle is a prophetic parody, as it were, of this future world; the parody precedes the original.

14 See chapter 1.

15 Meyer Schapiro, "Nature of Abstract Art" [1937], in *Modern Art: 19th and 20th Centuries. Selected Papers* (New York: George Braziller, 1968), 200.

16 "Ces Fétiches divins ne sont autre chose que le premier objet matériel qu'il plaît à chaque nation ou à chaque particulier de choisir et de faire consacrer en cérémonie par ses prêtres: c'est un arbre, une montagne, la mer, un morceau de bois, une queue de lion, un caillou, une coquille, du sel, un poisson, une plante, une fleur, un animal d'une certaine espèce, comme vache, chèvre, éléphant, mouton; enfin tout ce qu'on peut s'imaginer en pareil." Charles de Brosses, *Du culte des Dieux Fétiches ou Parallèle de l'ancienne Religion de l'Égypte avec la religion actuelle de Nigritie* [1760] (Paris: Librairie Arthème Fayard, 1988), 15.

17 Karl-Heinz Kohl, *Die Macht der Dinge: Geschichte und Theorie sakraler Objekte* (Munich: C. H. Beck, 2003), 201.

18 *African Negro Art,* exh. cat., ed. James Johnson Sweeney (New York: Museum of Modern Art, 1935), cat. no. 489.

19 "Von der Autonomie der Kunstwerke … ist nichts übrig, als der Fetischkarakter der Ware, Regression auf den archaischen Fetischismus im Ursprung der Kunst." Theodor W. Adorno, "Ästhetische Theorie," in *Gesammelte Schriften,* vol. 7, ed. Gretel Adorno and Rolf Tiedemann (Frankfurt am Main: Suhrkamp, 1972), 33.

20 Dieter Daniels, *Duchamp und die anderen: Der Modellfall einer künstlerischen Wirkungsgeschichte in der Moderne* (Cologne: DuMont, 1992), 219–220.

21 In his important book on Surrealism in the 1930s, Steven Harris suggests that this quasi-triptych may represent sexual fetishes (the woman), economic fetishes (the collection box), and religious fetishes (the Virgin Mary; Dalí had earlier proposed an exhibition of "Catholic fetishes"). Steven Harris, *Surrealist Art and Thought in the 1930s: Art, Politics, and the Psyche* (Cambridge: Cambridge University Press, 2004), 53–54, 70–71.

22 Georges Bataille, "L'esprit moderne et le jeu des transpositions" [1930], in *Œuvres complètes, I: Premiers Écrits 1922–1940* (Paris: Gallimard, 1970), 273.

23 "Indem an Dingen ihr Gebrauchswert abstirbt, werden die Entfremdeten ausgehölt und ziehen als Chiffern Bedeutungen herbei. Ihrer bemächtigt sich Subjektivität, indem sie Intentionen von Wunsch und Angst in sie einlegt." Theodor W. Adorno, letter to Walter Benjamin, August 5, 1935, in Adorno/Benjamin, *Briefwechsel 1928–1940,* ed. Henri Lonitz (Frankfurt am Main: Suhrkamp, 1994), 151–152.

24 "...es verschwinden also auch die verschiedenen konkreten Formen dieser Arbeiten, sie unterscheiden sich nicht länger, sondern sind allzusammt reduciert auf gleiche menschliche Arbeit, abstrakt menschliche Arbeit." Marx, "Das Kapital" (see note 12), 72.

25 John Roberts, *The Intangibilities of Form: Skill and Deskilling in Art After the Readymade* (London/New York: Verso, 2007), 27–29.

26 Giorgio Agamben, *The Coming Community,* trans. Michael Hardt (Minneapolis, MN: University of Minnesota Press, 1993), 9–11.

27 Benjamin Buchloh has defined the Modernist work of art as both " the *exemplary* object of all commodity production and the *exceptional* object of withdrawal and resistance that denies and resists the universality of that reign"; this dialectic of the exemplary and the exceptional was deconstructed in the 1960s and 70s by artists such as Marcel Broodthaers, who realized that the integration of art into the culture industry meant that art's exceptional status had become a sham, mere ideology. See Benjamin Buchloh, "Marcel Broodthaers: Open Letters, Industrial Poems" [1987], in *Neo-Avantgarde and Culture Industry: Essays on European and American Art from 1955 to 1975* (Cambridge, MA: MIT Press, 2000), 70. However, in a different register, Broodthaers resuscitated Buchloh's dialectic of the exemplary and the exceptional, which is characteristic of the modern and the contemporary work of art, not only of a narrowly defined modernism.

28 Roberts, *Intangibilities of Form* (see note 25), 21–25. That "Mr. Mutt ... created a new thought for that object" (the urinal-become-fountain) is stated in an anonymous text no doubt (co-)authored by Duchamp, "The Richard Mutt Case," in *The Blindman,* no. 2 (1917), unpaginated.

29 In his stimulating essay, *On (Surplus) Value in Art* (Rotterdam: Witte de With; Berlin/New York: Sternberg Press 2008), Diedrich Diederichsen distinguishes between the work of art's "everyday value" and its "speculative value," but everything in art conspires to erase this distinction.

30 In part because of their glorification of labor, Anselm Jappe terms Negri and Hardt's work "the last masquerade of traditionalist Marxism." Anselm Jappe, *Die Abenteuer der Ware: Für eine neue Wertkritik* (Münster: Unrast, 2005), 235.

31 Eagleton, *Ideology of the Aesthetic* (see note 10), 209. The term "pseudo-concrete" is used by Karel Kosik in his *Dialectics of the Concrete,* originally published in Czech in 1963.

32 For more on Marx's readings in fetishism, see Hartmut Böhme, *Fetischismus und Kultur: Eine andere Theorie der Moderne* (Reinbek: Rowohlt, 2006), 331–312.

33 The symbol occurs in both Hegel's philosophy of art and of religion, in contrast to the fetish, which had no claim to being even crude art.

34 See Sven Lütticken, "After the Gods," in *New Left Review* 30 (November/December 2004): 90–94.

35 G. W. F. Hegel, "Vorlesungen über die Ästhetik" [1817–1829], vol. 1, in *Werke,* vol. 13 (Frankfurt am Main: Suhrkamp, 1986), 393–466.

36 Ibid., 395.

37 Ibid., 393, 411.

38 Eagleton, *Ideology of the Aesthetic* (see note 10), 208.

39 "Denn bedeutsam und erwecklich wird das Symbol eben durch jene Incongruenz des Wesens mit der Form und durch die Überfülle des Inhalts in Vergleichung mit seinem Ausdrucke." Friedrich Creuzer, *Symbolik und Mythologie der alten Völker, besonders der Griechen* vol. 4.3, 3rd ed. (Leipzig/Darmstadt: Carl Wilhelm Laske, 1843), 530. In this third German edition, which started publication in 1836, the theoretical part of Creuzer's work closes the last volume as a theoretical appendix. In Guigniaut's French version, it opens the first volume, as it did in the original German 1810–12 edition. This French edition was published from 1825 onwards; the volume collecting all the plates saw the light of day in 1841.

40 "Dort [Symbol] ist momentane Totalität; hier ist Fortschritt in einer Reihe von Momenten. Daher auch die Allegorie, nicht aber das Symbol, den Mythus unter sich begreift, dessen Wesen das fortschreitende Epos am vollkommensten ausspricht, und der nur in der Theomythie, wie wir unten sehen werden, sich zum Symbolischen zusammenzudrängen strebet." Ibid., 441.

41 Ibid., 534–535.

42 Hegel, "Ästhetik" (see note 35), 393, 415–416.

43 "So wie es einerseits aus der Welt der Ideen, wie aus dem vollen Glanze der Sonne abgestrahlt, sonnenähnlich heissen kann, einen Platonischen ausdruck zu gebrauchen, so ist es hingegen durch das Medium getrübt, wodurch es in unser Auge fällt." Creuzer, *Symbolik* (see note 39), 530.

44 "Des idées pures, revêtues de formes corporelles, tels sont proprement les symboles ..." Frédéric Creuzer, *Religions de l'antiquité, considérées principalement dans leurs formes symboliques et mythologiques*, vol. I.1, translated from the German, revised in part, completed and developed by J. D. Guigniaut, (Paris/Strasbourg/London: Treuttel and Würtz, 1825), 26.

45 Naomi Klein, *No Logo* (London: HarperCollins, 2000), 28.

46 For the difficult relation between the Surrealists and the French Communist Party as well as the role of the Surrealist object in this relationship, see Harris, *Surrealist Art and Thought* (see note 21), throughout.

47 The quotation is at the beginning of Breton's "Situation surréaliste de l'objet" [1935], quoted in ibid., 153.

48 Ibid., 44–47.

49 Rosalind Krauss, *"A Voyage on the North Sea": Art in the Age of the Post-Medium Condition* (London: Thames & Hudson, 1999), 9–20.

50 Clement Greenberg, "Review of Exhibitions of Hedda Sterne and Adolph Gottlieb" [1947], in *The Collected Essays and Criticism 2: Arrogant Purpose, 1945–1949* (Chicago: University of Chicago Press, 1986), 188–189.

51 Barnett Newman, "Open Letter to William A.M. Burden, President of the Museum of Modern Art" [1953] and "Remarks at the Fourth Annual Woodstock Arts Conference" [1952], in *Selected Writings and Interviews*, ed. John P. O'Neill (Berkeley: University of California Press, 1992), 38, 245. Intriguingly, Duchamp's 1918 painting contains the shadow of a screwdriver, as well as those of a number of known readymades.

52 Barnett Newman, "The First Man Was an Artist" [1947], in ibid., 159.

53 "Kunst absorbiert die Symbole dadurch, dass sie nichts mehr symbolisieren .... Die Chiffren und Charaktere der Moderne sind durchweg absolut gewordene, ihrer selbst vergessene Zeichen." Theodor W. Adorno, "Ästhetische Theorie" (see note 19), 147.

54 Leo Steinberg, *Other Criteria: Confrontations with Twentieth-Century Art* (New York: Oxford University Press, 1972), 77–78.

55 Caroline A. Jones, *Machine in the Studio: Constructing the Postwar American Artist* (Chicago: University of Chicago Press, 1996), 162.

56 "Die Einfühlung in die Ware stellt sich der Selbstbeobachtung oder inneren Erfahrung als Einfühlung in die anorganische Materie dar; neben Baudelaire ist hier Flaubert mit seiner *Tentation* Kronzeuge." Walter Benjamin, letter to Theodor W. Adorno, December 9, 1938, in Adorno/Benjamin, *Briefwechsel* (see note 23), 385. The reference is to another episode of the *The Temptation,* but the episode of the gods also has a strong "inorganic" feeling.

57 For more on the death of Le Poittevin see Flaubert, letter to Maxime Du Camp, April 7, 1848, in *Correspondance,* vol. I, ed. Jean Bruneau (Paris: Pléiade, 1973), 493–494. For a detailed analysis of Creuzer's impact on Flaubert's *Temptation,* see Jean Seznec, *Les sources de l'épisode des dieux dans La Tentation de Saint Antoine (première version, 1849)*, Paris, 1940. The medium through which Creuzer's work was transmitted to Flaubert (and Le Poittevin) was J. D. Guigniaut's French translation/adaptation, which appeared in several volumes between 1825 and 1851.

58 Sigmund Freud, *Moses and Monotheism*, trans. Katharine Jones (New York: Random House, 1939), 61.

59 There are three versions of *La Tentation de Saint Antoine,* dating from 1849, 1856, and 1874. Flaubert did not publish the first version after a negative reception by his friends; he reworked it in 1856, but the result was still not satisfactory, leading to a much more substantial rewrite in the 1870s. *The Temptation* finally saw the light of day in this form. The previous versions were published posthumously. See, for instance, *Œuvres complètes de Gustave Flaubert,* vol. 4 (Paris: Louis Conard, 1910). For an analysis of the different versions, see Gisèle Séginger, *Naissance et métamorphoses d'un écrivain. Flaubert et* Les Tentations de saint Antoine (Paris: Honoré Champion, 1997).

60 Without himself questioning the classicist norm, Jean Seznec notes that Flaubert has chosen certain "oriental" gods "for their very ugliness or deformity." Jean Seznec, *The Survival of the Pagan Gods: The Mythological Tradition and Its Place in Renaissance Humanism and Art* (Princeton, NJ: Princeton University Press, 1953), 252.

61 As Edward Said said of Flaubert and Nerval: "On the one hand, therefore, the scope of their Oriental work exceeds the limitations posed by orthodox Orientalism. On the other hand, [their work] quite consciously plays with the limitations and the challenges presented to them by the Orient and by Knowledge about it." Edward W. Said, *Orientalism* (New York: Pantheon Books, 1978), 181.

62 Gustave Flaubert, *La Tentation de Saint Antoine* [1874 edition], in *Œuvres complètes de Gustave Flaubert,* vol. 4 (Paris: Louis Conard, 1910), 149–157. The emphasis on the contrast between early religious symbols and later plastic symbols is one instance in which the *Temptation's* implication in nineteenth-century Orientalism manifests itself, but to a much greater extent than Flaubert's more lurid exercises in Orientalism, *Salammbô* and *Hérodias*, *The Temptation* not only deconstructs its manifest subject matter, but also its own ideological context. To stress the point once more: in Flaubert's best work, the *intentio operis*—to use Umberto Eco's useful term—is far from identical with the *intentio auctoris*. Flaubert was a social reactionary who embraced Louis Napoleon's Second Empire and dismissed emerging socialism with the sneer "Always slogans! Always gods!" but the textual strategies of his art of rewriting point beyond the limitations of Flaubert as a historical subject.

63 Ibid., 134.

64 "Alors défilent devant eux, des idoles de toutes les nations et de tous les âges, en bois, en métal, en granit, en plumes, en peaux cousues." Ibid., 118.

65 "et il voit passer à ras du sol des feuilles, des pierres, des coquilles, des branches d'arbres, de vagues représentations d'animaux; puis des espèces de nains hydropiques; ce sont des dieux." Ibid., 118–119.

66 See Frank Paul Bowman, *French Romanticism: Intertextual and Interdisciplinary Reading* (Baltimore: Johns Hopkins University Press, 1990), 164f.

67 Hirst himself turned out to be a participant in the consortium that had bought the skull, thus reducing the whole matter to one of marketing strategy.

68 Hirst's *Golden Calf* was made especially for an auction of new Hirst works at Sotheby's.

69 http://arts.guardian.co.uk/news/story/0,,1779919,00.html.

70 Ironically, such a question is immediately coopted by the work: it adds complexity, meaning, and hence value.

71 "... un code généralisé de signes, un code totalement arbitraire (faictice, fétiche) de différences." Jean Baudrillard, *Pour une critique de l'économie politique du signe* (Paris: Gallimard, 1972), 100. Baudrillard criticizes Marx for conceiving of fetishism as "une force qui reviendrait hanter l'individu." It is true that Marx used metaphors referring to occultism and "primitive" religion in his iconoclastic attack on the illusions in which capitalism wraps the subject, but his analysis was no less structural—although not, of course, structuralist—for all that. Baudrillard's attack here seems more directed at a certain debased Marxism, which in turn "fetishizes" the notion of the fetish, and whose analysis itself reverts to quasi-magical incantations. It is also true that in Marx's early work in particular, the "estrangement" from man's essence is bemoaned, but while such essentialist rhetoric may now strike us as naïve and potentially dangerous, the dreaded accusation of essentialism is often used, by Baudrillard and others, against any discourse that tries to name and right social wrongs, that seeks to gauge and use opportunities for change. There needs to be a distinction between rigid notions

of a narrowly defined ideal state, and a critique of the present state of affairs, in the name of a possible alternative.

72 For Deleuze's take on the simulacrum, see *Logique du sens* (Paris: Les Éditions de Minuit, 1969), 292–324.

73 Jean Baudrillard, *Pour une critique* (see note 71), 59–194.

74 Ibid., 64.

75 During the course of the 1970s, as he distanced himself from Marxism, it became increasingly obvious that Baudrillard's work was underpinned by hysterical mourning for a lost reality. In a fine example of the pot calling the kettle black, Baudrillard accused Marxism of nostalgia for pre-capitalist economies, a nostalgia for an oneiric reality before the universal rule of exchange, before alienation, while his own narrative of an increasing loss of reality certainly went hand in hand with such a nostalgia. Baudrillard's own utopia were pre-modern economies of "symbolical exchange," in which objects were not exchanged as abstract commodities but as part of a network of symbolical obligations, anchored in a hierarchy that is sustained by the gods (or, in certain tribal societies, the ancestors, who are seen as ever-present). Here the symbolic is not a platonic archetype, but part of enacted social obligations. On the capitalist market, such symbolical obligations are replaced by equivalence; this means that, as this market penetrates societies more and more, reality is lost and simulation takes over.

76 David Joselit, *Feedback: Television Against Democracy* (Cambridge, MA: MIT Press, 2007), 5.

77 W. J. T. Mitchell, *What Do Pictures Want? The Lives and Loves of Images* (Chicago: University of Chicago Press, 2005), 156.

78 Ibid.

79 Bruno Latour, "Why Has Critique Run out of Steam? From Matters of Fact to Matters of Concern," in *Critical Inquiry* 30, no. 2 (2004): 225–248, http://criticalinquiry.uchicago.edu/issues/v30/30n2.Latour.html.

80 Aleksandr Rodchenko, letter, spring 1925, quoted in Kristina Kiaer, *Imagine No Possessions: The Socialist Objects of Russian Constructivism* (Cambridge, MA: MIT Press, 2005), 1, 199.

81 Gerald Raunig, *Kunst und Revolution: Künstlerischer Aktivismus im langen 20. Jahrhundert* (Vienna: Turia + Kant, 2005). Raunig argues against the model of the revolution as one radical break and in favor of a long chain of events produced by "transversal" connections between different fields, activism in particular.

82 Sekula's diagrams were made during a lecture/discussion event with Sekula and Noël Burch concerning their film script project, *A Forgotten Space*, November 21, 2003.

83 Flaubert, *Tentation de Saint Antoine* (see note 62), 156.

84 "Hegel gerieth daher auf die Illusion, das Reale als das Resultat des in sich zusammenfassenden, in sich vertiefenden, und aus sich selbst sich bewegenden Denkens zu fassen, während die Methode vom Abstrakten zum Concreten aufzusteigen, nur die Art für das Denken ist sich das Concrete anzueignen, es als ein geistig Concretes zu reproduciren." Karl Marx, "Einleitung zu den 'Grundrissen der Kritik der Politischen Ökonomie'" [1857/58], in *Marx/Engels Gesamtausgabe (MEGA)*, part 2, vol. 1.1 (Berlin: Dietz, 1976), 36. English translation by Martin Nicolaus: Karl Marx, *Grundrisse: Foundations of The Critique of Political Economy* [1857/58] (London: Penguin, 1993), 101.

85 Anselm Jappe uses the term *Realabstraktion*, on the basis of a passage in the first edition of *Capital*. Jappe, *Abenteuer der Ware* (see note 30), 35–36. It is marginally interesting to note that Mondrian, who rejected the term *art concret*, often spoke of "abstract-real" art, though he of course did not conceive of the reality of abstraction in terms of exchange.

86 "...l'abstraction de tout travail particulier et l'abstraction générale de la production d'ensemble se traduisent parfaitement dans le spectacle, dont le *mode d'être concret* est justement l'abstraction." Guy Debord, *Societé de Spectacle* (see note 11), 30. English translation by Donald Nicholson-Smith at http://www.cddc.vt.edu/sionline/si/tsots01.html.

87 "In dessen universalem Vollzug [des Tausches], nicht erst in der wissenschaftlichen Reflexion, wird objektiv abstrahiert." Theodor W. Adorno, "Gesellschaft" [1965], in *Gesammelte Schriften*, vol. 8: *Soziologische Schriften I*, ed. Rolf Tiedemann (Frankfurt am Main: Suhrkamp, 1972), 13. See also Fredric Jameson, *Late Marxism: Adorno; Or, The Persistence of the Dialectic* (London/New York: Verso, 2007), 35–42.

88 Vilém Flusser, "Auf dem Weg zum Unding," in *Medienkultur* (Frankfurt am Main: Fischer, 1997), 185–189. Flusser does not differentiate between things and objects; he uses the term "thing" for both, arguing that the number of "un-Dinge" has increased exponentially.

89 Stephen Moss and John Henley, "Crunch Time," *The Guardian*, September 17, 2008, http://www.guardian.co.uk/business/2008/sep/17/recession.labour.

Chapter Four

LIVING WITH ABSTRACTION

The new religion is faith in life. The new religion is for those capable of abstraction. For Realists like to have a concrete idea of God.
Piet Mondrian[1]

The problem with the spectacle is not with what is shown, but with what remains invisible. If the interplay of commodities is merely a distraction from a fundamentally aniconic structure, this raises the question of the relation between the "real abstraction" at the heart of capitalism and the abstract art that emerged after 1910; isn't the modern work of art fundamentally abstract, a pseudo-concrete commodity, regardless of whether a specific painting consists of squares and rectangles or represents cute kittens? As the budding Situationists once put it: "As uninteresting as obsolete postage stamps, and offering as little variation as these, literary or artistic productions are now signs of nothing but abstract commerce."[2] Formal abstraction thus would seem to offer no privileged insight into a society where abstraction is triumphant.

Furthermore, as Meyer Schapiro noted, there are problems with theories that derive abstraction in art either from the forms of industry or from "the abstract nature of modern finance, in which bits of paper control capital and all human transactions assume the form of operations on numbers and titles," since abstract art did not emerge in the most industrially advanced nations or in the main centers of finance—and moreover, many early abstract artists positioned their work squarely in opposition to what they perceived as the materialism of modern society.[3] One way out of this quandary is offered by Adorno's argument that formal abstraction was the result of a new "interdiction" of representation, which stemmed from the imperative for the work of art to absorb its "deadliest enemy, exchangeability," resisting abstraction by representing it negatively.[4] Abstract art is thus positioned as perhaps the modern art par excellence—its "windowless monads" showing the abstract nature of society by refusing to represent its glimmering surfaces, or even its dark underside, returning a blank stare rather than attempting to adjust traditional representation to a post-traditional world. In this respect, it is not surprising that capitalism created a double abstract effigy for itself in the guise of the World Trade Center, consisting of two "zips" reminiscent of Barnett Newman's compositions. On September 11, 2001, Islamist iconoclasm hit a structure which suggested that the capitalist West, attacked for its idolatrous materialism, may in fact be abstract with a vengeance—as much beyond representation as the monotheistic deity. Brecht famously remarked that a photo of the Krupp factories does not manage to show anything of the processes going on inside, or of the nature of industrial capitalism; if anything, post-industrial capitalism is only more resistant to representation.[5] No wonder that Baudrillard proclaimed the "abolition of the spectacular."[6] In our abstract spectacle, images and objects are but momentary manifestations—or incarnations—of a digital *logos*.

For his 2002 poster project commemorating the 9/11 attacks, Hans Haacke produced an edition of monochrome white posters from which the silhouettes of the Twin Towers had been cut out. These were glued onto New York walls, the underlying printed matter partly visible through the outlines. For the design of his "negative" poster, Haacke used an advertisement for a Broadway production from the *New York Times Magazine* as a background, and on the walls of the city fragments of posters and advertisements—often for shows, films, or records—were likewise visible in the towers' silhouettes (fig. 4.1). Although ostensibly commemorating September 11, 2001, the project effectively examined the problem of the destroyed building itself, which had visualized the abstract, aniconic tendency of the advanced spectacle in the form of a "spectacular" icon. As an image of deterritorialized streams of capital, the eradicated World Trade Center in Haacke's project becomes the empty frame for commodity-images, which, according to Marxian theory, are themselves pseudo-concrete manifestations of abstract exchange-value. But the World Trade Center was not only a manifestation of monetary abstraction; it showed conceptual abstraction becoming as real as exchange. In the 1970s, Baudrillard used the Twin Towers as the spectacular effigy of a capitalist system that had passed beyond the pyramid to the punch card, into the digital. "The buildings are no longer obelisks, but trustingly stand next to one another like the columns of a statistical graph."[7] Since this remark is made in a passage that expounds upon the binary code and its "superstructural" equivalents such as opinion polls, which must be answered with either yes or no, it seems that Baudrillard reads the towers as double icons of binary capitalism.

Part of Baudrillard's theoretical assemblage was a quasi-Situationist emphasis on the becoming-image—the becoming-crocodile—of the commodity. In an interesting passage, Baudrillard frames his theory of the image in terms of iconoclasm and "iconolatry." He argues that iconoclasts were possessed by "metaphysical despair"; their real fear was not that images deflect worship from God onto themselves, but rather that there is no God behind the images, that the divine referent is lost. In a striking turn of phrase, Baudrillard characterizes images as "murderers of the real."[8] Modern culture attempted to curtail this danger by imposing rules of representation, but in the end this was to no avail, and simulation triumphed. Strictly speaking, this simulation is no longer iconic. Even while Baudrillard writes about the image with an iconoclast's metaphysical despair, his real contribution was to suggest that the image is no longer itself. Whereas the symbol was a concept of the image, a *linguistic fantasy of the visual*, the *logos* that underpins the images of advanced capitalism is both post-visual and post-linguistic. Baudrillard argues that the interplay of quasi-symbolic logotypes and brands results in a system of pure difference—which is to say: of equivalence—meaning that capital abstracts itself *beyond the visual*. The medium of this abstraction is digital; it is the binary *logos* of pure difference, of 0/1, of yes/no. To be sure, the Twin Towers' nearly identical character makes Baudrillard's allegorization of the World Trade Center rather forced; if anything, they can be read as two "ones," with the empty space between them functioning as "zero."

It is relevant to note that in his design, Haacke used a New York Times advertisement for the musical *42nd Street* as a background, a montage advertisement of drawn, typographic and photographic elements which looks like a digital version of 1920s and 30s photomontage. Such photomontage—pioneered by the Russian Constructivists and soon popular among avant-garde advertising designers—integrated photographic elements into compositions influenced by Suprematism and Constructivism, thus prefiguring the *becoming real* of conceptual abstraction in the digital economy, as embodied by the World Trade Center, that structure designed to function as an image of what may be beyond picturing. Now that this double icon of ultimate abstraction is gone, what ways are there to get beyond the surfaces of the image-objects surrounding us, to chart our abstract spectacle?

THE ABSTRACT WOR(L)D, CONCRETELY

While only industrial capitalism allowed for truly "universal implementation" of the exchange system, doing away with traditional limitations, transforming God-given hierarchy into mobile capital, monetary abstraction itself predates capitalism by a long time. Creuzer's ample use of images from coins recalls that ancient coins were often stamped with images of deities, and the possible interrelation between the distribution of coins and the emergence of more abstract concepts of the gods has offered various authors highly suggestive material for historical and anthropological speculation.[9] Whether the monotheistic God as such represents an abstraction in relation to pre-monotheistic gods is subject to debate; Margalit and Halberthal emphasize that the relationship of the Yahweh of the Torah to the Israelites is presented as that of a jealous husband to his fickle wife.[10] A tribal deity with a distinct personality, Yahweh is not some abstract philosophical concept; this personalization of God would continue, in one form or another, in most Mosaic religions. Nonetheless, the ban on images facilitated the formation of more abstract conceptions of the deity that exacerbate his unrepresentability.

One would expect the questioning of representation in modern art, and especially its rejection in abstract art, to have occasioned a serious and prolonged interest among religious circles; aside from a few exceptions, such as the Cologne-based Jesuit Friedhelm Mennekes with his Kunst-Station Sankt Peter, this has not been the case. The 1997–1998 affair involving a Catholic propaganda poster based on Barnett Newman's painting *Who's Afraid of Red, Yellow and Blue III* suggests that often, abstract art's complex ties to the monotheistic tradition are completely ignored. Newman's painting, in the collection of Amsterdam's Stedelijk Museum, became a *cause célèbre* in the Netherlands when a psychologically unhinged man slashed the red surface that constitutes the bulk of the composition. On the poster, intended for display in schools, the archdiocese of Utrecht mimicked the damaged Newman painting, but with slash marks intersecting to form a cross. (The cuts on the real Newman painting had been roughly parallel.) The caption read "Who's Afraid of God?" The church was sued by Stichting Beeldrecht, a Dutch organization administering copyright on behalf of artists, for infringing upon Newman's—or his widow's—copyright. The judge refused to accept the church's defense that the use was parody and therefore a case of "fair use." In response, the church had the proportions altered and the yellow "zip" was replaced with a green one (fig. 4.2).

What makes this poster difficult to read—and therefore interesting—is Christianity's, and particularly Catholicism's, divergent approach to representation based on the notion of the Incarnation. Are we to surmise that the red surface stands for an aniconic God, that of Islam, or, more pertinently in Newman's case, of Judaism? Is the slashed crucifix an attack on the unrepresentability of the deity—a Catholic attack on an abstract God? Or is the poster simply an indictment of modern art as empty, irredeemably profane and meaningless unless stamped with the mark of the cross? It does not appear that the bishopric had any interest in examining the complex relationship between modern—particularly abstract—art and monotheism. In a report written by the bishopric's then-public relations officer, the dominant motive seems to have been a rather juvenile desire to get back at modern art, to provoke an art world that is seen as constantly insulting religion.[11] It is telling that this dispute had to be settled in court: religious controversies aside, it is the secular Second Commandment forbidding "copyright infringement" that most hinders the creative or critical use of images in today's society.

The relationship between modern art and monotheistic iconoclasm is highly complex and mediated. We have already seen that Carl Andre ascribed to himself "a temperance of dissatisfaction deriving from the history of Protestant dissent in Europe" in a letter to Sol LeWitt (who would later follow in Barnett Newman's footsteps by designing a synagogue).[12] However, when he created his mature work, Andre had abandoned the faith in which he had been brought up; the same had been true of Mondrian and most of the other early abstract artists. Rather than laying down dogma, Mondrian's writings seek to create a discursive context for a painterly practice likely to be misunderstood and rejected. Furthermore, this practice is decidedly post-Calvinist in that it presents art as being not in any way subservient to religion, but rather as a separate form of access to the universal—access by plastic means. Mondrian's aniconism, and that of Modernist abstraction in general, is thus a revival or return to monotheistic aniconism in a context mediated by Theosophy, Symbolism, and the rediscovery of Medieval art. In 1913, at a time when he was moving through Cubism toward his mature Neoplasticism, Mondrian painted a copy of the "primitive" fifteenth-century *Avignon Piétà*: here we see the incarnate and crucified Word lying in the arms of Mary, an elongated but clearly physical body. Christ's face, like all other faces except that of a patron on the left, is surrounded with a golden halo. Whereas his halo consists of beams of light emanating from his face, those of Mary, John, and the Magdalene consist of concentric circles on which their names are inscribed; they merge with the sky, which is golden as well.

Although this copy was commissioned by a collector, it was peculiarly appropriate for Mondrian, providing him with an opportunity to study the work's dialectic of naturalistic detail and abstraction.[13] In his own work, he would push toward further abstraction, in order to free the universal from its particular imprisonment in all-too-human forms, arguing that art can be a "direct plastic expression of the universal" only if such surface symbolism is left behind. In his writing, Mondrian disparaged "symbolical art," using the term "symbol" to denote conventional meanings imprisoned in circumscribed forms, such as the Christian cross. Nonetheless, a phrase such as that of the "direct plastic expression of the universal" is, in fact, very much in accordance with idealist definitions of the symbol as the absolute or an idea manifesting itself in a form, thus creating a synthesis of the ideal and the real.[14] Abstract art creates a new plastic expression by juxtaposing color and line, horizontal and vertical, outwardness and inwardness, nature and spirit, individual and universal, female and male; it gives a determinate or concrete expression to the universal by putting "purified" forms and colors in rhythmic compositions.[15] In this way, it represents the refusal to abstract beyond the visual, to become conceptual. Even though Mondrian opened his groundbreaking 1917 essay with the statement that "life is becoming more and more abstract," he took care to point out that his art stands "between the absolute-abstract and the natural or the concrete-real. It is not as abstract as abstract thought, and not as real as tangible reality. It is aesthetic, living plastic representation: the visual expression in which each opposite is transformed into the other."[16]

Mondrian's adherence to the archaic and stubbornly material medium of easel painting implies a conservative protest against the onward march of abstraction—a decision to confront the concept with its refuse, with corrections and imperfections, with blotched and botched areas of paint. As a young man, Mondrian collaborated with his father, a Protestant teacher who devised didactic allegorical compositions; a print composed by Mondrian Senior in 1874 is called *Revolution or Gospel.* In the early 1890s, Piet painted an allegorical tableau for his father's school, following an iconographic program devised by the latter, which showed an assembly of objects including a bible and crucifix, and the inscription "Uw woord is de waarheid"—"Thy word is truth."[17] This is the Calvinist triumph of the written word, rather than of the Word as *Logos* incarnate: the composition is an emblem that is not allowed to go too far beyond its pre-programmed meaning. By contrast, even if Mondrian's mature work is accompanied by voluminous writings and would thus seem to consist of "painted words," the relationship between word and image (or non-image) has shifted decidedly.

Mondrian's writings are suffused with Hegel, mediated through the work of the Dutch Hegelian Bolland.[18] However, in his refusal to make the final leap into what Mondrian called "abstract thought," into the concept, Mondrian refuses to follow Hegel to the point of the "end of art" and its replacement by philosophy. Hegel argued that the break of Christian art with the "equilibrium" of antique forms represented Spirit triumphing over matter and moving on to greater self-realization, which meant a triumph of the concept over visible form. For Hegel, the concept or notion [*Begriff*] is "the truth of being," an active principle that manifests itself objectively.[19] Hegel defines an *idea* as the "absolute unity of a notion and its objectivity," of the ideal and the real. "The Idea is the *adequate Notion,* that which is objectively *true*, or the *true as such*."[20] However, the notions through which philosophy expresses the idea are no more abstract than the ideas, for they are not merely formal categories imposed on being; they are the active principles of being, and therefore not abstract, but determinate. Hegel's trajectory of Spirit was a philosophical translation of the Christian narrative of God's incarnation, so beloved by Cologne's Catholic caliph. In becoming man and being crucified, God gave mankind a crash course in dialectics; He revealed Himself as Spirit precisely by having the Son—that image of the invisible—become man, by exiling Himself into nature.[21]

Here we are no longer dealing with an abstract, transcendent God, but with a determinate one—just as Hegelian philosophy does not deal with abstract, formal categories, but with concepts or notions that are the active principles of being, "the truth of being." Creating a dialectical movement of notions means making the step from necessity to freedom, into the realm of the absolute idea. But positing that the concept is "the truth of being" clearly *is* to abstract from particulars and to relegate what cannot be subsumed under this abstraction to the realm of mere appearance, of contingency; a reality which does not correspond to a notion is mere appearance, something accidental and contingent.[22] The becoming-determinate of Spirit, then, rings hollow. As enacted in Hegel's philosophy, it transforms reality and casts aside what it cannot absorb into conceptual abstraction. Theodor W. Adorno was to examine the remainder of this operation—the refuse of the concept, the non-identical remainder of philosophical abstraction. Art, which for Hegel was replaced by philosophical concept, came to play a crucial role for Adorno, for whom modern art was precisely about *resistance* to the concept. Modernism in art amounted to a fight for the rights of the "non-identical" in the face of the triumph of the concept—which Adorno, against Hegel, sees as an abstraction.

The concept is modern art's closest enemy. Art operates by latently magical procedures harking back to the dawn of humankind: it is fundamentally mimetic. In this way, "art is a correction of conceptual knowledge."[23] However, if art is to be successful, it should not engage in an "abstract negation of reason," but absorb the remainder of triumphant reason, its non-identical Other, into its "immanent necessity" that is: into its mimetic appropriation of rational procedures.[24] Art, in other words, is "reason which criticizes itself, without escaping from its grasp...."[25] It is reason turned against itself. This is why works of art are quasi-linguistic; they are hieroglyphic writings whose code has been lost.[26] When artist Peter Halley decoded abstract art as being "nothing other than the reality of the abstract world" and "simply one manifestation of a universal impetus towards abstract concepts that has dominated twentieth-century thought," he was effectively placing abstraction in a quasi-Hegelian trajectory, in which Spirit first manifests itself in sensuous forms, and later in philosophical concepts.[27] For Halley, abstract forms apparently amount to a conceptualization of the visible. The above shows this to be a fundamental misinterpretation of historical abstraction—and yet, have recent decades not witnessed an increasing re-coding of art?

Mondrian's 1928 *Tableau-poème: textuel* is a rare case in which the artist integrated text into his art (fig. 4.3). In this gouache and ink drawing on paper, a Michel Seuphor poem has been integrated into a typical Mondrian composition, though not especially elegantly; two of the poem's lines are broken off rather clumsily at the end.[28] Even if the piece can be said to prefigure Conceptual art in its use of graphically arranged language and in being suitable for reproduction in various formats, the piece retains traces of its hand-made nature, and the text is a poem. In Modernist poetry, and Modernist literature in general, language itself is turned against conceptual thinking through perpetual de- and reconstruction. Compare, by way of contrast, recent pieces by Joseph Kosuth titled *Mondrian's Work,* in which graphic reproductions of Mondrian compositions are inscribed with quotations from Mondrian's writings (fig. 4.4). While the principle may seem similar to *Tableau-poème: textuel* at first sight, it is in fact diametrically opposed: here, statements by Mondrian become "content" for a managerial approach to language, one that effectively reduces a sustained writing effort to sound bites; these are then integrated into compositions that are used as typographic clichés. The quasi-language of abstract symbols is transformed into the coded oppositions of Flusserian "programmed surfaces."

In one of Kosuth's 1960s photostat blow-ups of dictionary definitions, "abstract" is defined as "Separated from matter, practice, or particular examples, not concrete; ideal, not practical; abstruse."[29] *Abstruse* contemporary abstraction may be, but it is neither lacking in concreteness nor in practicality—nor indeed is it separated from matter. However, just as abstraction has become an ever more pervasive presence, as it becomes increasingly incarnated, it is once again projected on the Islamic Other, externalized as incompatible with Western visuality.

ISLAMIC ABSTRACTION

To Western theorists, Islam has often appeared as the abstract negation of the world, whereas the West is identified with an incarnated and plentiful visual culture. While the Israelite God had a paternal, tribal relationship to his people, and the Christian God took on human form to die for the sake of mankind, Islam has long been marked by an abstract relationship to a transcendent deity, manifesting itself above all in language—even though the Arabic of the Qur'an is sometimes characterized as still being anchored in oral culture and thus less abstract than one might think.[30] Nonetheless, Hegel considered Muslims to be "dominated by abstraction," in contrast to

Christianity as a religion of Spirit incarnate: "Abstraction ruled the Muhammadans, whose goal was to establish an abstract worship, and this goal they pursued with the greatest enthusiasm. This enthusiasm was *fanaticism*, that is to say: enthusiasm for something abstract, for an abstract thought that exists in a relation of negation to the existing order."[31] In today's media, this abstract negation of existence is interpreted mostly as a negation of western democracy, the "free word," and the "free market," but the relation between Islamic and "Western" abstraction is rather more complex.

The notion of Islam as the religion of abstraction goes some way toward explaining Cardinal Meisner's response to Gerhard Richter's new window for the Cologne cathedral, which caused a German media scandal in 2007 (fig. 4.5). After fruitless experiments with figurative motifs, Richter had decided to adapt the principle behind his earlier works consisting of grids of rectangular color fields. In works such as *4096 Colors* (1974), Richter submitted the rigor of the grid to the laws of chance: the distribution of the 4,096 unique tones across the structure is aleatoric. For the church window, Richter placed squares of colored glass in a grid held together by silicone, rather than the traditional lead. In his design for the cathedral's south transept, Richter mirrored some parts of his chance-based "composition," so that symmetries emerge; however, these mostly remain in the viewer's optical unconscious, being only really apparent in the plans and in reproductions. Apart from the scale of the window and the number of squares, this "hiddenness" of the symmetries has to do with the surprising intensity of the colors, especially at sunny moments. This is, above all, what sets Richter's window apart from the old abstract windows in its vicinity; Cologne cathedral contains numerous abstract examples with ornamental patterns and muted colors. Compared to these, Richter's window refuses to be mere background, and looks—as many critics noted—somewhat like a pixelated flat screen. Perhaps it is this aggressive quality, and the fact that the primary context for this piece is provided by Richter's "autonomous oeuvre," that made the cardinal forget about the presence of old abstract windows. Meisner claimed that an abstract window in a cathedral is misplaced. Catholicism is a religion of the Incarnation, not of transcendence; in his original off-the-cuff remark about Richter's window, which was widely reported in the media, Meisner opined that it would be more suitable for a mosque.[32]

In a subsequent newspaper article, Meisner explained that Christ has descended "as a mediator into the center of our world" (*als Mittler in die Mitte unserer Welt*), and therefore churches belong in the center of the city.[33] But while the great cathedrals are still located in the geographic center of their respective cities, do they still remain spiritual centers? In his article, Meisner claims that societies that "banish god from their center" become "inhuman." His proof are the "two forms of dictatorship" produced by the last century; "Man's dignity is jeopardized when God is abolished and man is put in his place as sole measure; human life then loses its worth."[34] Secularization leads straight to the gulag. This is the voice of reactionary Catholic *Kulturkritik,* which happily reduces National Socialism to the desire to place "man" (*den Menschen*) in the center. The Holocaust, then, had little to do with an ideology that wanted to purify the collective *Volkskörper,* or body of the people, from alien elements; it was simply the logical consequence of the modern rebellion against God, which must necessarily reduce man to the level of beasts.

In his cynical ideological instrumentalization of Nazism, Meisner conveniently omits its links to the very discourse he espouses. During an earlier mass, Meisner had intoned: "Where culture is severed from worship, cult becomes rigid ritualism and culture degenerates. It loses its center."[35] While most responses focused on the verb "entartet," which is now forever linked to Nazi repression of "degenerate art" (*entartete Kunst*), Meisner's insistence upon the "loss of the center" is perhaps more interesting. The art historian Hans Sedlmayr, who coined the phrase, was a member of the Nazi party in the 1930s and at the time of the 1938 *Anschluss* of Austria had rhapsodized about the South German baroque style as being completely distinct from the Italian baroque, amounting to a purely German *Reichsstil,* which created "a new, German center" for Europe.[36] During and after the war, Sedlmayr would reformulate the question of the center and its loss in Catholic rather than fascist terms; his best-selling book *Verlust der Mitte* (*Loss of the Center),* argued that the Enlightenment, culminating in the traumatic event of the French Revolution, saw man rebel against God and his place in creation. Man puts himself in the place of God, which means that the great *Gesamtkunstwerke* of the past, the great churches and palaces with their decorations, are no longer possible.[37] The arts disintegrate and the image of man in visual art, created in God's own image, becomes horribly distorted or effaced altogether. The center folds.

By presenting modernity as intrinsically satanic, Sedlmayr silently suggested that Nazism was a trifle. This undoubtedly soothed his readers' souls: for what is Auschwitz, compared to the horrors of a Mondrian? The success of *Verlust der Mitte* and its sequel, *Die Revolution der modernen Kunst,* in post-war Germany suggests that Sedlmayr sounded a reassuringly familiar note. This was *entartete Kunst* lite. In 1951, Sedlmayr was appointed professor of art history in Munich—where Benjamin Buchloh was among his reluctant students. Ironically, an artist who is crucial to Buchloh's critical-historical project has long professed an allegiance to Sedlmayr's analysis: from the 1960s to the present, Gerhard Richter has repeatedly stated that Sedlmayr had been correct in diagnosing a loss of center. The time of kings and of God-ordained hierarchy was indeed over, and as a consequence art became formless. Richter has always considered the term used to denote 1950s European gestural abstraction, *art informel,* to be applicable to his own work, and by extension to modern art in general.[38] However, the artist should affirm and explore this situation, rather than be seduced by reactionary nostalgia.[39] Richter "detourned" Sedlmayr's discourse by pressing it into the service of a skeptical and questioning artistic practice. Since the 1960s, he devised a number of strategies to cope with what he sees as the absence of valid forms in modernity. The putative absolute nature of the squares and grids employed by modernists is as arbitrary as the chance that Dadaists and Fluxus artists put into the service of art, and Richter managed to combine the two extremes in his color charts.

Here we are dealing with Adorno's "new interdiction" of representation, not the old one; Richter sees his work as the product of capitalist modernity, in which, as Marx and Engels put it, everything that was solid melts into thin air. In a crude and moralizing idiom, Sedlmayr's thesis on the loss of center made a similar point. The cardinal's equation of abstraction with the religious Other would therefore appear to be singularly irrelevant. Or should one read his remark to the effect that Islam itself is a decentering force, a force of abstraction threatening to shatter the Cathedral-centered old towns of Europe? Islam, then, would eerily mirror capitalism's mode of operation: both introduce change, both challenge Christian hierarchies. For all the leftist criticism of economic abstraction, Marx and the thinkers in his wake have always presented such abstraction as a double-edged sword: while the abstract reality of capitalism must be criticized and fought, because workers are deprived of the product of their labor, capitalism has also been a liberating force by extracting and abstracting people from "traditional" bonds of servitude, from feudal shackles (a process which was, of course, also violent and destructive). Both Islamists and Enlightenment fundamentalists regard the Muslim *umma* as the complete Other to western society, the only essential difference being that Islamists regard as liberating what Enlightenment fundamentalists consider patriarchal and oppressive. However, one can posit that there is, in fact, a crucial parallel between capitalism's effect on the societies in which it takes hold and the way in which Islam nullifies or thoroughly transforms existing social bonds when introducing someone into the community of believers.

"Oriental" carpets are exemplary objects that show Islamic abstraction as historically implicated in the de-territorializing forces of exchange, since these vehicles of Islamic art were sold to and collected in Europe. The abstract patterns on such carpets became prototypical artistic commodities in the West. For centuries, and precisely in the centuries that led from early mercantile capitalism to industrial capitalism, oriental carpets were abstracted from their context and sold to Europeans. To study them as specimens of "Islamic abstraction," without taking this into account, is to miss the point. De Rijke/de Rooij's 2002 series of photographs of Islamic carpets emphasizes this secondary abstraction: the photographs consist of life-size black-and-white reproductions of carpets surrounded by white borders (fig. 4.6). Long after they were exported to Europe, de Rijke/de Rooij imported these rugs from the Rijksmuseum collection into the white cube by means of black-and-white photography, thus exacerbating their abstraction from their context to such a degree that a qualitative change sets in. Not simply presented as precious aesthetic objects that enter into more or less organic relationships with other precious objects, the carpets here are transformed into photographic ghosts of themselves, and presented as gallery works on a scale grown to dominance with the rise of the New York School of the 1950s. Not only is the size of these carpets comparable to New York School paintings, but in most cases the main elements of the composition also have a "deductive" relationship to the rug's edges. However, the rugs are more complex and less bold than New York School painting, containing more detail and more deviations from the deductive principle.[40]

If history is, as Henri Focillon once stated, not "a neatly plotted series of harmonic tableaux" but rather, "throughout its entire course, variety, exchange and conflict," then anachronistic juxtapositions of—for instance—ancient Islamic and modern art should not be decried in advance as ahistorical. Neither, however, should formal similarities be fetishized.[41] De Rijke/de Rooij articulate the relationship between carpet and painting, between ornament and abstraction, between Islamic and modern/contemporary art as one of repetition and difference rather than one of pseudomorphic identity. The latter road was ultimately taken by the curators of *Documenta 12* in 2007, who regurgitated Roger Fry-style formalist comparisons and abstracted from all historical and cultural specifics. Because of this, their inclusion of a number of old Islamic artifacts only seemed to affirm the image of Islam as the religion of abstraction par excellence.

De Rijke/de Rooij's conceptual photographs exacerbate the carpets' status as abstract commodities by turning them into highbrow art pieces, promoted by critical and theoretical texts that function as genteel sales talk; this is both their enabling condition and their structural limitation.[42] In 1985 Guillaume Bijl performed an anticipatory desublimation of these pieces, as it were, by transforming a space in Amsterdam's Stedelijk Museum into an *Oosterse Tapijtenhandel,* a shop for oriental carpets. In his "transformational installations," Bijl collapsed the distinction between art markets and other markets, between artistic and non-artistic spectacle; in this case, he created the impression of a carpet shop with minimal means: mainly the carpets themselves, some potted plants, and lights. As in actual carpet shops, some rugs were displayed horizontally, but some were fixed to the walls—evoking, as de Rijke/de Rooij's work does, art-theoretical debates on horizontality versus verticality in the work of Jackson Pollock. In staging this fake carpet sale, Bijl's piece ironically suggests that *Documenta 12*'s "dialogue" between various abstract and ornamental compositions, which also included a huge ancient carpet mounted on a wall, is one that mainly takes place on the level of prices, of exchange value.

Inadvertently, Gregor Schneider's *Cube Venice 2005* made the same point. Originally, Schneider wanted to temporarily erect a large black cube on Saint Mark's Square in Venice as a modernist remake of the Ka'aba, recalling Venice's historical role as an interface between the West and the Orient; when this project could not be realized because of local political opposition and alleged fear of Islamist violence, Schneider took it on the road, eventually erecting his black volume next to the Hamburger Kunsthalle. The artist's relentless pragmatism may have undermined the original site-specific significance of his piece, but transforming his cube into a moveable commodity suggests that the "migration of forms" is, in fact, a continuous decentering, a decoding of ancient social and cultural structures that results in the unstable *umma* of global capitalism.[43] Like Bijl's carpet sale, the travails of the *Cube* indicate that the real encounter takes place not in forms, but in the *informal* realm of global capitalism's decentering structures—on the plane of abstraction that is the market. As much as certain ideologues want us to see Islam as the abstract and veiled Other, we are all natives of abstraction; a far from otherworldly abstraction that is central to our de-centered world.

CODE AS CURRENCY

If the rich and complex patterns of the Islamic carpet pay homage to the Creation, while mostly refraining from depicting living creatures and moving into abstraction so as not to violate the ban on representation, the modern carpets and other textiles created by Anni Albers and others at the Bauhaus represent the triumph of a different kind of abstraction: even though they drew inspiration from Islamic and other ornaments, their work shows "abstract thought" becoming operative in the form of industrial technology. The Bauhaus textile shop was equipped with a Jacquard loom, a machine invented in 1801, which can be "programmed" using punched paperboard sheets; the placement of the holes determines the composition woven into the rug. The Jacquard loom, which would provide inspiration to the pioneers of computer technology, can be seen as a primitive, mechanical graphic computer. By using it to weave straight-lined compositions of interlocking color bands and planes, rather than any figurative or biomorphic motif, Bauhaus artists rendered the program explicit, as it were. Some of these works appear oddly pixelated and digital, much more so than Richter's window; thus they seem to prefigure the arrival of a technology that would make it even easier to incarnate abstraction in the form of programmed surfaces. For media theorist Lev Manovich, the Jacquard loom prefigured the mid-twentieth century integration of two distinct lines of development:

that of visual media and that of computing, their integration resulting in digital "new media" which transform photographic or filmic images into raw materials that can be altered at will.[44]

Abstract art was based on the supposition that abstracting from visible appearances enabled one to reach a higher truth, but now abstraction penetrates society to the core. This has radical consequences for abstract painting: the dream of a quasi-language of abstract forms, which would create a truer picture of being than the one produced by representational conventions, becomes obsolete. In this regard, it is interesting that Theo van Doesburg and many artists in his wake—though not his erstwhile ally, Mondrian—renounced the term abstract art, opting instead for *concrete art*. Reasoning that abstract forms as such are also concrete and sensuous is not unlike Mondrian's resistance to ultimate abstraction; what was new in the van Doesburg-style *art concret* was an emphasis on rational construction with the aid of mathematical formulas. Concrete art à la Max Bill or Richard Paul Lohse is already "programmed," rather than composed, and in the 1960s and 70s artists associated with the *art concret* tradition would be among the first to embrace computers for art-making, inaugurating the triumph of the abstract concept turned operative code. Concrete art thus inaugurated a regime in which conceptual thinking indeed became the "truth of being," by not only assimilating, but actively transforming the material world to an unprecedented degree. In one crucial respect, Sol LeWitt's work from the 1960s and 70s is quite similar to *art concret*: formal abstraction becomes the permutation of simple elements, and lines are combined in various ways until all possibilities are exhausted. Rather than making specific compositional choices, LeWitt established parameters that function as a program to generate forms.

In the late sixties, when LeWitt characterized the idea as a "machine that makes the art," he was effectively mimicking the corporate attitude toward patents and brands, which are "machines for making products"—the latter activity could possibly be subcontracted to others, just like LeWitt would soon have assistants all over the world.[46] Carl Andre framed the implication of Conceptualism in the economic regime in rather stark terms, stating that advertising is the mother science of Conceptual art and that "a work of Conceptual art has to do with a work of material art the way a stock certificate has to do with a steel mill."[47] In recent years, a number of authors have analyzed

Conceptualism in relation to an economic regime associated with notions such as post-Fordism and immaterial labor—a regime in which "Abstract thought"—as Paolo Virno paraphrases Marx—"has become a pillar of social production."[48] In other words: conceptual abstraction itself becomes increasingly operative and concrete, largely leaving behind language as the master medium of abstraction in the process. In Baudrillard's hysterical discourse, this is the replacement of the concept as the medium of abstraction by "the generation by models of a real without origin or reality."[49]

Andre focused his attacks on Conceptual art's use of written words, stating that "THE LATEST ART MOVEMENT IS AN ATTEMPT TO DRIVE OUT ALL ART & REPLACE IT WITH LANGUAGE."[50] The prominence of language in Conceptualism can be seen as a form of archaism in the face of the onward move of conceptual abstraction, which increasingly leaves the natural languages behind as it moves from philosophical notions to the mathematical abstractions of modern science, and from the blueprints of industrial technology to the programs of the digital age. In the process, it becomes increasingly operative and transformative. Hegel's philosophical version of the incarnation of the word as the determinate concept was prophetic, but what happens in advanced capitalism can be characterized instead as abstraction itself becoming determinate, the *abstract becoming concrete*. Or rather: the abstract becoming concrete *once more*, since—as Marx and his followers noted—exchange value is already a "real abstraction." Perhaps history can be graphically represented not only as the merger of different lines of abstraction, but also of abstraction's concretion. In advanced capitalism, concept and coinage reveal their historical complicity, as "abstract thought" itself becomes as concrete as exchange. With an iconic nod to the "actually existing socialism" of the old Soviet Bloc, one might call this merger of two forms of real abstraction—of monetary and conceptual abstraction—"actually existing abstraction." To us, it is what the alleged socialism of the Warsaw Pact was to the people living in its member countries—our horizon.

Marx already noted that money, liberated from precious metals in the form of paper currency, becomes a pure sign.[51] This process was essentially complete when the gold standard was abandoned in the early 1970s, when Broodthaers made his own experiments with the value of gold.[52] In his "Dollar Bill" paintings from the early 1960s, Andy Warhol had already desublimated the grids of geometrical abstraction by filling them in with dollar bills. In an act of defiant reductionism, formal abstraction is decoded in terms of monetary abstraction—and this act creates symbolic value, which is, in turn, translated into market value. Such practices tend to turn the physical object into a stand-in for its own value: the object is a materialization of its price. In this respect, Yves Klein's legendary 1957 exhibition in Milan, in which eleven more or less identical blue monochromes were offered for sale at different prices, is crucial.[53] The monochrome is the end of painting as formal articulation, and here, structure is not integral to an individual painting, but a matter of abstract relations between different pseudo-concrete objects. Much more radically than in Warhol's case, in which smudges and other imperfections give an individual aura to each painting, Klein's work becomes conceptual: the concept of differently priced paintings is the real work of art. In this sense, such work represents a break with earlier abstract art, which had *refused to take the leap into the conceptual*—and it effects this break, prophetically, by suggesting that monetary abstraction is ultimately identical to conceptual abstraction. In the process, the concept has become a technocratic *logos*, a post-linguistic code propelling capitalist expansion—Adorno's "purposive logic" of old.

Although Adorno and Horkheimer wrote very cogently about the technological and technocratic turn of "enlightened" reason, Adorno often reverts to a somewhat dated conception of knowledge as being philosophical and encoded in language. Of increasing importance during the nineteenth and twentieth century is the transformation of *Begriffliche Erkenntnis*—philosophical, discursive *logos*—into scientific discourse and experiments. Even as it resisted the theoretical concept, at various moments, modern art showed its implication in the emerging science that would eventually leave linguistic concepts behind, or relegate them to the status of impoverished approximation. Recent research emphasizes the role of optical science in the emergence of abstract art.[54] Particularly interesting is the use, in nineteenth-century optical research, of colors and patterns to abstract the fundamental laws of perception from the plenitude of sensuous experience. Around 1800 some panels were prepared for Goethe's study of color, which could have passed for studies made by Bauhaus students more than a century later.[55] And is not the dissolving of particulars, and their conversion into interchangeable units—or as Mondrian might say, freeing forms from their limitations and putting them in "purer relationships"—precisely the modus operandi of the capitalist economy?

If real abstraction has been a reality for a long time, nonetheless something changes in what is variously referred to as post-industrial capitalism, post-Fordism, or the information economy. In becoming software that can be sold over and over again, the concept of real abstraction itself becomes currency. Information technology has enabled the abstraction of the money sign to go beyond Marx's paper currency. In the process, the concept becomes concrete and operational, as the operational concept is the ultimate commodity—the ultimate currency. This means that form changes its status. Under classic industrial capitalism, matter was "informed" by the use of rather inflexible processes involving molds or stamps with a limited number of forms, which were then often assembled into larger wholes.[56] Modern logos were two-dimensional versions of this, and their presence on commodities emphasized their "conceptual" status, turning them into strong brands. In the information economy, objects and surfaces are much more effortlessly coded and recoded; computer programs control equipment, which realize complex designs in two or three dimensions. In this context, with matter ever more penetrated by abstraction and therefore easier to "inform," the brand becomes continually more dominant, its powers to shape matter ever increasing.

Aside from *art concret*, Modernism by and large opposed industrial culture with a different approach to form: form was extracted from the material properties of a medium through personal confrontation with this medium. The new informational paradigm is so dominant that in art, too, form becomes design—that is to say, the implementation of a concept by coding or programming surfaces. This can already be seen in various forms of art from the 1960s, from Frank Stella's paintings to early experiments with computer art and Conceptual art's typography. This is not to say, of course, that such art is design, merely that it reflects, and to an extent reflects on, the status of design as the current paradigm of *Gestaltung*. In contemporary art, it is perhaps Liam Gillick who explores and exploits this paradigm change most radically. Gillick's 2005 show at the Palais de Tokyo, *Texte court sur la possibilité de créer une économie de l'équivalence*, was informed by what has become Gillick's master myth: his narrative about unemployed workers of a closed-down factory who transform the site of production into one of post-production by using it to generate ideas, instead of cars.[57] The formal elements—a floor with red glitter, an abstract landscape of cut-out metal mountain silhouettes, cages in sundry colors—relate to this narrative and to the workers' interventions in the factory and its environment, but without losing or dissimulating their status as speechless stand-ins, as contingent décor.

If one were to characterize abstraction in Adornian terms, as a mimetic absorption of the elements of capitalist technology in order to *rescue the mimetic itself* (for the mimetic is anachronistic in advanced industrial capitalism), one might argue that this mimesis of technological reason has become so complete as to become a *celebration* of capitalist technology and its purposive rationality. While this transformation became undeniable by the 1960s, the most convincing late-Modernist and Minimalist art still managed to infuse its quasi-design forms with a logic of its own, a logic excessive in its rigor. Seen as an object, Gillick's *Rescinded Production* (2008) is little more than a normalized, generic echo of 1960s practices, lacking both Judd's nominalist precision and the suggestiveness of LeWitt's quasi-automatized permutations; LeWitt's formalist concepts generated exhaustive permutations of formal possibilities that are suggestive of the changing circumstances of production in the 1960s in ways that elude Gillick's branded shapes. Ironically, this could be said to make Gillick's art rather Adornian in character; after all, for Adorno the shapes of modern art are *pseudo-signs* marked precisely by the failure—or refusal—to fully signify. However, Gillick's objects and installations are hardly allowed to develop an aesthetics of poverty on their own terms, for they function above all as props in the post-Fordist drama staged in Gillick's discourse.

In a passage paraphrased by Gillick in one of his texts, Maurizio Lazzarato has noticed that the rather hazy notion of immaterial labor in fact covers "*two different aspects* of labor. On the one hand, as regards the "informational content" of the commodity, it refers directly to the changes taking place in workers' labor processes in big companies in the industrial and tertiary sectors, where the skills involved in direct labor increasingly involve cybernetics and computer control (and horizontal and vertical communication). On the other hand, as regards the activity that produces the "cultural content" of the commodity, immaterial labor involves a series of activities that are not normally recognized as "work"—in other words, the kinds of activities involved in defining and fixing cultural and artistic standards, fashions, tastes, consumer norms, and, more strategically, public opinion."[58] Thus, immaterial labor comprises both post-linguistic coding and discursive practices that "translate" code into meaningful language.

If the "orthodox" Conceptualism of a Joseph Kosuth, with its emphasis on "ideas" that can be realized in a variety of seemingly indifferent forms and media, seems to be a platonic mystification of the role of "informational content" in the post-Fordist economy, the practices of artists such as Broodthaers, Graham and Smithson place emphasis not on the program, on the idea-turned-code, but on the other kind of immaterial labor, presenting art as infinite mediation and reflection, as discursive (or meta-discursive) art rather than Conceptual art. Gillick's work can be placed in this lineage, and it is in the problematic relation between his objects and his discourse that his work might be said to develop a dynamic that can be called aesthetic—a friction between relentlessly programmed forms and a discourse that is itself mimetic appropriation. Nonetheless, a kind of Platonism returns in Gillick's discourse, which tends to reduce complex processes to a few suggestive and reductive narratives and/or images. In Fredric Jameson's words, the public sphere constantly demands a traffic in tokens that it terms ideas, but which are really "idea objects," commodified fragments of theory—a production of ideas along the lines of Fordist car production.[59] Some forms of discourse offer less resistance to this mechanism than others, and some seem tailor-made for the process.

Obviously, contemporary conditions must be absorbed by the work of art if it is to be relevant, but this should not result in cartoon-like ideologizations of post-Fordism or immaterial labor. What matters in the end is the degree to which abstraction can be inhabited, the ways in which actually existing abstraction can be transformed by the demands of a life that is more than mere survival. Perhaps Krijn de Koning's befuddling and exhilarating presentation of relationships between old and new structures, which range from careful dialogue to blatant conflict, succeeds in intimating what it means to live with and in abstraction. The colored walls of his installations penetrate pre-existing architectural structures in often supremely illogical ways, affecting the sites and objects with which they engage in dialogue—a sink, for instance, may suddenly be situated at floor level. In the case of de Koning's exhibition at the Musée des Moulages, Lyon (2003), his structure emphasized the degraded status of antique idols in their guise as decayed plaster casts, which were presented as bulk goods, slapped together haphazardly and divided by pathways that functioned as abstract lines of flight (fig. 4.7).

These brittle simulacra were once made for an international market, but in their present dilapidated state suggest an excess of concretion and inertia; here as elsewhere, de Koning interrupts existing structures with new planes of abstraction in ways both alien and liberating. His work not only suggests that abstraction already penetrates all things, but also that this state of affairs may point beyond abstraction as we know it. What exists, exists to be tampered with; pushed to its limits and then still further. The obtuseness and imperfect readability of abstract structures is a symptom of a contemporary condition that is shot through with missed historical opportunities and forestalled futures, and functions as an incentive to abstract beyond existing abstraction.

CHARTING THE ABSTRACT WORLD

In the hyper-abstraction of conceptual capitalism, in which concept and currency both become code, the *logos* triumphs over the non-identical refuse that is sensory experience—to the extent to which the latter can no longer be fetishized as an oppositional force. This means, as Baudrillard was wont to emphasize, that the illusion of some lingering "authentic" realm of non-alienated experience must be given up. In the age of "social networking" sites such as MySpace, this has become more obvious than ever. Is there any point, then, in criticizing our abstract world? Modern critical discourse on abstraction has been accused—not least by Baudrillard—of romantic primitivism. Doesn't criticizing abstraction presuppose an ideal of aboriginal purity, a lost Eden untainted by abstraction? Recent artistic and intellectual practices suggest that there is an alternative: to intervene in actually existing abstraction; not in the name of some ideal of authenticity, but in order to transcend the limitations of this particular concretion of the abstract. The aim cannot be to oppose the abstract with "concrete facts," but rather, to make concrete the omnipresence of abstraction itself. In this context, the diagram has become a crucial tool in recent art.

The rise of the science of statistics, which played such an important role in the penetration of the social body by administrative reason, created a demand for visual information. In the late eighteenth century, by-now ubiquitous diagrams, timelines and bar graphs began to appear—often to make abstract economic data such as import and export figures more readily accessible. However, the positivist philosopher Otto Neurath considered these forms of statistics, which proliferated throughout the nineteenth century, insufficiently graphic. In the 1920s and 30s, working with the artist Gerd Arntz, Neurath created a system of "visual statistics," called ISOTYPE, in which rows of graphic signs—post-Creuzerian symbols—made it easy to compare quantities. Typically, such graphs compare numbers of workers, of unemployed people, or of industrial production in different countries or different decades. Rows of schematic cars, for instance, might be used to compare the number of automobiles on different continents; each car representing one million autos. By rendering statistical information visible, for ease of comparison, Neurath made the abstract concrete.[60] In recent years, Alice Creischer and Andreas Siekmann have remade sections of Neurath's picture atlas from the 1930s, updating ISOTYPE while doing away with its positivist and technocratic framework, attempting to make the contradictions of global capitalism visible.

However, in the intervening decades, the diagrammatic has moved on: while some of Neurath's charts show interrelations between various countries or different organizations, most are, in effect, bar graphs with an additional pictorial element. The emphasis is on quantity. In the post-war era, the most culturally prominent form of the diagram was the flow chart, which places emphasis on systemic structure rather than mass. Used to both program and navigate complex social and technological systems, these flow charts were open to critical appropriation. If diagrams are abstract machines that program reality, diagrammatic art hacks the machine and turns it against the reality it produces. Informed by cybernetics and semiotics, Stephen Willats pioneered this approach in his work of the 1960s and 70s; less explicitly but just as crucially, practices such as Haacke's and Allan Sekula's were also diagrammatic. Haacke charted the slumlord empire of Shapolsky and Co.; later, Sekula mapped the largely invisible streams of sea transport in his *Fish Story* project. In the 1980s, Peter Halley desublimated the squares and lines of modernist abstraction by reading them as the coded signs of a society in which abstraction is the norm, in which models produce reality. In his massive paintings with synthetic Day-Glo colors, abstraction became utterly diagrammatic, standing for hyper-capitalist society as a whole, without going into specifics. While his paintings were marketable luxury goods, they were clearly permutations of a basic concept, condensed and stretched in various ways, and filled in with different color schemes. Furthermore, Halley emphasized their incompleteness by combining the paintings with wallpapers and wall drawings containing flow charts adorned with words suggestive of social or technological processes—without ever exploring the implications of this suggestion.

In the 1990s, artists rejected this version of the diagrammatic in order to analyze specific networks and structures once again. With a penchant for conspiracy theory, Mark Lombardi traced the involvement of the Bush clan in various economic networks and their political interests, whereas the Parisian collective Bureau d'études sought to trace "world government," including state organizations and think tanks, and the affiliated "global laboratory" of surveillance and technology. In analyzing the "revolution of the sign" in El Lissitzky's work, T. J. Clark paraphrased its intention: "Do not map the world, transfigure it."[61] There is always danger that mapping will take the place of intervention, yet these days, tracing relations within today's regime of abstraction seems like a critical step towards conceiving alternatives, not to, but *within* abstraction. Actually existing abstraction cannot be the final word. In his *Hacker Manifesto*, McKenzie Wark detourns the "classic" leftist discourse on abstraction, by arguing for the revolutionary potential of abstraction: "To abstract is to construct a plane upon which otherwise different and unrelated matters may be brought into many possible relations. To abstract is to express the virtuality of nature, to make known some instance of its possibilities, to actualize a relation out of infinite relationality, to manifest the manifold."[62] In other words: one must not only make actually existing relations visible, but also actualize possible relations between matters that are usually kept separate, and break down neo-feudal hierarchies and inequalities programmed into actually existing abstraction.

In a lecture/performance in which he traced CIA flights in an increasingly intricate diagram, Walid Raad stressed that "revelations" about contemporary political or economic activities seem to have very little effect.[63] In any case, the intricate graphs Raad showed are difficult to read in detail, and while Bureau d'études uses a "pictographic grammar" of signs denoting various social and political actors, these are incorporated into charts of such bewildering, almost Piranesian quality that one wonders whether the abstract world is as much beyond representation as the Jewish or Muslim God.[64] In any case, it must be stressed that the ultimate abstraction is the ultimate concretion, that conceptual abstraction *informs* the material world ever more radically. Detourning Christian incarnation theology, Christina von Braun has argued that western history is marked by a progressive materialization of thought, and that the "incarnation" of *logos* in western science's interventions in matter does not mean "the process of abstraction has been annulled [aufgehoben], but rather that the *logos* actually controls matter, has subjugated matter."[65] Abstract reason has certainly made its mark upon matter; however, we are not dealing with a single incarnation, but with a purposive *logos* that segues in and out of forms—and which is always in the process of becoming concrete. In this sense, the digital image may indeed be like the Byzantine icon, making invisible data visible. But in contrast to the icon, many digital images do not acknowledge their invisible obverse; they want to appear as photorealistic as possible.

In this respect, modernist abstract art is a more legitimate successor to the icon, as Marie-José Mondzain has argued. Mondzain claims that western Catholicism's theory of the image is impoverished; the questions raised by the Son as the invisible image of God were properly pursued by eastern Orthodox theorists during the second iconoclastic crisis, in which the image was defined as "radically *independent of visibility*."[66] While the Son remained "indivisible and consubstantial" with God, by taking human form, Jesus Christ assimilated the *invisible image* that is the Son to the external image of God (man, fashioned in His image).[67] Thus, "the incarnation is nothing other than the redemption of the image by the image."[68] Christ is a double image, both an image of the Father and of man, but the first image predates his visibility; it is an invisible image. The defenders of the image could oppose iconoclasts, who accused images of trying to "imprison" God by "circumscribing" him in a line, by simply arguing that "*the iconic graph is neither a prison nor a tomb*," because the icon establishes a relation between different types of images, each shining through in the other; such is the economy of the icon.[69] Mondzain suggests that the paucity of both the Catholic approach—could she want any better confirmation than the Cologne and Utrecht affairs?—and its Protestant refutations could not help but push modern artists in a "Byzantine" direction, as modernity created problems that could not be solved with the tools of western Christianity. In this sense, modern art is Byzantine art returned, its de-symbolized symbols attempting to create images of the invisible.[70]

Monotheistic as well as Platonic theory was always marked by a slippage between visual and textual; while Mondzain used what is essentially a sophisticated form of Christian Neo-Platonism to suggest a post-hoc theory for the abstract symbols of early abstract art, her emphasis on the "invisible image" seems apposite in the current situation, in which we are dealing with a *logos* that is neither visual nor linguistic. Furthermore, her characterization of an economy in which iconic graphs time and again set "the visible and the invisible in relation with each other without any concessions to realism, yet without contempt for matter," seems like an apt description of contemporary diagrammatic practices.[71] Such practices, making modernist abstraction's diagrammatic leanings explicit, correct the illusionism of many digital images; they are the true icons of our abstract spectacle.

One Bureau d'études map of the "world government" is dedicated to "Monotheism, Inc.," which allows one to study the various economic entanglements of the monotheistic religions (fig. 4.8). From a central circle with the founding figures of the Abrahamic faiths, one can trace the investments, corporations, and foundations associated with these religions—such as the companies linked to the bin Laden family. All branches of the tree seem utterly compromised by secular dealings, each one more dubious than the next. The spectacle is infiltrated through and through by monotheistic capitalism. But isn't Bureau d'études' map a form of critical iconoclasm that hints at interventions in these structures—interventions that aim at a different order, that aim to abstract beyond this web of shady interests? The use value of such a bedazzling map is open to question; if anything, such a chart suggests that transparency and legibility are not necessarily the goal. While the global economic system must indeed be made more transparent and more legible, possible alternatives themselves are sketchy, imperfectly transparent—and this symptomatic obtuseness is potentially aesthetic. Conversely, aesthetic projects are potentially political, even while their trouble in achieving any political or social agency is, in turn, symptomatic of the current deadlock.

For Baudrillard and others, the reign of the digital ended the dialectic of sign and symptom; if everything is a matter of coded simulations, what room is there for symptomatic formations? But where there are signs, there are symptoms; we are not dealing with the perfect systems of cybernetic diagrams, but with an order that is lived; with codes that are enacted. If the World Trade Center was Baudrillard's perfect sign of the digital code, September 11 was the revenge of the symptom, hijacking and destroying the sign, and reminding us of the pressing need to intervene in actually existing abstraction. It is true that a simulating patient may produce "real" symptoms, as Baudrillard notes, but this is nothing new.[72] What matters is using the production of symptoms—however compulsive or contrived they may be—to intervene in contemporary capitalism, in which abstraction is continually being enacted, continually performed.

In Liam Gillick's video piece *Everything Good Goes* (2008), architectural forms appear on a computer flatscreen in a stylishly minimalist office, while the Mac mouse is manipulated by an operator who remains unseen—despite the mirror behind the monitor (fig. 4.9). Some recorded voicemail messages on contemporary labor play over the soundtrack. The building on the screen is a model of the Salumi meat factory in Godard and Jean-Pierre Gorin's 1972 film *Tout va bien*; of this film's ambitious attempt to analyze and criticize concrete abstraction in a neo-Brechtian way, next to nothing remains. Gillick not only glosses over actual production—and producers—of his own works of art, in keeping with the art world's general code of silence, but also seems to suggest that material production and conflicts over labor conditions are a thing of the (Fordist) past, a laughable anachronism barely deserving a fleeting thought over one's latte macchiato.[73] Neither discursive nor poetic, the disjointed and barely audible voiceover does nothing to complicate the image of disembodied sign production, which obscures the production of the machinery being used, the hidden world of server centers and their ecological implications, the potential execution of the design on the screen, and its implication outside the trendy office environment.

What does it mean to suggest that the production of cars is replaced by the production of ideas? Does the narrative of the factory then become something of a reductive cartoon, a line drawing traced over and over again? Is there difference in these repetitions? And what about the unseen laborer, who is rather less immaterial than Gillick's discourse and camera care to suggest? Digital *logos* is not only incarnate in images and objects, but also in laborers—in *performers*.

NOTES

1 Piet Mondrian, "A New Religion?" [ca. 1938/40], in *The New Art—The New Life: The Collected Writings of Piet Mondrian,* ed. Harry Holtzman and Martin S. James (Boston: Macmillan, 1986), 319.

2 "Aussi peu intéressantes que les timbres-postes oblitérés, et forcément aussi peu variées qu'eux, les productions littéraires ou plastiques ne sont plus les signes que d'un commerce abstrait." Michèle Bernstein et al., "Les Distances à garder," in *Potlatch,* no. 19 (April 1955). See *Guy Debord présente Potlatch (1954–1957),* Paris 1996, 144.

3 Meyer Schapiro, "Nature of Abstract Art" [1937], in *Modern Art: 19th and 20th Centuries. Selected Papers* (New York: George Braziller, 1968), 207.

4 "Von Anbeginn war ästhetische Abstraktion ...eher ein Bilderverbot." Theodor W. Adorno, "Ästhetische Theorie," in *Gesammelte Schriften,* vol. 7, ed. Gretel Adorno and Rolf Tiedemann (Frankfurt am Main: Suhrkamp, 1972), 40.

5 Bertolt Brecht, "Der Dreigroschenprozess" [1931], in *Dreigroschenbuch: Texte, Materialien, Dokumente* (Frankfurt am Main: Suhrkamp, 1960), 93–94.

6 "...l'abolition même du spectaculaire." Jean Baudrillard, *Simulacres et simulation,* (Paris: Éditions Galilée, 1981), 52.

7 "L'effigie du système capitaliste est passée de la pyramide à la carte perforée." Jean Baudrillard, *L'Échange symbolique et la mort* (Paris: Gallimard, 1976), 109. English translation by Iain Hamilton Grant: Jean Baudrillard, *Symbolic Exchange and Death* (London: Sage, 1993), 69. In his 1974 postcard edition, *Cosmos und Damian,* Joseph Beuys approached this structure in a resolutely archaizing vein, attempting to redeem the bar graph-like towers: Beuys printed the World Trade Center towers in yellowish tones—using a 3D postcard purchased in New York as a model—and inscribed them with the words "Cosmos" and "Damian," thus recalling the saints Cosmas and Damian, a pair of healers often represented in medieval sculpture. Yet by writing "Cosmos" instead of "Cosmas," Beuys did not so much replace the towers with (the names of) two specific saints, as with a vague intimation of pantheistic spirituality. If the postcard format is a nice contrast to the World Trade Center's megalomania, it is also symptomatic of the powerlessness of Beuys' symbolic intervention.

8 "... la puissance meurtrière des images, meurtrières du réel..."Baudrillard, *Simulacres et simulation* (see note 6), 16.

9 See, for instance, Christina von Braun and Bettina Mathes, *Verschleierte Wirklichkeit: Die Frau, der Islam und der Westen* (Berlin: Aufbau Verlag, 2007), 366–384.

10 Moshe Halbertal and Avishai Margalit, *Idolatry,* trans. Naomi Goldblum (Cambridge, MA: Harvard University Press, 1992), 9–35.

11 I refer to a report by Jan-Willem P. Wits, then press chief of the archbishopric, *Who's Afraid of God? Terugblik op een spraakmakende poster,* October 1998. Thanks to Marijke Kamsma, who designed the poster, for providing me with information, and thanks to Suzanne Tiemersma for her assistance.

12 Carl Andre, "Letter to Sol LeWitt" [1970], in *Cuts: Texts 1959–2004* (Cambridge, MA: MIT Press, 2005), 37.

13 Carel Blotkamp, *Mondrian: The Art of Destruction* (London: Reaktion Books, 1994), 60.

14 Piet Mondrian, "The New Plastic in Painting" [1917/18] in *The New Art—The New Life* (see note 1), 45–46, 49.

15 Even if the author experienced Mondrian first-hand during his final years, Victor Papanek's suggestion that Mondrian would have taken to working with computers is as far off the mark as his assertion that Mondrian "had decided to turn himself into a machine" during the 1920s. Victor Papanek, *Design for the Real World: Human Ecology and Social Change* [1971/84] (London: Thames & Hudson, 2006), 45.

16 Mondrian, "New Plastic in Painting" in *The New Art—The New Life* (see note 1), 28, 36.

17 Martin S. James, "Piet Mondrian: Art and Theory to 1917" in *The New Art—The New Life* (see note 1), 11.

18 Bolland's impact on Mondrian's thought is particularly pronounced throughout "The New Plastic in Painting," in *The New Art—The New Life* (see note 1), esp. 27–74.

19 G. W. F. Hegel, "Enzyklopädie der philosophischen Wissenschaften im Grundrisse," vol. I [1830], in *Werke,* vol. 8 (Frankfurt am Main: Suhrkamp, 1970), 304.

20 "Die Idee ist das Wahre *an und für sich, die absolute Einheit des Begriffs und der Objektivität.*" Ibid., 367. "Die Idee ist der *adäquate Begriff*, das objektive *Wahre* oder das *Wahre als solches*." G. W. F. Hegel, "Wissenschaft der Logik," vol. II, in *Werke*, vol. 6 (Frankfurt am Main: Suhrkamp, 1969), 462.

21 See G. W. F. Hegel, "Vorlesungen über die Philosophie der Religion," vol. II, in *Werke*, vol. 17 (Frankfurt am Main: Suhrkamp, 1969), 218–299.

22 "Der Gegenstand, die objektive und subjektive Welt überhaupt *sollen* mit der Idee nicht bloß *kongruieren*, sondern sie sind selbst die Kongruenz des Begriffs und der Realität; diejenige Realität, welche dem Begriffe nicht entspricht, ist bloße *Erscheinung*, das Subjektive, Zufällige, Willkürliche, das nicht die Wahrheit ist." Hegel, "Wissenschaft der Logik," (see note 20), 464.

23 "Kunst ist Berichtigung der Begrifflichen Erkenntnis." Adorno, "Ästhetische Theorie" (see note 4), 179.

24 Ibid., 73.

25 "Kunst ist rationalität, welche diese kritisiert, ohne sich ihr zu entziehen."Ibid., 87.

26 Ibid., 189.

27 Peter Halley, "Abstraction and Culture" [1991], in *Recent Essays 1990–1996* (New York: Edgewise Press, 1997), 27, 32.

28 Blotkamp, *Mondrian* (see note 13), 137, 145.

29 Joseph Kosuth, *Definition: Abstract (Art As Idea As Idea)*, 1967, collection Des Moines Art Center.

30 Von Braun and Mathes, *Verschleierte Wirklichkeit* (see note 9), 126–130.

31 "Die Abstraktion beherrschte die Mohammedaner: ihr Ziel war, den abstrakten Dienst geltend zu machen, und danach haben sie mit der größten Begeisterung gestrebt. Diese Begeisterung war *Fanatismus*, d.i. eine Begeisterung für ein abstraktes, für einen abstrakten Gedanken, der negierend sich zum Bestehenden verhält." G. W. F. Hegel, "Vorlesungen über die Philosophie der Geschichte" [1822/31], in *Werke*, vol. 12 (Frankfurt am Main: Suhrkamp, 1970), 431. Hegel's term for Muslims, *Mohammedaner* (Mohammedans or, in the contemporary spelling, Muhammadans), is now largely discredited as a polemical Christian term based on the notion that Muslims engage in idolatrous worship of Muhammad.

32 Meisner, it should be noted, said "a mosque or a house of prayer," the latter term suggesting a Jewish or Protestant place of worship, but it was the mention of the mosque that attracted the most attention. For Richter's response to the mosque comparison, see Georg Imdahl, "Meisner irrt sich ein bisschen," *Kölner Stadt-Anzeiger*, August 31, 2007, http://www.ksta.de/html/artikel/1187344877397.shtml.

33 Cardinal Meisner, "Wenn Gott nicht mehr in der Mitte steht," *Frankfurter Allgemeine Zeitung*, September 18, 2007, http://www.faz.net/s/RubC4DEC11C008 142959199A04A6FD8EC44/Doc~E7D0461E2A59D493A8DCD03956888 41F9~ATpl~Ecommon~Scontent.html.

34 "Sobald sie Gott abschaffen und den Menschen als Maß in ihre Mitte stellen, ist der Mensch in seiner Würde gefährdet und ein Menschenleben nicht mehr viel wert." Ibid.

35 "Dort, wo die Kultur von der Gottesverehrung abgekoppelt wird, erstarrt der Kultus im Ritualismus und die Kultur entartet. Sie verliert ihre Mitte." In "Meisner warnt vor Entartung der Kultur," *Focus online*, September 14, 2007, http://www.focus.de/politik/deutschland/koeln_aid_132896.html.

36 See the third part of Albert Ottenbacher, "Kunstgeschichte in ihrer Zeit. Hans Sedlmayr," http://www.albert-ottenbacher.de/sedlmayr/seite3.html.

37 Hans Sedlmayr, *Verlust der Mitte. Die bildende Kunst des 19. und 20. Jahrhunderts als Symptom und Symbol der Zeit* (Salzburg: Otto Müller, 1948). Sedlmayr doesn't speak of *Gesamtkunstwerke*, or the total work of art, but of *Gesamtaufgaben*, or total tasks/challenges (17–19).

38 Gerhard Richter, "Interview mit Hans-Ulrich Obrist 1993," in *Text: Schriften und Interviews*, ed. Hans-Ulrich Obrist (Frankfurt am Main/Leipzig: Insel, 1993), 245.

39 Richter first encountered Sedlmayr's *Verlust der Mitte* in the 1950s, when he was still studying at the academy in Dresden (letter to the author, September 9, 1999). See the references to Sedlmayr, including one in the course of a conversation with Buchloh, in *Text*, 72, 120, 139.

40 A related film by de Rijke/de Rooij, *The Point of Departure* (also 2002), is in color and scans one carpet from various distances and angles.

41 Henri Focillon, *The Life of Forms in Art* [1934], trans. Charles B. Hohan and George Kubler (New York: Zone Books, 1989), 141.

42 In other words: de Rijke/de Rooij's practice strategically inhabits a point of indifference, where critical exploration and commercial exploitation of the art world's mechanisms are all but indistinguishable, where critical reflection is abstract enough to function as marketing.

43 An official publication touts the work and the controversy as a prime example of "art in the age of global terrorism": *Cubes: Art in the Age of Global Terrorism* (Milan: Charta, 2006). Schneider has since moved on to wilder shores of shock by proposing to exhibit a dying man.

44 See Lev Manovich, *The Language of New Media* (Cambridge, MA: MIT Press, 2001), 21–26.

45 For more on *art concret*, see Jonneke Jobse, *De Stijl Continued: The Journal Structure (1958–1964). An Artists' Debate* (Rotterdam: 010 Publishers, 2005), 220–225.

46 For an analysis of LeWitt's linking of idea and machine within the context of the post-Fordist economy, as expounded in his "Paragraphs on Conceptual Art" (1967), see Sabeth Buchmann, *Denken gegen das Denken: Produktion, Technologie, Subjektivität bei Sol LeWitt, Yvonne Rainer und Hélio Oiticica* (Berlin: PoLYpeN, 2007), 48–54.

47 Carl Andre, "The Mother Science of Conceptual Art" [undated] and "Art and Dematerialization" [1972], in *Cuts* (see note 12), 84.

48 Paolo Virno, *A Grammar of the Multitude*, trans. Isabella Bertoletti, James Cascaito, Andrea Casson (Los Angeles: Semiotext(e), 2004), 63. The authors who have written most cogently on Conceptual art in the context of post-Fordism and immaterial labor are Alexander Alberro (*Conceptual Art and the Politics of Publicity* [Cambridge, MA: MIT Press, 2003]) and Sabeth Buchmann in her aforementioned book. My reflection on this issue has also been stimulated by recent texts in which my student Leen Bedaux analyzed the recent discourse on Conceptual art and further developed its analysis in terms of immaterial labor and post-Fordism.

49 "Elle [la simulation] est la génération par les modèles d'un réel sans origine ni réalité: hyperréel." Baudrillard, *Simulacres et simulation* (see note 6), 10.

50 Carl Andre, "Art is not a Linguistic Phenomenon" [1976], in *Cuts* (see note 12), 85.

51 Karl Marx, "Das Kapital: Kritik der politischen Ökonomie" [1872 edition], in *Marx/Engels Gesamtausgabe (MEGA)*, part 2, vol. 6.1 (Berlin: Dietz, 1987), 149–151.

52 See Natascha Sadr Haghighian's essay, "Immateriality and Oil," on the oil crisis, the abandonment of the gold standard in relation to immaterial labor, and the "dematerialization" of art in Conceptualism: http://www.possest.de/notaboutoil%20files/introtexts/immateriality%20and%20oil.htm. A similar comparison has been made in an essay by my student, Leen Bedaux.

53 Nuit Banai, "From the Myth of Objecthood to the Order of Space: Yves Klein's Adventures in the Void," in *Yves Klein*, ed. Olivier Berggruen, Max Hollein, Ingrid Pfeiffer (Ostfildern-Ruit: Hatje Cantz, 2005), 19.

54 See for instance, *Aux origines de l'abstraction*, exh. cat. (Paris: Musée d'Orsay, 2003).

55 See Jacques Le Rider, "L'héritage de Goethe: romantisme et expressionnisme," in ibid., 111–120.

56 Vilém Flusser, *Medienkultur* (Frankfurt am Main: Fischer, 1997), 222.

57 Liam Gillick, "A short text on the possibilities of creating an economy of equivalence" (2004), http://www.airdeparis.com/liam/2005/pdt/liam_gillick.htm.

58 Maurizio Lazzarato, "Immaterial Labor," trans. Paul Colilli and Ed Emery, http://www.generation-online.org/c/fcimmateriallabour3.htm. For Gillick's paraphrasing, see Liam Gillick, *Maybe it would be better if we worked in groups of three*, Hermes Lecture 2008 (Den Bosch: Hermes Lecture Foundation, 2008), 15.

59 Fredric Jameson, "Introduction: On Not Giving Interviews," in *Jameson on Jameson: Conversations on Cultural Marxism*, ed. Ian Buchanan (Durham: Duke University Press, 2007), 6.

60 For more on Neurath, see the "web file" relating to the project "After Neurath at Stroom in The Hague," with contributions by Steve Rushton and others: http://www.stroom.nl/webdossiers/webdossier.php?wd_id=2615745.

61 T. J. Clark, *Farewell to an Idea: Episodes from a History of Modernism* (New Haven, CT: Yale University Press, 1999), 291.

62 McKenzie Wark, *A Hacker Manifesto* (Cambridge, MA: Harvard University Press, 2004), 14.

63 Walid Raad's multimedia presentation, *I Feel a Great Desire to Meet the Masses Once Again*, has been given a number of times in various countries since 2005.

64 See http://utangente.free.fr/.

65 "…so leitete das Christentum die Inkarnation des Logos, die Verkörperung des Geistes, ein..."; "Dass Gott (oder das Wort) Fleisch wurde, heißt nicht, dass der Abstraktionsprozess wieder aufgehoben wurde, sondern es bedeutet vielmehr, dass der Logos tatsächlich die Materie beherrscht, die Materie unterworfen hat." Christina von Braun, *Nicht ich: Logik,*

Lüge, Libido (Frankfurt am Main: Neue Kritik, 1985), 110.

66 Marie-José Mondzain, *Image, Icon, Economy: The Byzantine Origins of the Contemporary Imaginary,* trans. Rico Franses (Stanford: Stanford University Press, 2005), 80.

67 Ibid., 81.

68 Ibid., 102.

69 Ibid., 93.

70 Ibid., in particular 88–91, where Mondzain refers to Malevich, Kandinsky, and Worringer.

71 Ibid., 84.

72 "Le simulateur est-il malade ou non, puisqu'il produit de 'vrais' symptômes?" Baudrillard, *Simulacres et simulation* (see note 6), 12.

73 It is curious that Gillick repeatedly refers to radical filmmaking from the 1970s by Jean-Luc Godard, the Dziga Vertov Group, Chris Marker, and the Groupe Medvedkine, and their struggles with the (un)representability of labor in advanced capitalism, while carefully sidestepping any concrete or detailed confrontation of such issues. For a recent project investigating the shadowy world of companies that specialize in producing pieces for Gillick and others, see Natascha Sadr Haghighian's *Solo Show.*

Chapter Five

VEILED REVELATION

Smash the images! Veil the virgins!
Tertullian, in Flaubert's *The Temptation of Saint Anthony*[1]

The country is being run by madmen who believe that the twelfth imam is about to return! They actually believe that!
From a conversation with an exiled Iranian, volunteering in a Dutch petting zoo

During her years in Holland, Ayaan Hirsi Ali wrote the script for a short film on the role of women in Islam, *Submission (part 1)*.[2] The 2004 film was directed by Theo van Gogh, the filmmaker and enfant terrible who for years dabbled in anti-Semitic rhetoric, which he then effortlessly transformed into anti-Islamic rhetoric; van Gogh famously described Muslims as backward "goat-fuckers." He paid with his life for *Submission* when he was stabbed to death on an Amsterdam street in broad daylight by a young fundamentalist, now famous as Mohammed B.[3] *Submission* shows a woman wearing a dark yet transparent veil, which reveals parts of her body upon which verses from the Qur'an on the submissive role of women have been written in ornate calligraphy. Here, the role of the camera in unveiling the body, the fight between veil and camera over visibility, is restaged with crypto-pornographic explicitness. The film's voiceover monologue contains harrowing stories of abuse and represents the veil as a prison, the innermost circle of an extremely restricted world. In many cases, this is undoubtedly true, yet Hirsi Ali and van Gogh reduce the veil's ambiguity and contradiction to a cartoon image, transforming veiled women into the faceless face of Otherness and refusing to address the obverse side of the violence cloaked by the veil: the violence of unveiling.[4]

Gestures of unveiling are an essential part of Enlightenment rhetoric. Nature, religion, the economy: all must be unveiled to have their secrets revealed. Hence the emergence of a small number of women donning full-body veils in major European cities over the last few years has been experienced as a radical contestation of the Enlightenment. Such veils function as screens upon which cultural anxieties and desires are projected—and not only from one side. In the process, Orientalist fantasies and fears are rekindled: associated with Islam, the veil becomes an emblem for Islamic/Oriental culture's Otherness and incompatibility with the West.[5] Under these conditions, Islam itself comes to be represented as an alluring, elusive, and vaguely threatening woman waiting to be unveiled.[6] Yet although the identification of the veil with Islam is a powerful one, various historians and theorists have pointed out that there is no exclusive or "natural" relationship between the veil and Islam. Not only were statues of goddesses often veiled in the Middle East and the Mediterranean, but wives were veiled as well, long before the advent of Islam. In these regions, the veil—which predates Islam and Christianity—often had social rather than religious connotations.[7] While the veiled image of a goddess signified the inaccessibility and Otherness of the sacred, the veil on a wife traditionally signified her status as a man's property in contrast to the unveiled prostitute. However, the veil can change its meaning: if it primarily signified that the woman was accessible only to her husband and inaccessible to the gaze (and touch) of others, the connotation of inaccessibility could be sacralized. This is what seems to have happened in Islam; while Christianity transformed marriage into a sacrament, Islam sacralized the female body by veiling it.[8]

Those women who fight against the imposition of the veil deserve every support, but the overt aim of "rescuing" women from a patriarchal regime can easily become a fashionable version of cultural colonialism, in which Islam is presented as the dark Other to European civilization. While it is clear that there are serious issues with women's rights in many Muslim societies even today, as well as among certain immigrant communities in Europe, the current fixation on the veil suggests that further issues are at stake, and that feminism is often instrumentalized to rather dubious ends—there have been plenty of strange alliances between feminists and Islam-bashing, right-wing Enlightenment fundamentalists who find their favorite *bête noire* in the veil. Lord Cromer, the British consul general in Egypt during the late nineteenth century, set a telling precedent: he ideologized the veil as a sign of Islamic oppression of women, while at the same time opposing universal suffrage at home.[9] Thus, an apparent engagement of women's rights can in fact be a reactionary instrumentalization of women's rights. Repeated images of veiled women serve to fortify the status quo; using the veil as Exhibit A, many authors present the integration of Muslim populations into "Western" history as unthinkable. When then-immigration minister Ella Vogelaar suggested that a "Judeo-Christian-Muslim" tradition might develop in Holland in the far future, the main response to her remark was vicious, right-wing furor.[10] The historicity of religions and their relationships is consistently denied; anti-Semites ranging from Martin Luther to Houston Stewart Chamberlain would be baffled by the current popularity of the epithet "Judeo-Christian" among those who wish to define and defend the essence of "Western civilization."

The Qur'an's prescriptions for the proper dress and behavior of women offer a wide scope for interpretation, and there is no unambiguous demand that hair or faces be covered.[11] However, it is equally true that many contemporary Muslims use the veil precisely to mark space which is beyond the grasp of the secular and sexual gaze. Ever since Sayyid Qutb, Islamists have regarded the comparative sexual freedom and sexualization of the public sphere as crucial symptoms of the new western idolatry. Not only is thought itself turned into an idol by western rationalists, as Qutb noted with horror; but even lower than that, westerners also idolize the body.[12] Perhaps this is a mere front for true idolatry: as Ali Shariati stated, sexual freedom is "part of a new exploitation, a type of limitless deception, which the impure system of western capitalism produces." Behind the seductive appearance of commodified sexuality lie "great idols and the three faces of the contemporary religious trinity: exploitation, colonialization, and despotism."[13] This may be true, but it is hard to avoid the feeling that Shariati is all too keen to attack sexual freedom as such. In this, he is close to Khomeini, whose *Little Green Book* opens with general attacks on imperialism and colonialism, only to delve into insanely detailed prescriptions for dealing with sexuality and "woman and her periods."

Nonetheless, in a moralizing, puritanical, and overly abstract way, Islamic thinkers have focused on the commodification of the human subject. In recent theory, this development is reflected upon according to the rubric of immaterial labor—when labor becomes less routine and demands more and more "soft skills," it grows increasingly akin to performance. Under advanced capitalism, abstraction is ultimately enacted; the becoming-real of abstraction culminates in the ultimate reality of human action and interaction. The abstract spectacle becomes performative.

ABSTRACT BODIES

Images of veiled women have become a minor genre in European newspapers. Photographs of Muslim women—either with headscarves or full veils—walking in front of billboards featuring scantily clad advertising vixens, drive home the point that the spectacle commodifies bodies just as it sexualizes commodities, and that Muslim women demonstrate their difference from the western economic and visual regime by shrouding themselves. The most potent images are of full-body veils such as the *niqab,* which leaves only the eyes visible through a narrow slit, and the Afghan burqa, which covers the eyes with an embroidered grille. In both cases, the human body is abstracted almost beyond recognition, in what seems to be a radical break with the "Western" glorification of the body and the capitalist scheme of visibility in general. After a group of radical Muslims allegedly plotted to kidnap and kill a British Muslim soldier on leave from Iraq was arrested in early 2007, British newspapers printed a photograph of a group of veiled women in Birmingham, one of them making a V-sign (fig. 5.1).[14] The veil here becomes a signifier for the "Muslim threat," a threat running deeper than mere terrorism. Perhaps the true threat is the veil itself; the occlusion of the face, the imposition of abstraction.

It is a fallacy to claim, as is often done, that all Islamic veils are instruments of oppression in every circumstance. Many women claim the veil for themselves, for a variety of—sometimes contradictory—reasons. Otto Neurath, who presented the vanishing of the veil in countries such as Turkey and Persia as an obvious sign of modernization and women's emancipation in *Modern Man in the Making*, would have been rather surprised at the sight of a woman demonstrator holding a placard with the words: "The veil is womens [sic] liberation."[15] For all the women who oppose the veil, there are countless others who adopt it to signify their Otherness, their non-identity. The libidinal economy of veiling and unveiling, of hiding and revealing, is highly complex. As a symbolic marker of difference, a concrete obstruction of the gaze and stimulation for the imagination, the veil can incite rather than kill off desire. In Atatürk's Turkey, the removal of the veil was experienced by some women as a *neutralization* of sexuality—a reminder that the liberal interpretation of the veil as evincing an unhealthy fear of sexuality is limited at best, even if today's Islamists essentially share this interpretation, railing as they do against western over-sexualization and presenting their interpretation of *hijab,* or "modest" clothing, as the remedy.[16] Like the self-styled "modesty patrols," which operate in ultra-orthodox quarters in Israel, the Iranian militias whose task it is to enforce a draconic dress code must be composed of erotomaniacs.[17] But not all veils are enforced. When the German archeologist and development worker Susanne Osthoff was released by her Iraqi kidnappers in December 2005, the German media rejoiced; when she decided to give an interview to the ZDF news program in a black *niqab*, sympathy transformed immediately into irritation and doubt about her sanity. Apparently, the niqab offered Osthoff some protection from the unwanted light of publicity at that particular moment; it was indeed an instrument of liberation, but at the same time it transformed Osthoff from "our Susanne" into "one of them"—less a person than an example of a powerful iconography.[18]

Like the black masks and clothes worn by the mythical "Black Bloc" of anti-globalist protest, the veil seems to signal a radical break in the spectacular order. In their video *Get Rid of Yourself* (2003), Bernadette Corporation investigates the Black Bloc, its strategies and its myths, at one point including an image of Malevich's *Black Square*—thus linking contemporary political contestation within and of the spectacle to modernist iconoclasm, which was itself, at least in Malevich's case, informed by anarchist political sympathies. While there is no more or less direct link in the case of the burqa as a performative prop, its use has a similar media effect; it is presented as a blackout of the visible, which amounts to a declaration of war on "western values." Using the veil as an abstract prop, some women rhetorically secede from the ruling regime of apparently unhindered visibility, effectively using it to *unveil* the limits of western liberalism—to reveal it as a sham, an ideology of exploitation. However paradoxical this may seem, the use of the veil in contemporary Islamism can thus be seen as an act of *unveiling*. At the same time, this act is a mystification—of women, of social relations, and indeed of Islam—that strengthens the Manichaean opposition between "the West" and "Islam." As a seemingly radical secession from the capitalist spectacle, the veil can be easily reabsorbed and neutralized, just as the media success of the Black Bloc shows that it functions as an ideal bogeyman.

In Peter de Wit's *Sigmund,* a popular daily Dutch comic strip, there are regular appearances by burqa-clad women, who are drawn as cone-shaped black blobs—dark voids in the field of vision. In one episode, two of these "burqa babes," seen from behind, stand in front of abstract paintings in a museum and effectively become part of the composition. One woman says to the other: "I don't like art when I can't see what it represents."[19] In this probably accidental variation on an old Ad Reinhardt cartoon, De Wit neatly encapsulates the strange structural homology between aesthetic modernism and Islamic culture in the contemporary imagination; both threaten to break with the apparently unhindered visibility often identified with "the West"—rejecting the abstract obverse of the spectacle's pseudo-concrete images. Islamic fundamentalists and Enlightenment fundamentalists alike attempt to exacerbate this divide. Both sides—defenders of "the West," as well as its enemies—identify western culture with a regime of total visibility, with an unhindered gaze whose favorite object has long been the female body. Hence, veils that cloak this body in mystery have come to signify a refusal to be subjected to (and by) the gaze of western public scrutiny. And yet, the burqa, a black speck in the field of vision, might stand as a surprisingly neo-modernist emblem. Just as modernist abstract symbols eventually revealed themselves to be differential signs, so the veil is a logotype standing for the Otherness of Islam.

In the Iranian town of Susa, there is a mural that shows a woman in Islamic dress, her face visible but body concealed and eyes modestly averted, accompanied by the slogan, in English: "A woman modestly dressed is as a pearl in it's [sic] shell" (fig. 5.2).[20] In Iran and elsewhere, strict interpretation of hijab has been forcefully imposed on women, in response to what conservative clerics see as the westernization and sexualization of Muslim societies during the early- to mid-twentieth century. The ideological counterpart to this exercise in public art was painted in 2003 on the side wall of an Amsterdam apartment building: a large mural of an undressed woman inspired by Jacob van Lennep's poem *Ode aan een roosje*. The poem's lines are splashed across the façade and across the body of the woman; a clothed man, presumably the author, floats over the text and the woman's legs. Although inhabitants of the neighboring buildings, many of them Muslims, were surveyed prior to the work's execution, (apparently responding in a predominantly positive way) once it had been completed, the mural was attacked both verbally and physically—with black paint. Struggling to remove this paint, the artist decided to pixelate the woman's pubic area, veiling the rose with an abstract grid.[21] Once again, abstraction is identified with Islam, this time with gendered connotations. A quasi-Richterian color grid appears to externalize abstraction, to cast the role of Islamic Other. Like the Peter de Wit cartoon, abstraction is considered fundamentally opposed to western "visual culture."

The contemporary status of the veil as a media myth that would have given Roland Barthes a field day has been challenged by a number of artists, including Natascha Sadr Haghighian; there has even been a group show on "veiling, representation and contemporary art."[22] Most of the work in this show deals with the Islamic veil in a rather illustrative way; a less straightforward approach is taken by Willem Oorebeek, whose *Blackouts* are lithographic prints that adopt the blackness characteristic of modernist art, from Malevich to Reinhardt to Stella, turning it into a veil superimposed onto media images. Starting from magazine pages and photographs, Oorebeek applies a layer of black ink through which the underlying images (and sometimes texts) can still be glimpsed, depending on the viewing angle. In another piece, which uses media images without a "blackout layer," Oorebeek includes a catalogue page of gray Gerhard Richter monochromes and a newspaper image of Michael Jackson shopping in Bahrain, wearing a facial veil and long black robes (fig. 5.3).[23] To the media, Jackson's veil could only be another unnatural, pathological attempt to break with the spectacle—even while Jackson and the media effectively cooperate in creating a spectacle of iconoclasm. The opposition between veil and visibility is thus a false one, and like the *Blackouts,* the image—which has been transformed into a wintery scene by a veil of white paint specks—subtly demonstrates this. Like other acts of iconoclasm, veiling creates new images, and whereas Oorebeek's layered erasures create a subtle dialectic of veil and visibility, gestures of veiling more typically result in a spectacular representation of Otherness.

Obviously, artistic practices that aim to develop a more complex semiology of the veil are rather powerless in the face of unchecked demagogy. A few years ago, it became popular to describe all art as performative, in the sense of Austin's speech-act theory: when a priest says, "I now declare you husband and wife," he is not describing a state of affairs but rather creating a new situation. His language is performative.[24] However, speech acts can fail: if the priest had been defrocked, or if some mistake had been made in the procedure, the words may be made null and void. In art discourse, the notion of performativity has often been little more than magical thinking. If all art is performative, then we can safely lean back and feel good. In the contemporary situation, the most successful performers, linguistic and otherwise, tend to be those interested in allowing the image wars to escalate ever further. The Dutch populist Geert Wilders, with his internet "film" *Fitna* (2008), is a case in point.[25] Insofar as they create an atmosphere of fear and distrust, the Enlightenment fundamentalists' discourse on (and mainstream western media's representations of) the veil as exemplifying Islam's Otherness are *performative;* they produce a new situation. The performative efficacy of artistic manipulations of the veil—if, by that, we mean a discernible impact on public discourse and opinion—is limited at best: it remains a largely dormant potential. However, this only makes the public articulation of some of these works' possible implications all the more important.

In recent years, Dutch artist Fransje Killaars—who switched from painting to textile installations in the early 1990s—has taken to draping her bedspreads, with their brightly colored grids, over tailor's dummies. Rather than articulating the cut of fashionable clothing, the dummies are covered almost completely by abstract and impractical full-body veils that draw attention to their materiality and sensuality—to their own surface and texture rather than to their status as obstructions of the gaze. Titled *Figures* and posed in groups, they form constellations that invite comparisons (fig. 5.4). Typically, Killaars also shows one or two dummies covered only from the neck down, the bedspread hanging as a cape. In contrast to the "burqa" *Figures*, the "cape" *Figures* use dummies whose heads have been removed; the cape is crowned by nothing. By "exposing" the veiled face as a void, these *acéphales* join the other works in privileging the cover over the covered, the veil over the veiled. Again, the veil is here linked to modernist abstraction, but with a crucial difference: whereas in the Roosje mural, pixelated squares clearly veil a censored "reality" underneath, Killaars' blankets are themselves the focus. At first, the works seem eminently readable as representations of full-body veils, but as sensuous signifiers draped over dummies, Killaars's *Figures* make the abstract veil visible as something integral to the figure, rather than a mere obstruction. The veil does not occlude the figure; it *is* the figure.

Thus, these pieces suggest the need to go beyond the abstract opposition between the Western body and the "oriental" veil; they suggest that media attention lavished on the veil projects the abstraction that is always being incarnated and re-incarnated in the body of the Western subject's Islamic Other. Are we not, as capitalist performers, selling our labor value and, ultimately, ourselves—becoming our own abstract doubles on the market? Veil-wearers, proponents, and opponents of the veil operate within a regime in which abstraction is incarnated in performers, in which codes function as scripts to be enacted. Driven to its limit, abstraction becomes theater and the pseudo-concrete commodity takes on human form; life becomes perpetual performance. As it is currently used, the burqa largely disavows its role as a prop in today's spectacle; to both sides it represents abstract negation, pure Otherness. The veil occludes the reality of enacted abstraction, the material reality of "immaterial labor." As instrumentalized by the two fundamentalisms, the veil veils the need for practices—aesthetic and/or political to differing degrees—that work in and against the status quo. Usually functioning as an obedient sign, its *symptomatic* status should be recognized and exacerbated. Can the veil, that indispensable semiotic prop in the fundamentalist spectacle, be made to abandon the script in which it functions?

LIVING COMMODITIES

In countries ranging from Turkey and Iran to Algeria, the increasing pressure on women to shed their veils during the early twentieth century (as part of western-style modernization) focused on women's appearance on the street in public life and as represented in photography. The two spaces are interconnected; as Parisa Damandan has noted, when the Pahlavi regime in Iran banned the hijab, "Women, who only a few decades earlier were visible in public as vague forms covered by *chadors* and veils, now deliberately put on clothes made of see-through material and with low necklines—even swimsuits, nightgowns and lingerie—to have their photographs taken."[26] The sheer speed of the transition and, in some cases, its imposition by a colonial ruler, meant that the liberation from the veil could also be experienced as a forceful subjection to the Other's—the camera's—gaze. The veil's removal also removed space for difference and withdrawal. The veil is, in a sense, the camera's polar opposite, photographic antimatter, a black hole in the realm of the Western visible. However, the archetypal nineteenth-century photographer, hidden behind his apparatus under a black cloth, points out an underlying similarity; both are blots on the visual field of others, seeing without being seen.[27]

A curious page from a 2007 issue of the German tabloid *Bild* juxtaposed a photo of a nude girl, accompanied by a "nudge nudge" text, with an ad for *Bild*'s latest prestige project: a deluxe Bible with Dürer illustrations, boasting the artist's famous study of praying hands on its cover.[28] Fighting Islamism with the Bible and naked chics—this could be the mission statement of many a right-wing tabloid. There's a certain logic to it. After all, isn't *Bild*'s bunny the distant offspring of the representational strategies developed in Dürer's time? And are these strategies even thinkable without Christianity, without the Incarnation?[29] However, as we have already argued, in today's spectacle we are no longer dealing with the unique incarnation of a divine *Logos*, but with a purposive rationality incarnated time and time again. The word has become a code that is stored, sold and re-sold, or leased. The unique incarnation of the Word has given way to the perpetual incarnation of technological *logos*—in digital programming, but in a more literal way also in genetic engineering. "If Christ is the *Logos* become flesh, this is the bit become biology," as Christina von Braun has said.[30] Biotechnology, however, is merely the culmination of a history in which abstract reason has increasingly become embedded and incarnated in human beings. Language itself, that rupture with the natural world, is fundamental in this regard, transforming the human animal from within; furthermore, various social formations have inscribed themselves on humans, quite literally in cases where slaves or serfs were marked as their owner's property.

As far as capitalism is concerned, we have already discussed Marx's definition of labor power as "labor in the abstract"; capitalism is built on the discrepancy between this abstract commodity and actual labor performed by the worker.[31] The main immaterial commodity was the only one most people had to offer on the market: their labor-power, a potential to do labor, which is treated more or less as a statistical average. The rows of identical and abstracted workers' figures in Neurath's and Arntz's visual statistics are a perfect representation of such "real abstraction." However, in the early *Philosophical and Economic Manuscripts*, Marx took his analysis further, claiming that the laborer himself effectively becomes a commodity. "Production does not simply produce man as a *commodity*, the *human commodity*, man in the role of *commodity*; it produces him in keeping with this role as a *mentally* and physically dehumanized being.—Immorality, deformity, and dulling of the workers and the capitalists.—Its product is *the self-conscious and self-acting commodity* ... the *human* commodity...."[32] Later Marx would not expand on this, perhaps considering the notion of a living commodity too poetic; neither would Debord. But the underdeveloped and abandoned Marxian concept of the living commodity seems apt for what is often termed post-Fordist capitalism, in which workers are increasingly ideologized, not as drones who sell their more or less interchangeable labor-power, but as creative, inspired individuals who bring something unique to the team. This goes not only for those who enact today's coded capitalism in jobs demanding "soft skills," but also for those who do purely technical work: at a company like Google, employees are encouraged to "be themselves," to spend time in play, which demands self-performance unlike the abstract roles required in the Fordist economy. Something more than interchangeable labor power is needed. The spectacle becomes a *performative spectacle*—or, in other words, a regime of immaterial labor.

Debord's notion of the spectacle is based on a theatrical metaphor, but in contrast to Italian Operaist Marxists, such as Paolo Virno and Antonio Negri, Debord did not expound at any length on the rise of post-Fordist "immaterial labor" as part of capitalism's trajectory of abstraction—of abstraction becoming increasingly pervasive and concrete.[33] Debord followed the traditional Marxian analysis of the commodity fetish, which focused on industrial goods, though it also encompassed services. Even in jobs where wages are standardized (and low), workers are increasingly expected to use their unique personality and qualities, though in a rather generic form and within certain limits. Their virtuoso performances, to use a term employed by Paolo Virno in this context, must still obey the general outline of a predetermined script; the contestation of the performative spectacle is not as easy as Virno's assurances of the inherently political nature of virtuoso performance seem to suggest.[34]

As Allan Sekula has argued, the post-industrial economy conveniently forgets that the dirty work is being subcontracted to other parts of the world, the rise of services and "creative industries" in the West means that classical *Modern Times*-type conveyor belt work is indeed on the wane there.[35]

No wonder that two Harvard Business School professors created a stir with a book claiming that in the "experience economy," every work is theater and every business a stage.[36] As anonymous services become performances, labor power must be enacted in a personalized way, by individual performers. This turns not only performance into a commodity, but ultimately, the performer himself as well. The performative turn is not only an ideological matter expounded in books and seminars; it is a performative ideology that penetrates actual working environments—meaning that social relations between people now appear not only as social relations between objects, as in classic commodity fetishism, but also *as social relations between people*. Human subjects have become their own spectral doubles, "living money," commodified self-performers enacting theological whims. Welcome to the performative spectacle, in which abstraction "incarnates" itself in programmed objects and images, and in a different way, in humans.[37] To be sure, human beings are not designed from scratch as other commodities are—no matter what desires and anxieties accompany gene therapy. However, in a very real way, human subjects have been *reprogrammed* over the past decades—subjected to the gospel of flexibility and life-long learning, they come to think of themselves as perpetually updated software.

Pioneering work in self-performance was done by modern celebrities—especially those created by the prototypical culture industry: Hollywood of the 1920s and 30s. Walter Benjamin noted that film actors sell themselves "mit Haut und Haaren, mit Herz und Nieren"—with all their organs, completely.[38] Compared to the workers considered typical by Marxian theory at the time, as a living commodity, the film actor presented a new type to Benjamin, who contrasted the progressive (Soviet) film practice he advocated with the artificial "cult-value" of the Hollywood-star system. Benjamin argued that cult value (which has its origins in the sacred and far from public status of religious cult images, which were often accessible only to priests and shown to the populace on specific days) was on the wane because of mechanical reproduction; however, Hollywood found a way to combine profusion with scarcity. Hollywood stars possessed a new kind of aura: the industrially produced glamour which Adorno would write about a few years later.[39] Similar to the way in which branded products emerged in the course of the twentieth century, the Hollywood star announces our economy. As with other commodities, the labor-theory of value increasingly seems to fail us with such living commodities. Granted, the amount of labor invested in performers like Jennifer Lopez, who reputedly has separate assistants to take care of individual parts of her priceless anatomy, is great—but while it partially enables her commercial success, is the labor invested proportional to the profit? For the vast majority of people, the imperative to become an ego-brand, a self-performer, does not lead to higher income; in some cases, quite the opposite. For those working for standardized wages, as well as those operating under precarious conditions on the freelance market, the self-branding that is an essential part of the performative market does not hold the promise of heightened surplus value. When it comes to labor, branding creates "value-added" brands à la Starbucks only for a limited group of entrepreneurs and stars (of star-entrepreneurs and entrepreneur-stars). For the others, it means that their lives are more completely colonized by exchange value.

If, in the 1960s and 70s, theorists and practitioners of performance art sometimes argued that performances are beyond commodification and capitalist recuperation, today's protagonists are less naïve and understand the performative turn of art to be an integral part of the performative enactment of capitalism's most avant-garde scripts. Tino Sehgal follows the logic of "dematerialization" to its limits, using striptease as a model for his own practice. To the fundamentalist, the striptease is beyond the pale, an example of sexual-commercial idolatry. Sehgal presents striptease as a form of dance that does not disguise its status as commodity: "what is specific about striptease is that it is generally done to be bought and sold. It is inherently commercial. It is a product like any other product, with one categorical difference: it is produced by a person transforming his or her actions."[40] In contrast to other service jobs that use objects (such as computers) or consist of the processing of objects, Sehgal argues that the striptease is almost wholly immaterial: the shedding of material ballast has become its very content. Despite the sexist connotations of striptease, something Sehgal clearly is uncomfortable with, it forms a perfect model for the future and for progressive performance art. Sehgal's works consist mainly of small surprises in art shows, actions which are generally carried out by the staff of the institutions concerned: a museum attendant who suddenly starts jumping up and down, for instance; someone rolling over the ground in slow motion; or a girl who unexpectedly sinks to the ground behind the visitor's back and breaks into song. Each of these acts concludes with a pronouncement of the title of the work and the name of the artist.

Even if these performances are successful commodities on the art market, their status is oddly dematerialized; Sehgal does not allow for photographic or video documentation of his pieces. The manifest reason for his anti-technological iconoclasm is ecological; to produce is to hasten the arrival of the ecological catastrophe. The fact that his neo-liberal ecotopia has barely anything to do with actual economic developments, in which industrial production continues to play a significant (if unsexy) role, turns it into a hypocritical fable—a magic mirror held up to the existing order. In their extremism, Sehgal's pieces still function as exemplary and exceptional commodities; they say a great deal about present economic conditions and ideological fantasies, even though Sehgal claims to oppose any model that is radically different from the existing economy. It is precisely extreme obscurantism that makes Sehgal's practice interesting; the ban on photography results in numerous pictures of Sehgal "interpreters" interrupting their performances by holding their hand in front of the camera, thus cultivating mystique. The aniconism is a ploy to generate an aura, to revert exhibition value into cult value. That Sehgal sells his pieces through oral, rather than written, contracts veils his work's complete implication in an economy of abstraction, in which the performative is the implementation of often invisible scripts or codes. His archaism is fodder for discourse, his pieces have their destiny in language; they seem designed less for providing an experience then for being easy to summarize. In this way, Sehgal is the perfect artist for an economy in which abstraction is incarnated time and again in bodies/subjects that are themselves as abstract as other commodities—and whose master codes are difficult to unveil.

In his attempt to formulate a "New Left theology," the young Terry Eagleton argued that both Christianity and Marxism are forms of (revolutionary) praxis aimed at creating a future "transfigured society" in which the animal, bodily side of the human being is reconciled with its being-in-language, which has shattered the original animal identity with the world.[41] For all the limitations of this early work by Eagleton, it is intriguing in its portrayal of the human being as an unhappy body and language, a portrayal that forecasts Eagleton's later view of the commodity as a "mere symbol of itself, an entity whose meaning and being are entirely at odds and whose sensuous body exists only as the contingent bearer of an extrinsic form."[42] No wonder the human subject, already at odds with itself, is so open to commodification. If the human commodity is a grotesque parody of the utopia posited at the end of history—with certain crucial differences—by Christians and Marxists alike, the twin poles of the commodity and of utopian redemption must be placed in a constellation with a third: the work of art, the eccentric and exemplary commodity that, at times, manages to deconstruct or intensify the promise of aesthetic reconciliation in such a way that it functions as an indictment of the present rather than its ideological veil.

Once Rodchenko demanded that things become comrades; this demand, which is an aesthetic demand pushed to the point of the political, should also be applied to humans, to *sans-papiers* and offshore workers—and to that enemy within and without, the Muslim. At first sight, Islam seems to accentuate the split between bodily being and language, since the Word is not incarnated but present in a Holy Book—even though this book can itself take on quasi-human characteristics, such as on an Indonesian children's DVD in which the Qur'an comes alive in the shape of a cartoon-like puppet. More relevant is the ritualistic coordination of sacred text and body in prayer and ritual, which plays a significant role in Islam; that there are too many cases in which this takes the form of violent imposition of dogma on the body, as suggested by Hirsi Ali's *Submission*, is the drama of an Islam in the grips of conservatism on the one hand and militant Islamism on the Other. We have already argued that the latter, in particular, is complicit with the performative spectacle, in which its veils function as mysteriously disquieting props.

Can there be a political poetics of the veil that intervenes critically in this fundamentalist spectacle? One work that points in this direction is Julika Rudelius' video *Forms* (2000), in which two women walk through the city; they wear a fairly conservative *hiijab*, but their faces are not fully veiled. However, after a cut in the film, the viewer realizes the women's faces are not entirely visible; they appear to be semi-veiled, wearing stockings pulled over their heads. The result recalls the pixelation of criminal suspects on TV, and suggests that the division between visibility and invisibility, between what is "freely" apparent and what is veiled, is not that transparent. Such a work is not hugely visible or efficacious in a mainstream political sense, nor should one expect it to be. However, like non-art performances such as Susanne Osthoff's, it intervenes in the current regime of visibility by focusing attention on the veil's symptomatic status. As an aesthetic meditation on and reconfiguration of the performative spectacle, such a piece can and should be supplemented by political interventions in this regime.

APOCALYPSE SOON

In Lidwien van de Ven's engagement with the ubiquitous iconography of the veil, two forms of iconoclasm meet. In an exhibition in Paris in 2006, van de Ven showed a photograph she had taken outside the French embassy in London, featuring veiled women protesting against an anti-veil ruling affecting French schools. This and a few other images were pasted directly onto the wall; in the second stage of the exhibition they were painted over with a thin coat of white paint, below which the images were still perceptible (fig. 5.5). Both obscuring the photographed veils and giving them a new visibility, van de Ven conferred the media myth with an ambiguously physical status, at once unreal and ethereal. A partial erasure, van de Ven's gesture made the veil-image visible again—visible as an iconoclastic act in its own right, an act whose political potential must be activated in ways that surpass (and even go against) its intentions. Van de Ven's delayed application of paint transforms the exhibited snapshot into a layered time-image; the image changes over time, becoming crypto-cinematic.

As Boris Groys has argued, film often engages in a *paragone* with other, static media.[43] By setting images in motion, film distinguishes itself from the immobile graven images of old, and montage theorists such as Eisenstein and Benjamin praise film for its iconoclastic "shattering" of the static universe. As Groys demonstrated in his analysis of iconoclastic scenes in various films—the toppling of statues in Eisenstein's *October* is a famous example—twentieth-century cinema again and again revisits scenes portraying the destruction of "idols." Remarkably, Freud conceived of Moses's reaction to the idol of the golden calf in quasi-cinematic terms: to help make his point about the moment Michelangelo depicted in his Moses statue, Freud had a draftsman make a series of line drawings of the different stages in Moses's reaction to the dance around the golden calf. Horst Bredekamp has drawn attention to the similarity of these curious drawings to film stills.[44] Above all, however, one is reminded of chronophotographs such as Muybridge's: a segmentation and sequencing of moments, rather than a movement-image. It is Freud's writing, more than the images, which gives life and movement to the statue; turning the Moses into a movement-image.

As the medium of the twentieth-century Western gaze par excellence, film is also a medium of iconoclastic unveiling; it erodes old social structures and taboos in its staging of the world and the body. On an ontological level, Deleuze also considered film to be liberating in its destruction of static representations—those idols of the sluggish mind.[45] In many ways, *Cinema 1* and *Cinema 2* are sequels to and applications of Deleuze's earlier book on Bergson; the cinema books read like retreads of *Bergsonism* interspersed with cinephilic passages. Deleuze uses Bergson to wage war on the human proclivity to imprison being and duration in static representations; in spatial time, Western representation turns the pure difference of becoming into spatialized (and thus relative) difference, into the manageable clockwork-time of modern life. Bergsonian-Deleuzian natural history is based on an ontologization of memory: "Everything happens as if the universe were a tremendous Memory."[46] From personal memory, it is but a step to a cosmic memory inherent to being itself: "It is a case of leaving psychology altogether. It is a case of an immemorial or ontological Memory. It is only then, once the leap has been made, that recollection will gradually take on a psychological existence: 'from the virtual it passes into the actual state …'"[47]

By contrast, for many Marxian thinkers cinema only created spurious movement. Benjamin, for one, considered the creation of "artificial cult value" in the form of Hollywood stars to be a betrayal of film's emancipatory potential; rather than exposing viewers to the shock of the montage, Hollywood created new cult images, and the fundamentally auratic and static cult(ure) of the star. Critical theorists such as Benjamin also attacked modern mass culture in general for relapsing into cyclical, "mythical" time: the time of commodified culture is that of a return of the same, rather than of history. The frenzied innovation of advanced capitalism is subject to a deeper political stasis; its dynamism barely masks its eternal returns.[48] In capitalism, movement itself becomes oddly static. This was also a crucial element of Debord's theory of the spectacle; his disdain for media and film theory—even as a filmmaker himself—is only consequential. However, both Deleuzian and Debordian conceptualizations of film fail to do justice to the cinema's complex role in the spectacle, its oscillation between liberating impulses and their curtailment.

Analysis of the time of spectacle as quasi-cyclical amounts to a critical appropriation of dominant discourse; usually the colonial Other was seen as devoid of history, in the grips of cyclical sameness. If Marxian intellectuals switched perspectives so as to critique western capitalism and its fetishes, contemporary Enlightenment fundamentalists once more portray the Oriental Other, more specifically the Muslim Other, as existing in a "sealed time," an apocalyptic vision cut off from all intellectual and political developments necessary to the modern (Western) world. Not infrequently, the spectacle itself was disguised in oriental clothing or veils. A case in point is the work of Loïe Fuller, whose *Serpentine Dance* and its many variants were triumphantly successful in the late nineteenth century, constituting the ultimate cinematic blossoming of the veil—Fuller's dances were a popular subject for early film producers, such as Edison and Lumière, although they had to make do with her imitators.[49] Closely allied with Art Nouveau, Fuller devised dances in which her body became the moving armature for whirling drapes (fig. 5.6). As a pulsating movement-image, Fuller, whose body was largely obscured by her costume, desexualized the Orientalist trope of the dance of the seven veils. As Rhonda Garelick has argued, watching Fuller move like an abstract organism under colored lights must have been like watching a scintillating commodity on display—a living, abstract commodity.[50] The pulsating, repetitive nature of the performance folded time back onto itself. While this may be conservative, Fuller's refusal to think in the binary terms propagated by much of the discourse on the veil is not without benefit: with Fuller, one can hardly make distinctions between moments of veiling and of unveiling. In Fuller's work, the apocalypse is postponed ad infinitum.

"Apocalypse," a term derived from the Greek, means unveiling: the truth is revealed, the seals are opened. In recent years, media have repeatedly reported on the "apocalyptic vision" that purportedly inspires Iranian president, Mahmoud Ahmadinejad: "that Shiite Islam's long-hidden 12th Imam, or Mahdi, will soon emerge—possibly at the mosque of Jamkaran—to inaugurate the end of the world."[51] Speculation has been ripe on how Iran's nuclear plans fit into this vision. This is Debord's "compromise between myth and history" in optima forma: contemporary socio-political developments are seen in eschatological terms. Yet this is hardly a prerogative of Islam. Ronald Reagan appointed Hal Lindsay as his advisor—an evangelist who believed he was living in "end times," and who interpreted all events, particularly in the Middle East, in this light.[52] Christian fundamentalist influence on the George W. Bush administration has also received much attention. While some who claim incompatibility between Islam and "the West" do so by fetishizing the Enlightenment, others (usually Christian democrats) refer to the "Christian nature" of Europe. That these two constructions exist happily side-by-side may betray a fundamental collusion between them: perhaps both parties, the liberals and the Christians, tacitly presuppose that Christianity, which is already based on the myth of a dying God—Christ dying on the cross like a common thief—has inherent potential for secularization and thus for historicization, in contrast to "absolutist" Islam and its purely religious, eschatological sense of time.

Against this, Tariq Ramadan argues that in relation to the sources, "the scope for the exercise of reason and creativity is huge," that faith always has to be situated within a historical and social framework, and that Islam exhorts the Muslim to be fully in the world and in the society in which he lives.[53] Ramadan still wants to contain the "exercise of reason and creativity" within the framework of Islam, while the Enlightenment fundamentalists' refusal to grant Islam any reason—or creativity—is clearly ideology at its purest. It should not be assumed, either, that reason is a priori compatible with sixth-century revelation. Nietzsche argued that from the Reformation onward, Christian morality had destroyed Christian dogma and faith; what Islamic reason might do to dogma remains to be seen. The cleric Abdolkarim Soroush, who was actively involved in the Iranian Revolution, has become a critic of the conservative official state theology, arguing that the Qur'an must be regarded as historically and socially specific—the book being influenced by its author, Muhammad, who was more than just a passive medium for the divine word.[54]

It is crucial to note that such iconoclasm is not an abstract negation of Soroush's faith, but the consequence of a religion he considers to be aligned with reason and therefore open to criticism and historical change. For him, Islam certainly does not exist in a "sealed time." Like iconoclasm, religion in general should not be left to those who cannot handle it.

LIBERATING TIME

Since the 1990s, a counter-cinema has emerged in the form of film and video art made for galleries and museums, often going to great lengths to create the opposite of frantic, contemporary blockbusters. Mainstream film has abandoned the project of liberating time from static representation, which Gilles Deleuze saw as progressing from classic Hollywood to the post-war cinema of Neo-Realism and the Nouvelle Vague; contemporary art appears to have resuscitated this project.[55] De Rijke/de Rooij's film *Of Three Men* (1998) is perhaps one of the defining films of this gallery-based counter-cinema, exhibiting its good qualities along with its fundamental problems. The film shows the interior of an Amsterdam mosque, formerly a Catholic church built in the 1920s in a rather bulky and sober modernist-historicist style. The interior has been stripped of its Catholic paraphernalia; chandeliers and an empty floor complete the visual transformation. The film mostly focuses on the changing effect of the light filtering through the windows; this light is largely artificial, and changes quickly. The association with seventeenth-century church interiors by Saenredam and others is assumed—yet de Rijke/de Rooij do not constitute a linear progression from Saenredam to modern art in order to inscribe themselves in it. By treating the mosque in a formal way, as the receptacle of a light show, de Rijke/de Rooij suggest that a mosque is a potential place of enlightenment—or Enlightenment—and reflection, like the seventeenth-century Dutch churches that have been transformed into cultural centers and spaces of debate.

Not only overlaying a church with a mosque and its diverging connotations, *Of Three Men* also juxtaposes the iconoclastic fury of seventeenth-century pictorial representations of space with modern artistic iconoclasm. Before the mosque is shown in the beginning of the film, the image is black; then it appears that the camera's view has been blocked by some men in dark cloaks. This opening recalls a convention sometimes used in Hollywood films for disguising cuts by having black clothing or a dark object momentarily block the view, but its length and position in the beginning of the film also recall examples of modern artistic iconoclasm such as Guy Debord's first film, *Hurlements en faveur de Sade* (1952), which consisted mostly of a black screen. *Of Three Men* thus effects a montage between Islamic aniconism and modern art, in a subtle and forceful critique of the discourse that deems mosques spaces of pure iconoclastic Otherness, incompatible with the allegedly secular order of visibility that rules European cities. It also creates a montage of still image (or non-image) and filmic time-image, fetishizing art as a realm of contemplation and true experience, and creating an all-too Manichaean opposition to the spectacle in which art itself is implicated. The liberation of time promised by such art remains farcical, as long as it does not use the ideology of the aesthetic for more than a confirmation of art's symbolic capital.

Arnoud Holleman's video work *Museum* (1997) and the ensuing legal imbroglio exemplify the difficulties of film within the art world. Holleman appropriated the French gay porn film *Musée hom* by Jean-Daniel Cadinot, which is set in a museum filled with (plaster casts of) mainly antique sculptures that are being studied by comely young men, who are themselves eyed by uniformed security guards; at times, instead of white casts, real bodies show up on pedestals (fig. 5.7). Missing from Holleman's version is the actual pornography; what remains is a ballet of gazes.[56] In its use of plaster casts, the original film gives a pornographic twist to the *paragone* tradition, in which film directors demonstrated the superiority of their medium to sculpture; Cadinot's original film even contains a humorous episode in which a visitor reveals one of the sculptures to be a plaster cast, which is then smashed. When Holleman wanted to sell the work and contacted Cadinot about the rights, the latter felt his own status as an artist was denied, his film relegated to source material and puritanically "censored"—even while Holleman argued that, far from censoring gay sexuality, he was in fact emphasizing Cadinot's desublimation of the aesthetic experience by showing the gaze to be utterly sexualized. In this respect, *Museum,* with its sexualized idols, is far more subversive than much contemporary film and video art, yet its shaky legal status is a reminder that capitalist copyright law amounts to a secular Second Commandment—thou shalt not re-use, quote, or appropriate. In this way, moving images are subjected to the rule of taboo and stasis. The liberation of time, then, cannot be a purely cinematic question: it touches on the whole edifice of pseudo-cyclical time.

Writing in prison in the early 1980s, Antonio Negri stated that capitalism tends to reduce all labor to merely quantitative, measured time, to a state in which "*Complexity is reduced to articulation, ontological time to discrete and maneuverable time.*"[57] A truly liberated time, Negri asserts, would break with this regimentation in favor of qualitative and collective production.

"Liberated time is a *productive quality.* It is a productive rationality torn away and isolated from the command that analyzed this rationality and extorted it from the time of life."[58] For Negri, then, the true liberation of time cannot be just cinematic, simply a matter of movement-images freeing *being.* Rather, it must be situated within capitalism's transformations. With the rise of immaterial labor in post-Fordism, what Debord called the pseudo-cyclical alteration between work and free time erodes, and time is no longer segmented and discrete. Thus the extreme colonization of time, in what we have termed the performative spectacle, is potentially liberation—as it becomes clear that time is indeed a productive quality, the time-of-life. There is an obvious messianic streak in such attempts to find the seeds of liberation in the very regime to be vanquished, but this is nothing to be ashamed of: secularist blackmail by those who turn the persistence of religious motifs into damning accusations must be resisted.

The leftist appropriation of Schelling's late Catholic philosophy of potency or potentiality, by Agamben and Žižek in particular, is exemplary in its activation of the dormant or repressed political aspects of a philosophical-religious body of thought. In his late work, Schelling fiercely opposed Hegelian logocentrism, arguing that Hegel's practice of dialectics remained merely logical, that Hegelian philosophy—starting from the idea—can never come to terms with the actual act of creation and actual history.[59] This is Schelling's starting point: the more than conceptual step from nothing to something, or from a state of potentiality into actuality, *ad actam,* which was the one thing Hegel could never explain. Schelling theorizes this step by positing an interplay of three *Potenzen,* of powers or potencies, which are three aspects of God: pure *Seinkönnen* (what-can-be) or the subject, pure *Sein* (being) or the object, and the subject-object that is the *Geist.* In the absolute, before creation, these potencies were latent. They were activated by a primordial, divine act, a transition from latent *Wille* (will) to active *Wollen* (wanting) around which Schelling's late work circles.

In this process, the potencies become active persons, the persons of the Trinity: Father, Son, Spirit. Freely using scholastic terminology, Schelling, who had converted to Catholicism, makes the Christian-Trinitarian structure of this thinking much more explicit than Hegel. While it is only the Christian revelation in which the divine persons fully reveal themselves, the ground for this revelation was prepared throughout history in a succession of mythologies. This was a *natural* process, because it is a causal chain of events in the human mind, rather than a direct divine revelation. Mythology as a succession of gods—as historical polytheism—is shaped by the interplay of the three potencies, but these now act as purely natural causes. Man, Schelling argues, wanted to freely rule over the three potencies, but instead he came to be ruled by them. Slowly extracting himself from his fallen state, the succession of gods enabled the human mind to rise to a level where, finally, man is ready for the true Revelation.[60] In this bizarre theogony, which can be seen as the positive answer to Flaubert's dismal parade—yes, they are dead gods, but they are dead now precisely because they prepared us for the one true God!—there is, unsurprisingly, no place for Islam.

Schelling's neo-theological outlook angered those young radicals who flocked to hear the former boy wonder of the German language in Berlin in 1841. Feuerbach, Arnold Runge, Bakunin, Marx, and Engels were either attending the lectures themselves or following them via their friends' reports, and the reaction was one of dismay.[61] To them, the theologizing Schelling simply seemed to be the philosophical mouthpiece of the reaction that had swept Europe after the Napoleonic era. But with some historical distance, Schelling often appears as a Christian version of Feuerbach, a closet radical, a Christian materialist: he argues that when the third potency, the potency of Spirit or *selbstbewusstes Können,* comes to the fore with the arrival of Christianity, this complete penetration of the real by the ideal—by Spirit—spells the end of the supernatural and a triumph of "free, self-conscious human knowledge."[62] More generally, in a context in which deterministic versions of Marxism positing revolution as a historical necessity have been discredited, thinking in terms of potentiality can open up a horizon of possibilities in the fundamentalist spectacle and its own version of historical necessity—its rigorous regime of cyclical innovation.

Unfortunately, the reception of Agamben's writings on potentiality in particular, especially in the art world, often leads to wallowing in abstract potentiality that functions as intellectual escapism. Agamben himself recalls that Schelling labeled a potentiality that cannot pass into action *blind*.[63] Is not the problem precisely that our beloved potentialities remain just that—symptomatic indications of blocked histories? To be sure, one might argue that if art is not to squander whatever qualities it has, it must never make the step *ad actum*; yet what is called for is not so much the erasure of difference, as the creation of overlaps and alliances between different admixtures of potentiality and actuality. A cult of pure potentiality is complicit with a culture in which the apocalypse has become secularized under the name of global warming.

We live in a culture in which radical social change is far less easy to imagine than the secularized apocalypse of global ecological collapse.[64] Multiplexes teem with disaster movies about catastrophic climate change, or viruses that turn New York into a ghost town. When even the economic meltdown of 2008 and 2009 does not lead to contestation of the gospel of growth, of capitalist expansion, it becomes obvious that the free market cult takes on an apocalyptic tone in the register of the most reactionary and mystifying fundamentalism—whose objections to tampering with Creation focus on abortion rather than on the conditions that cause global climate change, which, when seen through a millenarian prism are yet another sign of "end times."[65]

Where does this leave the critical thinking that much of contemporary monotheism seems intent to disavow? Terry Eagleton quotes Konrad Lorenz to the effect that "the great dangers threatening humanity with extinction" are "direct consequences of conceptual thought and verbal speech."[66] Critique, whether religious or secularized, is therefore always fundamentally complicit with this condition; from Moses to Marxism, the genealogy of critical thought is inextricably linked to that of the purposive rationality that is destroying the fabric of life. In this condition, critiquing images is anything but an exercise in iconophobia, since contemporary images are the product of a technological *logos* that forever steps in and out of visibility, incarnating itself at will. The ultimate image of this *logos* may well be the human body, altered by the genetic therapies that increasingly reprogram it, as well as by unpredictable changes effected by pollution and exposure to synthetic substances. In such a situation, the critique of idolatry is identical to the critique of instrumentalized reason; its aim must be to trace potential transformations of video work commodities—beyond the living death that is the fundamentalist spectacle.

***

The installation *Greenwich Degree Zero* by Rod Dickinson and Tom McCarthy consists of doctored documents—printed matter, a film—which purportedly substantiate the anarchist bombing of Greenwich observatory on February 15, 1894 (fig. 5.8). On that day, there was indeed an attempted bomb attack, plotted by an anarchist who was also a police informer—but it failed. The episode inspired Joseph Conrad's novel *The Secret Agent*. By "correcting" history and showing a pillar of smoke rising over Greenwich Observatory, Dickinson and McCarthy obviously evoke 9/11, thus countering the tendency to see that day as the day on which a sudden eruption of violence that is utterly alien to "the West," occurred, as well as anchoring it in a history of violent contestations intrinsic to capitalism.

What is particularly interesting in this regard, however, is that the Greenwich Observatory foreshadows the World Trade Center's dialectic of visibility and invisibility as the concrete and thus destructible manifestation of an abstract system: after all, Greenwich Observatory was home to the Prime Meridian, which meant that ships all over the world determined their longitude in reference to the heart of the British Empire, enabling the global flow of goods controlled by colonial empires through a tool supplied by modern geography. State, market, and science conspired to cast an abstract grid across the globe.

Like contemporary streams of digital capital, this historical abstract grid materialized in a prominent and vulnerable structure, an idol waiting to be smashed. The smoldering Greenwich Observatory captured on film in the installation shows an imaginary past; shot in the style of early cinema, it suggests that this attack would have been a media event on par with 9/11, and no doubt instrumentalized in a similar way. That the man responsible was a police informer recalls conspiracy theories about the 9/11 attacks; in both cases we seem trapped in a world of pseudo-events, a world in which terrorism conspires with its opponent to strengthen the status quo. The looped film, a static shot, suggests grim Debordian time, an industrial version of eternal return—but Dickinson and McCarthy's reading and viewing room also suggests that history may still be rewritten.

NOTES

1 *"Brisez les images! voilez les vierges!"* Gustave Flaubert, *La Tentation de Saint Antoine* [1874], in *Œuvres complètes de Gustave Flaubert,* vol. 4 (Paris: Louis Conard, 1910), 61.

2 "Submission" is a literal translation of "Islam," which means submission to God; for Hirsi Ali, of course, the term primarily refers to the oppression of women.

3 In Holland, the media do not publish the names of suspects and convicted criminals, even though this is now an anachronism. Because when it comes to prominent court cases and convictions, it is easy to find full names online.

4 When Hirsi Ali criticizes the silence of "moderate" Muslims in cases of violence against women, she has a point, insofar as there is hardly a vibrant critical public sphere in large parts of the Muslim world, which has suffered a catastrophic intellectual and cultural decline over the last centuries. Hirsi Ali's criticism becomes demagogy when she uses decontextualized Qur'an suras—equivalents for which can be found in many other holy books—to suggest that Islam as such is primitive and beyond reform, and that essentially no Muslim thinks that practices such as brutal punishments for rape victims should be condemned. As Tariq Ramadan rightly points out, he and others actually do condemn such practices, as well as the jailing of a hapless teacher who allowed her pupils to name a teddy bear Muhammad. As a result, they have become persona non grata in many countries. Moreover, their criticism may actually make some difference in the long run—in contrast to Hirsi Ali's diatribes, which seem excessive and unilateral.

5 In many ways, contemporary discourse on Islam is the contemporary version of nineteenth-century Orientalist discourse famously analyzed by Edward Said in *Orientalism*; the analysis of Orientalist interpretations and characterizations of Islam plays an important role in Said's book, and is quite revealing under present conditions. Said himself notes the persistence of Orientalist tropes in "contemporary" studies of Islam; Edward W. Said, *Orientalism* (New York: Pantheon Books, 1978), 300–301.

6 On the cover of a book by two Christian authors titled *Unveiling Islam* (Ergun Mehmet Caner and Emir Fethi Caner, *Unveiling Islam* [Grand Rapids, MI: Kregel Publications, 2002]), the viewer's gaze is met by a dark-haired woman whose head is partially wrapped in a white cloth; the veiled woman becomes the personification of "Oriental" Islam. Historically, truth and nature were often shown as female figures in the process of being unveiled. For representations around 1800 of a sculpture of Isis or Nature—sometimes depicted in the guise of the Artemis of Ephesus—being unveiled, see: Jan Assmann, *Moses der Ägypter: Entzifferung einer Gedächtnisspur* (Munich: Hanser, 1998), 186, 205. In the contemporary version, at stake is the unveiling of something seen as falsehood and unnatural.

7 Christina von Braun and Bettina Mathes, *Verschleierte Wirklichkeit: Die Frau, der Islam und der Westen* (Berlin: Aufbau Verlag, 2007), 52–59.

8 Ibid., 101–102.

9 Ibid., 311–313.

10 For Vogelaar's original statement in an interview with Trouw, July 14, 2007, see http://www.trouw.nl/achtergrond/deverdieping/article1649720.ece. Vogelaar was finally forced to resign in November 2008, the victim of both a lack of media savvy and, significantly, her opposition to prevailing anti-multiculturalist rhetoric.

11 The most relevant suras are 24:31, 33:53, and 33:58–69. Sura 33:53 states that visitors to the Prophet's house should speak to his wives from behind a hijab, which here refers to a curtain or partition in the interior of the house.

12 Ian Buruma and Avishai Margalit, *Occidentalism: The West in the Eyes of Its Enemies* (London: Penguin, 2004), 117.

13 Ali Shariati, *Fatima is Fatima*, http://www.iranchamber.com/personalities/ashariati/works/fatima_is_fatima2.php.

14 See, for instance, *The Sun* (London), Thursday, February 1, 2007, 8–9.

15 A photograph of women holding this and other slogans, taken at a demonstration in Jack Straw's constituency of Blackburn on October 14, 2006, can be found—for instance—here: http://www.theage.com.au/news/world/taking-cover/2006/10/15/1160850812211.html. Neurath's remark on the veil is in *Modern Man in the Making* (New York/London: Alfred A. Knopf, 1939), 115.

16 Von Braun and Mathes, *Verschleierte Wirklichkeit* (see note 7), 65. One Australian imam called rape victims "bare meat"; they should have stayed at home, rather than expose themselves to the male gaze.

17 If the Iranian regime *really* wanted to desexualize the public sphere, they should do the opposite; rather than terrorizing women with draconic sartorial rulings, which leads to a fetishistic sexualization of the tiniest hint of hair or any attractive sexual feature that can be glimpsed or guessed at, they should go about creating the most extreme pornocracy in history.

18 The interview with anchorwoman Marietta Slomka—whose blonde hair provided optimal contrast to Osthoff's black garment—was broadcast on December 28, 2005.

19 The "burqa babe" installments of *Sigmund* have been published in Peter de Wit, *Burka Babes* (Amsterdam: Uitgeverij De Harmonie, 2007).

20 The Susa mural was made known to me by Frank Denys.

21 See the statement by artist Rombout Oomen on http://www.romboutoomen.eu/category/archief-archives/.

22 *Veil* (2003), touring exhibition curated by Jananne Al-Ani, David A. Bailey, Zineb Sedira, and Gilane Twadros, inIVA. *Veil: Veiling, Representation and Contemporary Art*, exh. cat. (Cambridge, MA: MIT Press, 2003).

23 Willem Oorebeek, *Bigger Higher Leader!*, exh. cat. (Ghent: S.M.A.K., 2007), 27.

24 J. L. Austin, *How to Do Things with Words: The William James Lectures delivered in Harvard University in 1955* (1962 [1955]), ed. J. O. Urmson and Marina Sbisà, 2nd ed. (Oxford: Oxford University Press, 1980). For more on the reception of Austin, see Judith Butler, *Excitable Speech: A Politics of the Performative* (London/New York: Routledge, 1997); Peggy Phelan, *Unmarked: The Politics of Performance* (London/New York: Routledge, 1993), 146–166; Erika Fischer-Lichte, *Ästhetik des Performativen* (Frankfurt am Main: Suhrkamp, 2004), 31–42.

25 For months, the Dutch media were in a state of hysteria over Wilders's announcement that he would make "a film" attacking Islam; in the end, a shoddily edited video clip was uploaded to the Liveleak website on March 28, 2008, only to be taken off the next day for "security reasons." It later reappeared, then disappeared once more.

26 Parisa Damandan, "The Development of Portrait Photography in Isfahan," in *Portrait Photographs from Isfahan: Faces in Transition, 1920–1950* (London: Saqi Books, 2004), 47.

27 Von Braun and Mathes, *Verschleierte Wirklichkeit* (see note 7), 24–31.

28 *Bild*, Wednesday, October 4, 2006.

29 For more on the incarnation in relation to Western representation, see Marc De Kesel, "Malerei als Verbrechen," in *De Witte Raaf*, no. 96 (March 2002),http://dewitteraaf.stylelabs.com/web/flash/content.asp?struct_id=8&pagetype=search&language_id=2&pagecount=1&site=DWR_site.

30 "... Ist Christus der Fleisch gewordene *logos*, so handelt es sich hier um das Biologie gewordene Bit." Von Braun and Mathes, *Verschleierte Wirklichkeit* (see note 7), 46.

31 Karl Marx, "Das Kapital: Kritik der politischen Ökonomie" [1872], in *Marx/Engels Gesamtausgabe (MEGA)*, part 2, vol. 6.1 (Berlin: Dietz, 1987), 76.

32 "Die Production producirt den Menschen nicht nur als eine *Waare*, die *Menschen-waare*, den Menschen in der Bestimmung als Waare, sie producirt ihn, dieser Bestimmung entsprechend, als ein ebenso *geistig* wie körperlich *entmenschtes* Wesen—Immoralität, Mißgeburt, Hebetismus der Arbeiter und d[er] Capitalisten. Ihr Product ist die *selbstbewusste* und *selbstthätige Waare* ... die *Menschen*waare ..." Karl Marx, "Ökonomisch-Philosophische Manuskripte" [1844], in *Marx/Engels Gesamtausgabe (MEGA)*, part 1, vol. 2 (Berlin: Dietz, 1982), 249. English translation from http://www.marxists.org/archive/marx/works/1844/manuscripts/second.htm.

33 Paying homage to Debord, Paolo Virno has attempted to take the notion of the spectacle beyond its Debordian account; see Paolo Virno, *A Grammar of the Multitude*, trans. Isabella Bertoletti, James Cascaito, Andrea Casson (Los Angeles: Semiotext(e), 2004), 59–61.

34 Ibid., 52–56.

35 This is the central argument of Sekula's project *Fish Story*, as well as subsequent works.

36 B. Joseph Pine II and James H. Gilmore, *The Experience Economy: Work is Theater & Every Business a Stage* (Boston, MA: Harvard Business School Press, 1999).

37 The phrase "living money" is Pierre Klossowski's; *La Monnaie vivante* (Paris, Éric Losfeld Éditeur, 1970).

38 Walter Benjamin, "Das Kunstwerk im Zeitalter seiner technischen Reproduzierbarkeit" [1935–1937], in *Gesammelte Schriften* I.2, ed. Rolf Tiedemann and Hermann Schweppenhäuser (Frankfurt am Main: Suhrkamp, 1991), 492.

39 Theodor W. Adorno, with George Simpson, "On Popular Music," in *Studies in Philosophy and Social Science,* IX (New York: Institute of Social Research, 1941), 17–48.

40 Tino Sehgal, untitled text in *Now What? Artists Write!,* ed. Mark Kremer, Maria Hlavajova, Annie Fletcher (Frankfurt am Main: Revolver; Utrecht: bak—basis voor actuele kunst, 2004), 170.

41 Terry Eagleton, *The Body as Language: Outline of a 'New Left' Theology* (London: Sheed & Ward, 1970), 12.

42 See chapter 3.

43 Boris Groys, "Iconoclasm as an Artistic Device: Iconoclastic Strategies in Film," in *Iconoclash: Beyond the Image Wars in Science, Religion, and Art*, exh. cat., ed. Bruno Latour and Peter Weibel (Karlsruhe: ZKM, 2002), 282–295.

44 Horst Bredekamp, "Sigmund Freud und das bewegte Bild," in *Kino im Kopf: Psychologie und Film seit Sigmund Freud,* ed. Kristina Jaspers and Wolf Unterberger (Berlin: Bertz+Fischer, 2006), 30–37.

45 Jacques Rancière has aptly characterized Gilles Deleuze's two-part book on cinema as an "essay in the classification of signs in the manner of natural history," arguing that Deleuze is, in the end, not so much concerned with film, as he is with a philosophy of nature—with a Bergsonian philosophy of becoming and duration, in which the images of cinema are seen not as representations, but as "light-matter in movement," as "events of luminous matter." Jacques Rancière, *La Fable cinématographique* (Paris, Seuil, 2001), 147–148.

46 "Tout se passe comme si l'univers était une formibable Mémoire." Gilles Deleuze, *Le bergsonisme* (Paris: PUF, 1966), 76. English translation by Hugh Tomlinson and Barbara Habberjam: Gilles Deleuze, *Bergsonism* [1966], (New York: Zone Books, 1991), 77.

47 "Il s'agit de sortir de la psychologie. Il s'agit d'une Mémoire immémoriale ou ontologique. C'est seulement ensuite, une fois le saut fait, que le souvenir va prendre peu à peu une existence psychologique: 'de virtuel il passe à l'état actuel ...'" Ibid., 52; trans. ibid., 57.

48 See the section "Die Langeweile, ewige Wiederkehr," from "Das Passagen-Werk," in *Gesammelte Schriften* V.1, ed. Rolf Tiedemann (Frankfurt am Main: Suhrkamp, 1991), 156–178.

49 For an analysis of Fuller's complex relationship to cinema, and the films made of her imitators, see Giovanni Lista, *Loïe Fuller, danseuse de la Belle Époque* [1994] (Paris: Hermann, 2006), 347–381.

50 Rhonda K. Garelick, *Electric Salome: Loïe Fuller's Performance of Modernism* (Princeton, NJ: Princeton University Press, 2007), 34.

51 Jackson Diehl, "In Iran, Apocalypse vs. Reform," *The Washington Post,* May 11, 2006, http://www.washingtonpost.com/wp-dyn/content/article/2006/05/10/AR2006051001791.html.

52 See, for instance, Nancy Gibbs, "Apocalypse Now," *Time,* July 1, 2002, http://www.time.com/time/magazine/article/0,9171,110120701-265419,00.html.

53 Tariq Ramadan, *Western Muslims and the Future of Islam* (Oxford: Oxford University Press, 2004), 35.

54 It bears note that the mild intransigence of a Soroush is not in any way less "Islamic" than the regime in Iran, which—in their penchant for identifying fundamentalist regimes and movements with Islam as such—is what Enlightenment fundamentalists would have us believe.

55 For Deleuze, see *Cinéma 1: L'Image-mouvement* (Paris: Les Éditions de Minuit, 1983) and *Cinéma 2: L'Image-temps* (Paris: Les Éditions de Minuit, 1985).

56 Holleman also removed night shots and exterior views. This paragraph is based on a 2008 lecture/performance text by Holleman, *On ne touche pas.*

57 Antonio Negri, "The Constitution of Time" [1981], in *Time for Revolution,* trans. Matteo Mandarini (New York/London: Continuum, 2003), 27, 49. Negri argues that, since, in advanced capitalism nine-to-five jobs become rarer, until "the entire time of life has become the time of production" (29), the reduction of time to abstract measure, to clockwork-time, becomes more problematic, bringing the liberation of time nearer. However, as Negri himself noted,

capitalism tries to defuse this situation by—as per the above quote—once more imposing the reduction of ontological time to measured time, on a larger scale and more completely than before.

58 Ibid., 120.

59 For more on Schelling's late-period criticism of Hegel, see, for instance, the Berlin version of the lectures on Revelation, delivered in 1941/42, known through Paulus's transcript, published as F. W. J. Schelling, *Philosophie der Offenbarung 1841/42,* ed. Manfred Frank (Frankfurt am Main: Suhrkamp, 1977), 121–139.

60 Hence, Schelling's later *Philosophie der Mythologie* prepares the groundwork for *Philosophie der Offenbarung* (Philosophy of Revelation).

61 See the selection of letters included in Schelling, *Philosophie der Offenbarung* (see note 59), 479–581.

62 The system of the three potencies is discussed and developed throughout the late *Philosophie der Mythologie* and *Philosophie der Offenbarung,* repeatedly delivered as lectures during the 1830s and 40s and published posthumously by Schelling's son, as well as in the Paulus transcript (see note 59). In works of his earlier *identitätsphilosophische Phase*, such as *Philosophie der Kunst* (1802), Schelling had already developed a different system of potencies.

63 Giorgio Agamben, *The Coming Community,* trans. Michael Hardt (Minneapolis, MN: University of Minnesota Press, 1993), 35.

64 Fredric Jameson made an observation to this effect in *The Seeds of Time* (New York: Columbia University Press, 1994), xii; Slavoj Žižek has published a number of variations of it.

65 http://www.neaiga.org/global_warming.htm.

66 Eagleton, *Body as Language* (see note 41), 14.

ILLUSTRATIONS

Popular post-9/11 Internet meme

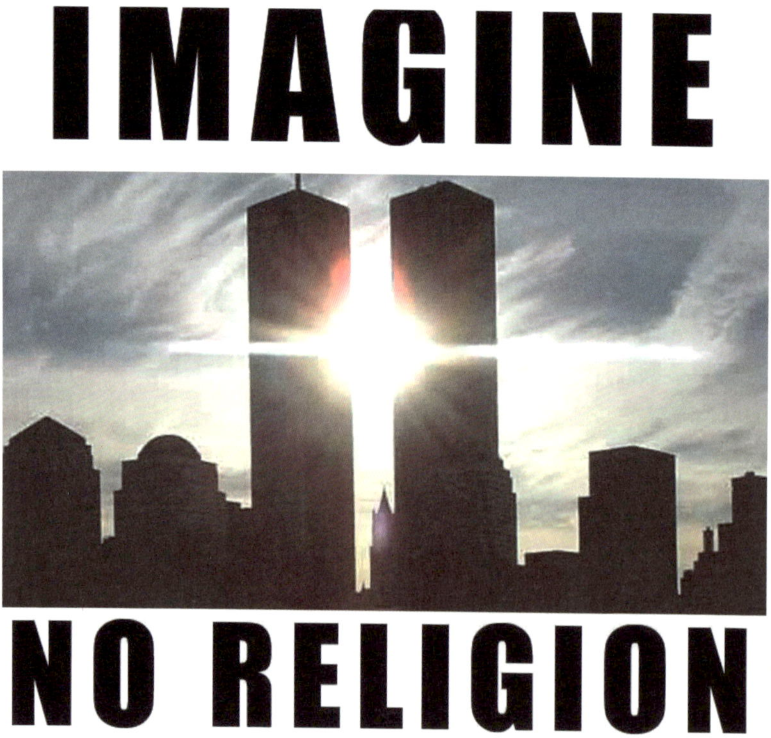

FIG. 0.1

Thomas Dworzak, from the series "Afghanistan," 2002

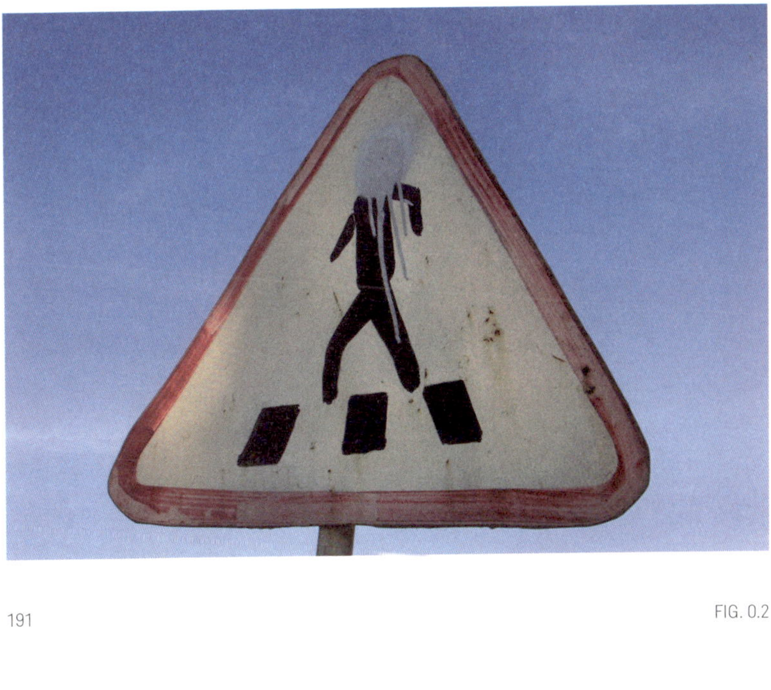

FIG. 0.2

Asger Jorn, *Brisez le cadre qui étouffe l'image*, 1968

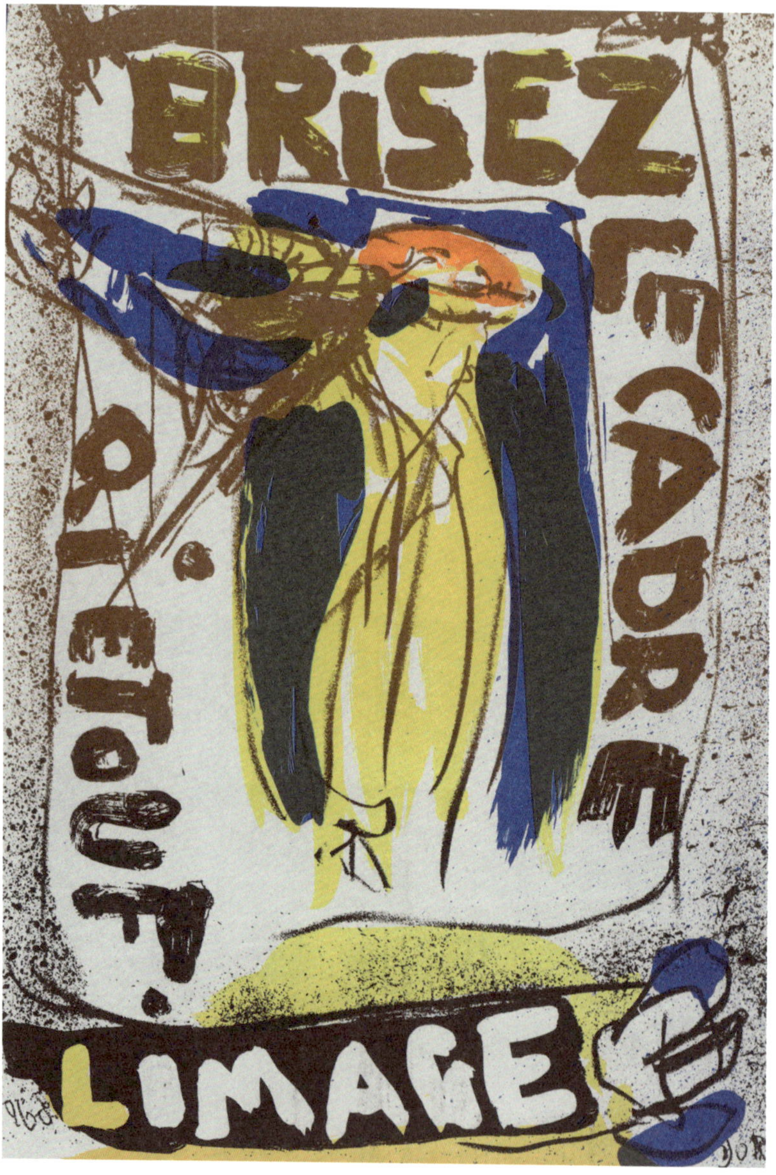

FIG. 1.1

Michelangelo, *Moses*, 1515 (detail)

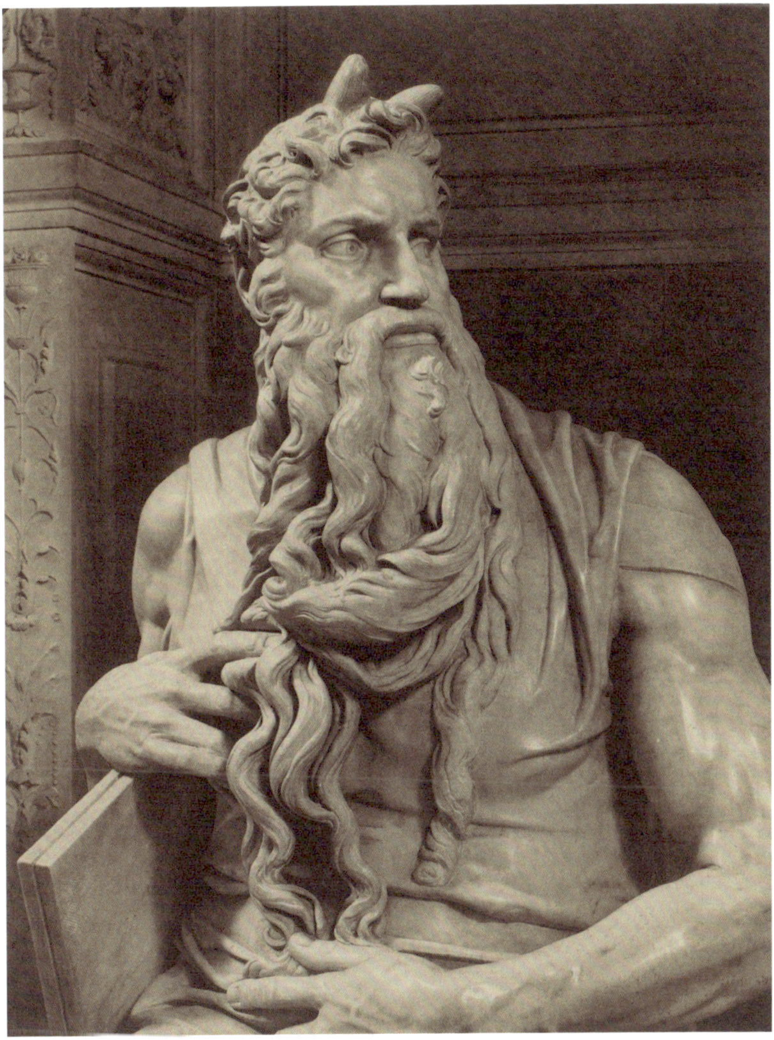

FIG. 1.2

Gert Jan Kocken, *Madonna with Child and donors, Zwolle. Defacement 16 June 1580*, 2005

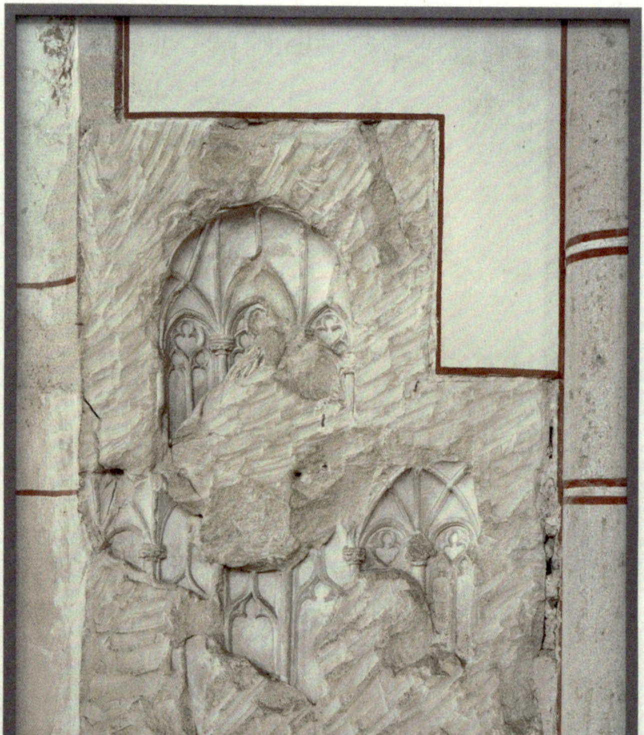

FIG. 1.3

Gert Jan Kocken and Krijn de Koning, installation at Capri, Berlin, 2006

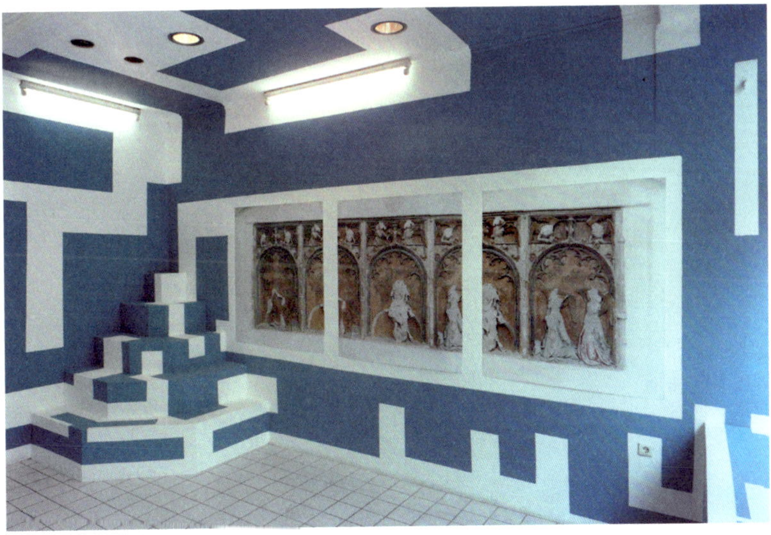

FIG. 1.4

Hubert Robert, *La Salle des Saisons au Louvre*, 1802–03

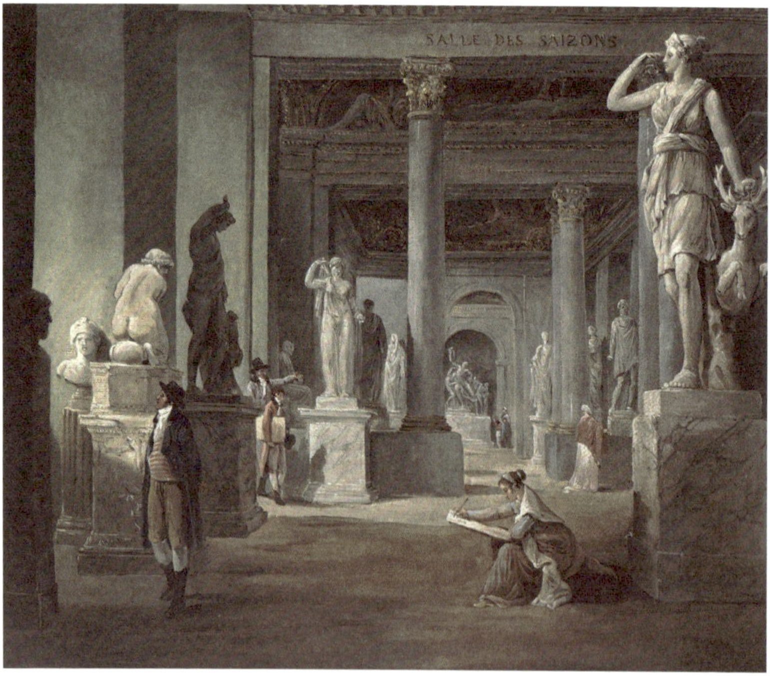

FIG. 1.5

Ludwig Philippson, Hebrew Bible, 1854
From the collection of Sigmund Freud

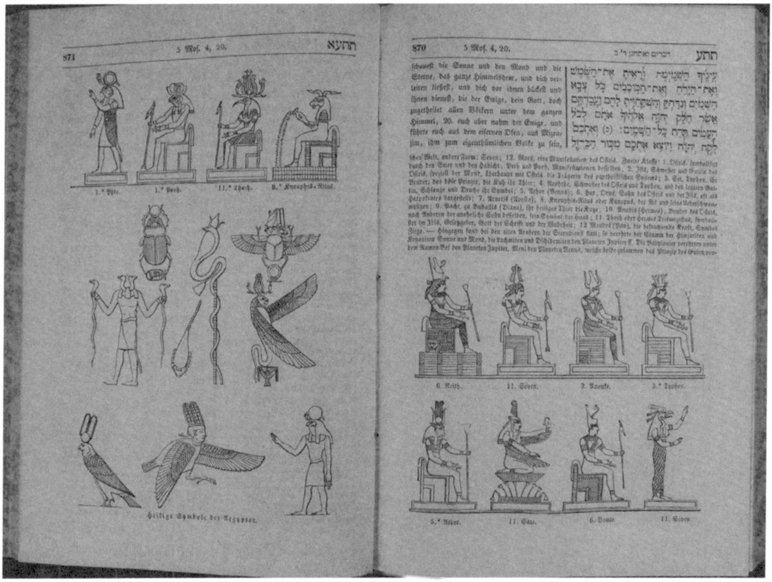

FIG. 1.6

Gert Jan Kocken, *New York, Tuesday, September 11, 2001*, 2004

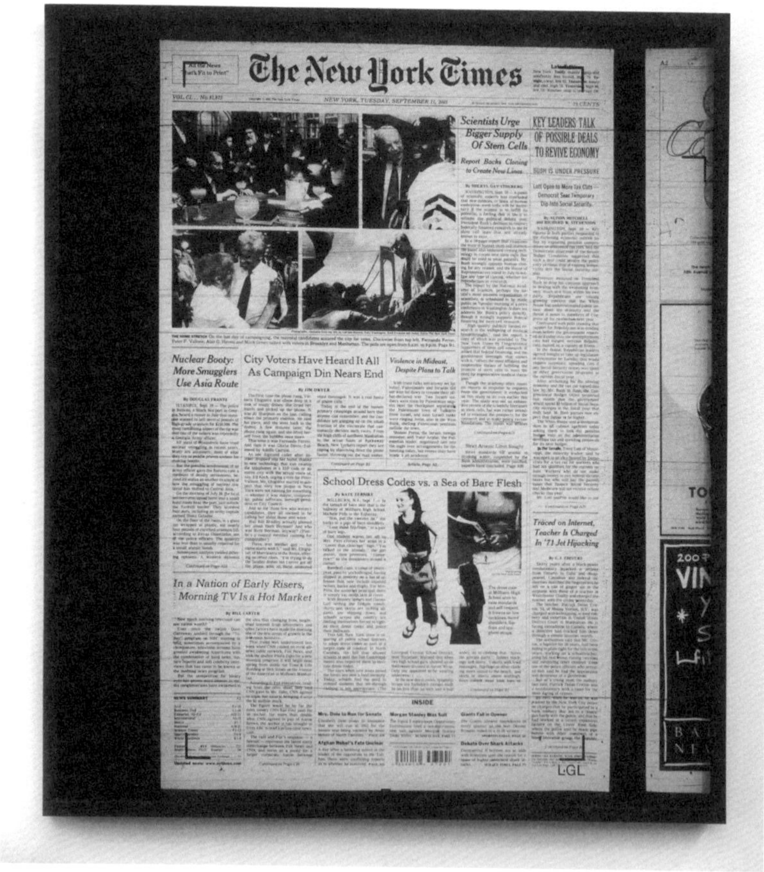

FIG. 1.7

Rosemarie Trockel, *Untitled (Doppelkreuz)*, 1993

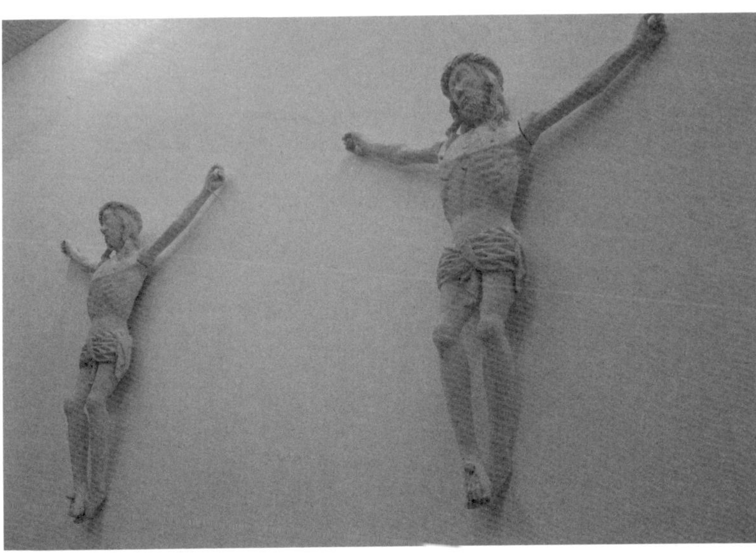

FIG. 1.8

Fig. 85 from Mike Kelley's catalogue, *The Uncanny*, 1993

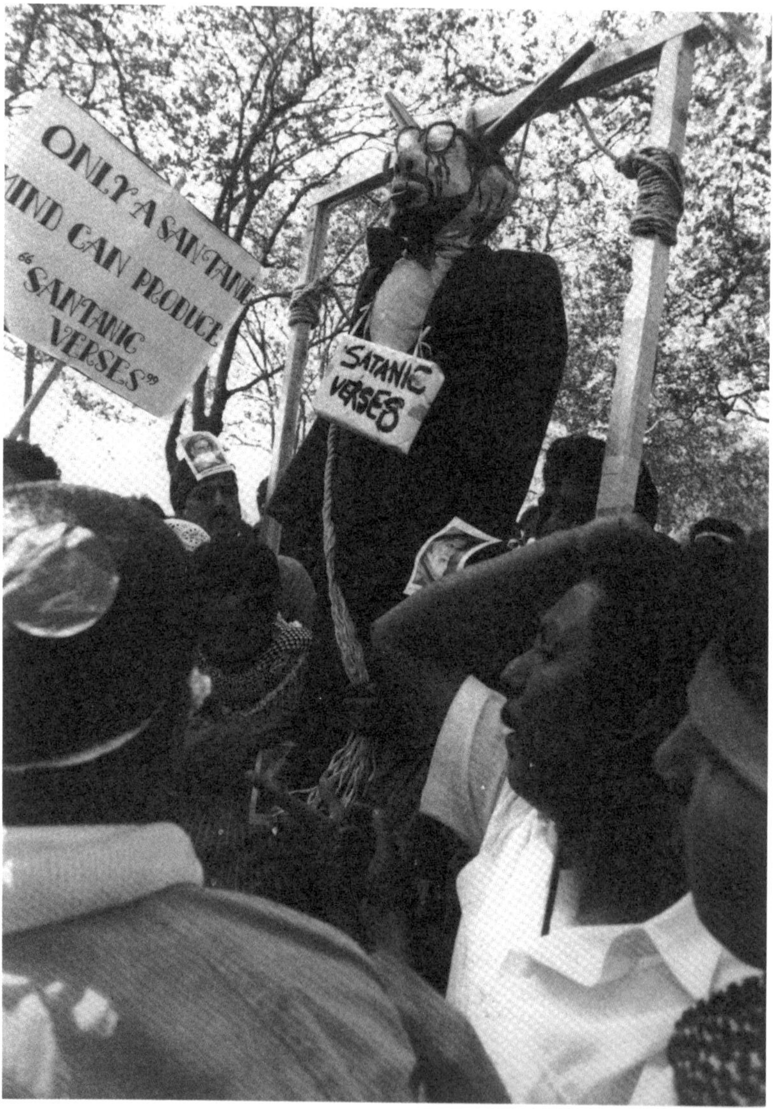

FIG. 1.9

Guy Debord, *Réalisation de la philosophie*, 1963

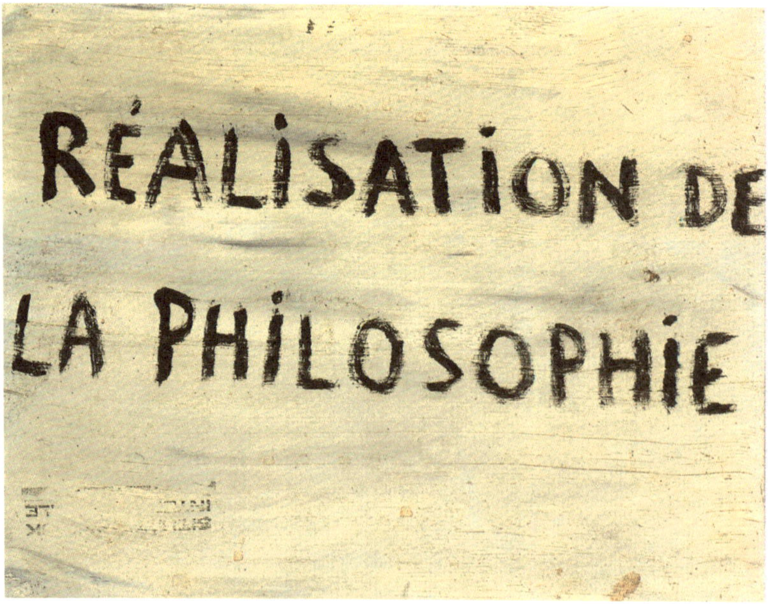

FIG. 2.1

Détournement of Jean-Léon Gérôme's *Pollice Verso,* 1872

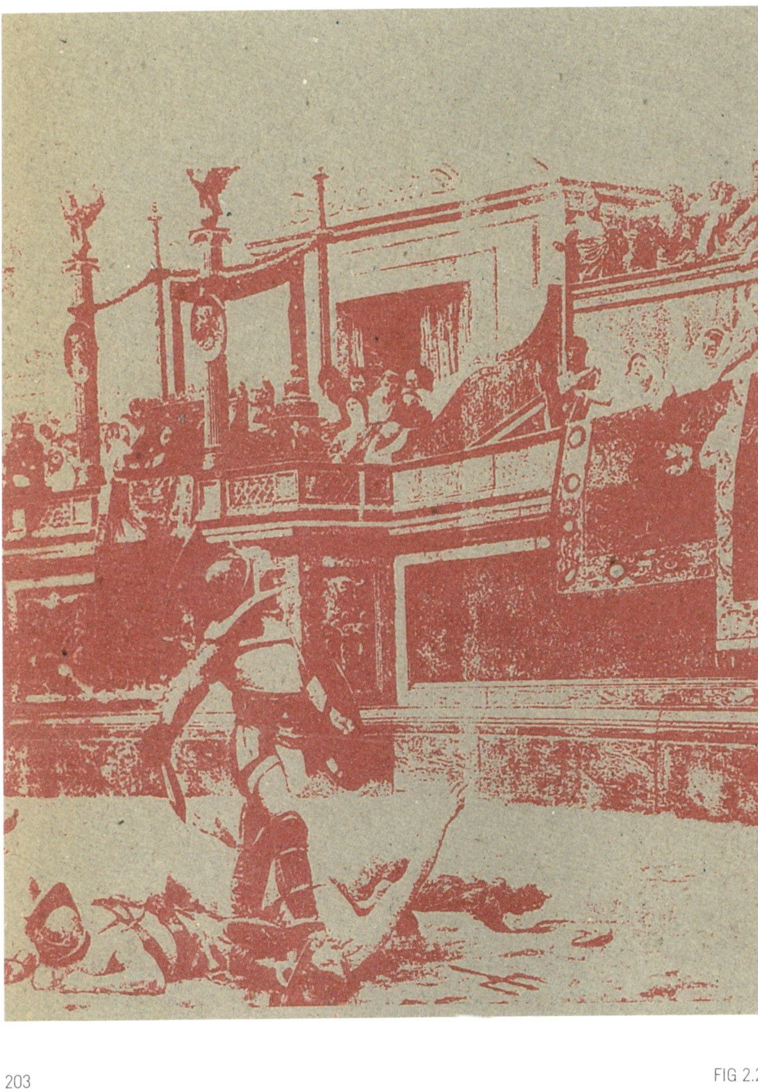

FIG 2.2.

Set of Alexandria built for the film *Cleopatra*, directed by Joseph L. Mankiewicz, 1963

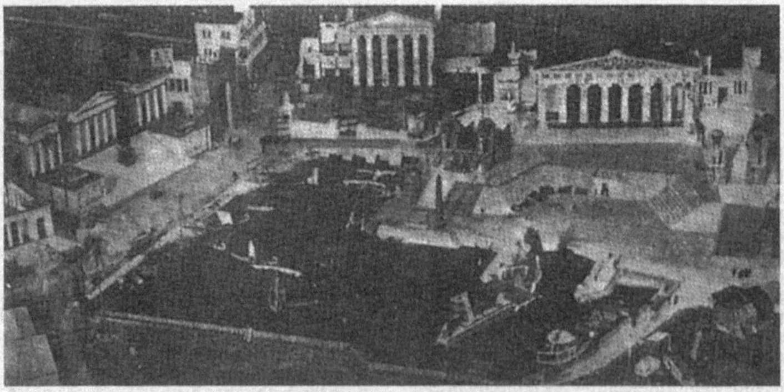

Le décor et son usage. Quatre historiens et plusieurs centaines de millions, dit-on, ont été employés, cette année, pour reconstruire une partie de la ville d'Alexandrie dans une lande d'Angleterre. Mais c'était pour qu'Elizabeth Taylor y jouât Cléopâtre. L'actrice étant malade, on ne put tourner le film, ni rien faire d'autre du terrain. Finalement, Alexandrie a été livrée aux flammes.

FIG. 2.3

Ben-Hur, directed by Fred Niblo, 1925

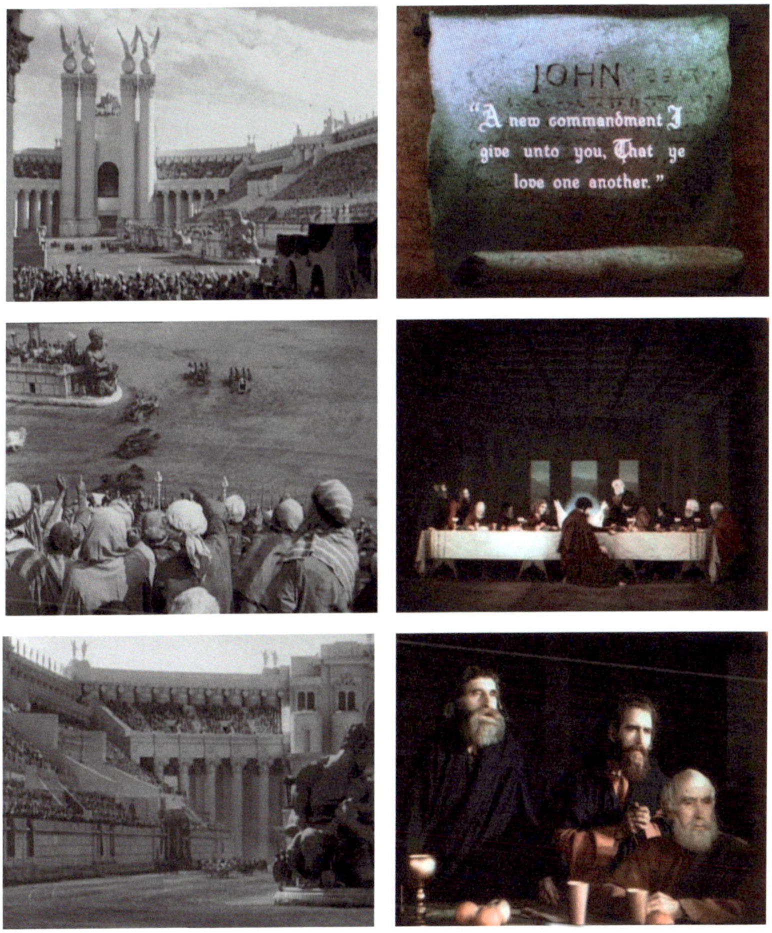

FIG. 2.4

Arnoud Holleman, *Staphorst*, 2003

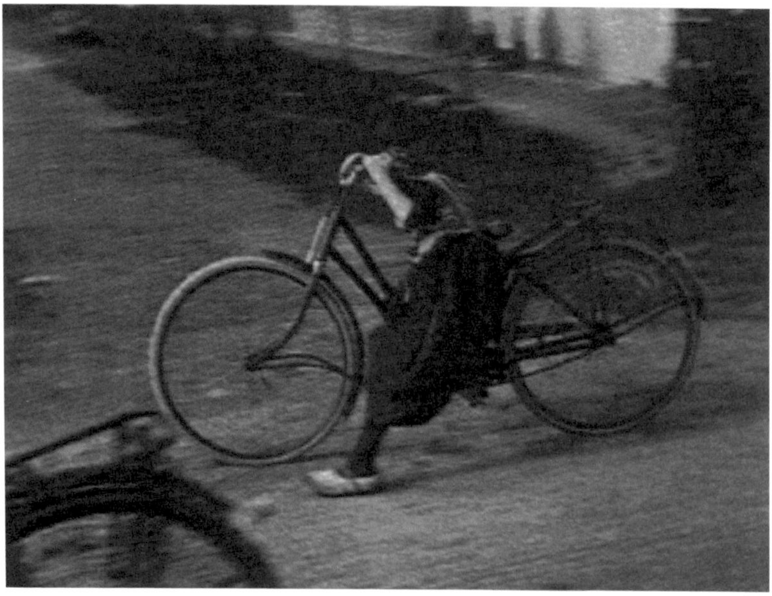

FIG. 2.5

Gholamhossein Derakhshan, *Calligraphers*, first half of the twentieth century
From Parisa Damandan, *Portrait Photographs from Isfahan*, 2004

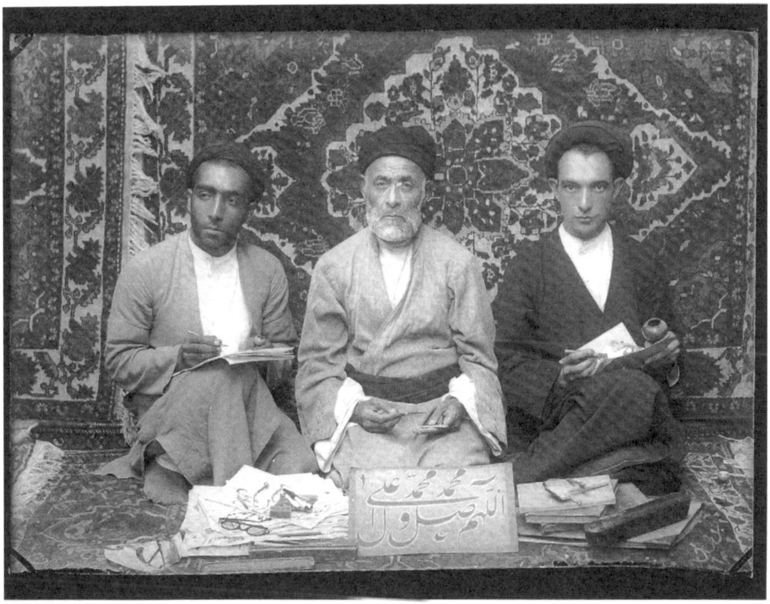

FIG. 2.6

Natascha Sadr Haghighian, *Empire of the Senseless Part I*, 2006
Installation view

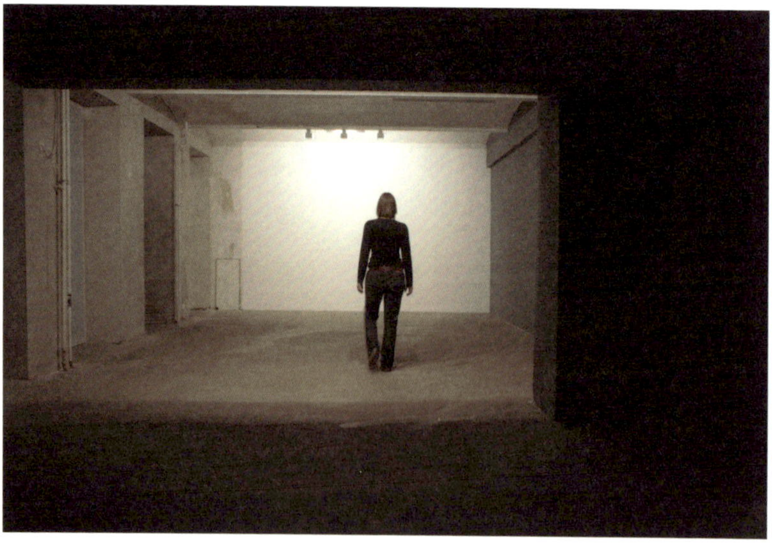

FIG. 2.7

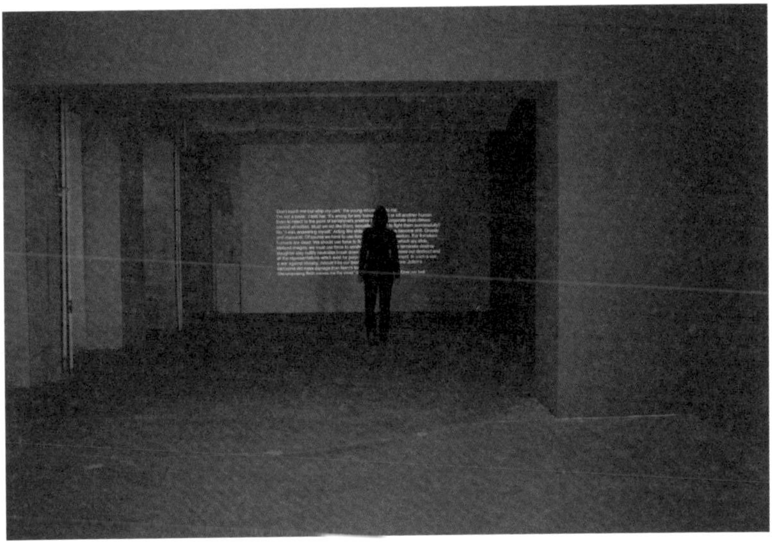

FIG. 2.7.1

Sean Snyder, *Index No. 078 (Primary Interest Component, US Department of Defense)*, 2007

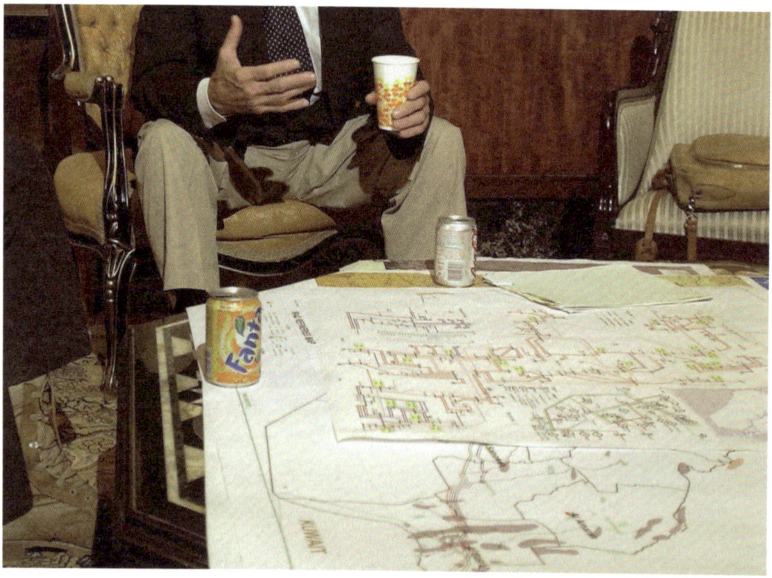

FIG. 2.8

Subject / Caption:
Secretary of Defense Donald H. Rumsfeld is briefed by Ambassador Paul Bremer in Iraq.

Date:
Sept. 4, 2003

Photo Credit:
Tech. Sgt. Andy Dunaway, U.S. Air Force.

Image File Data

Size: 16.9 Mb
Width: 3008 Pixels
Height: 1960 Pixels

FIG. 2.8.1

Omer Fast, *Godville*, 2005

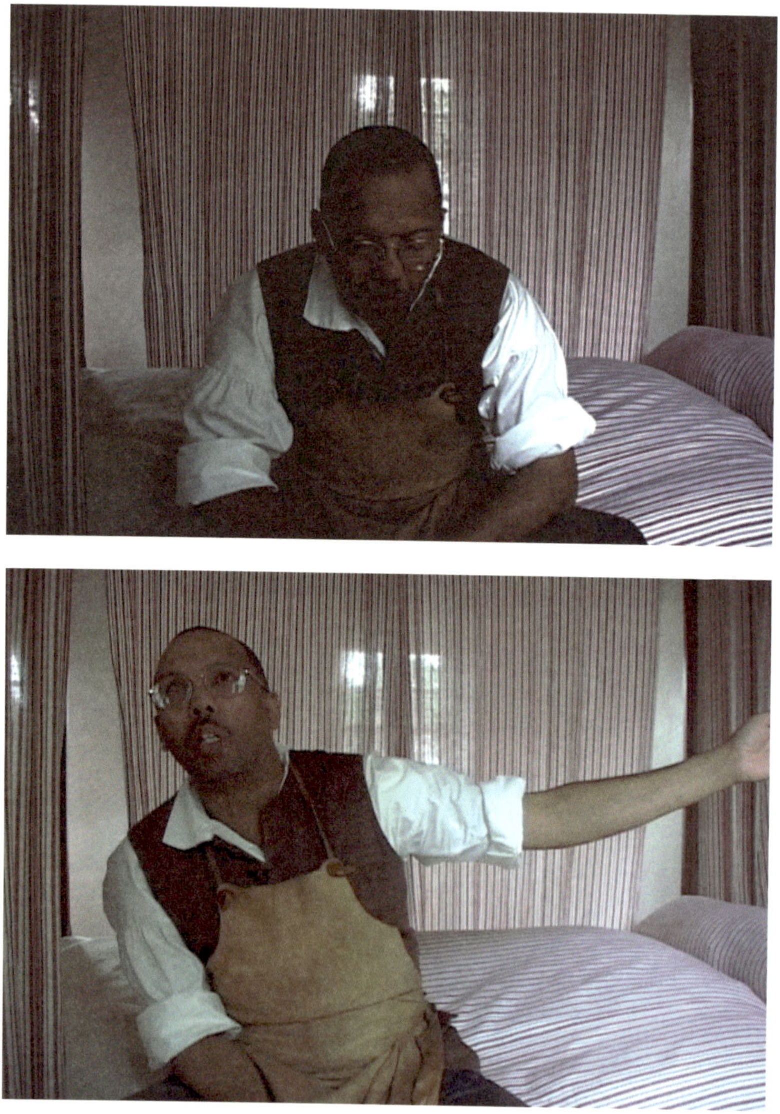

FIG. 2.9

Carl Andre, untitled text piece, *Art-Rite #14*, Winter 1976/77

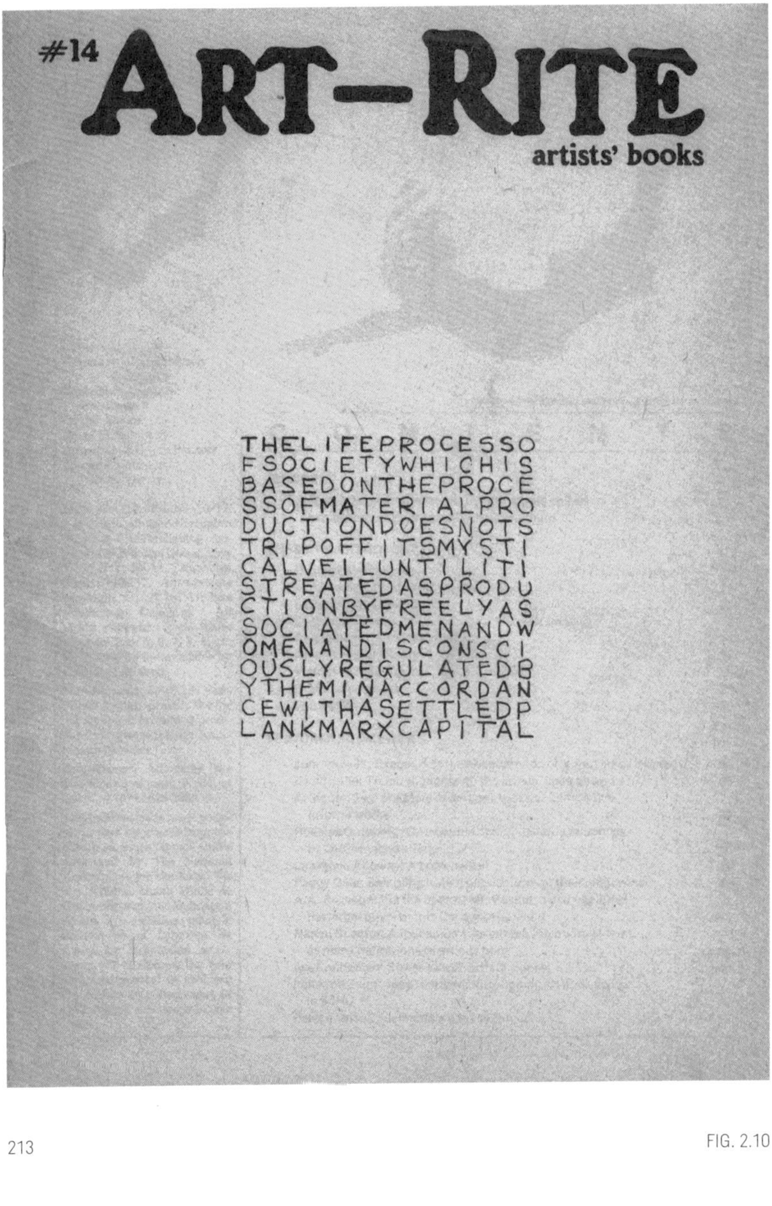

FIG. 2.10

Liebig trading card, 1928

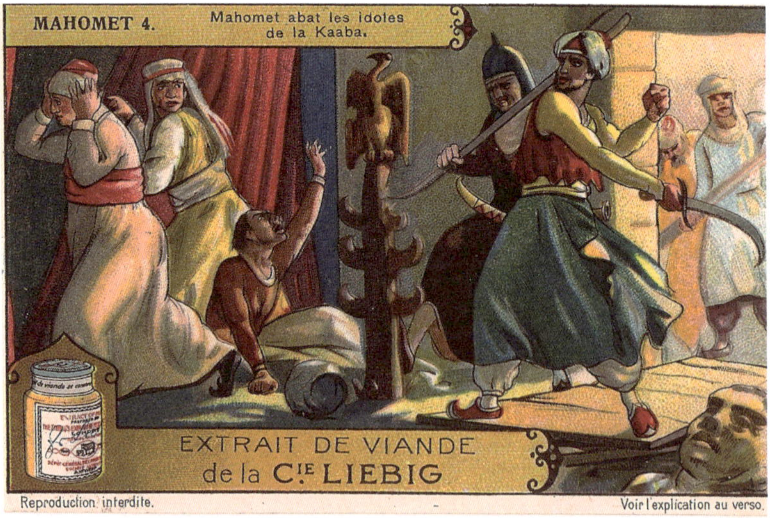

FIG. 3.1

“Fetish” with calabash and shells, Belgian Congo

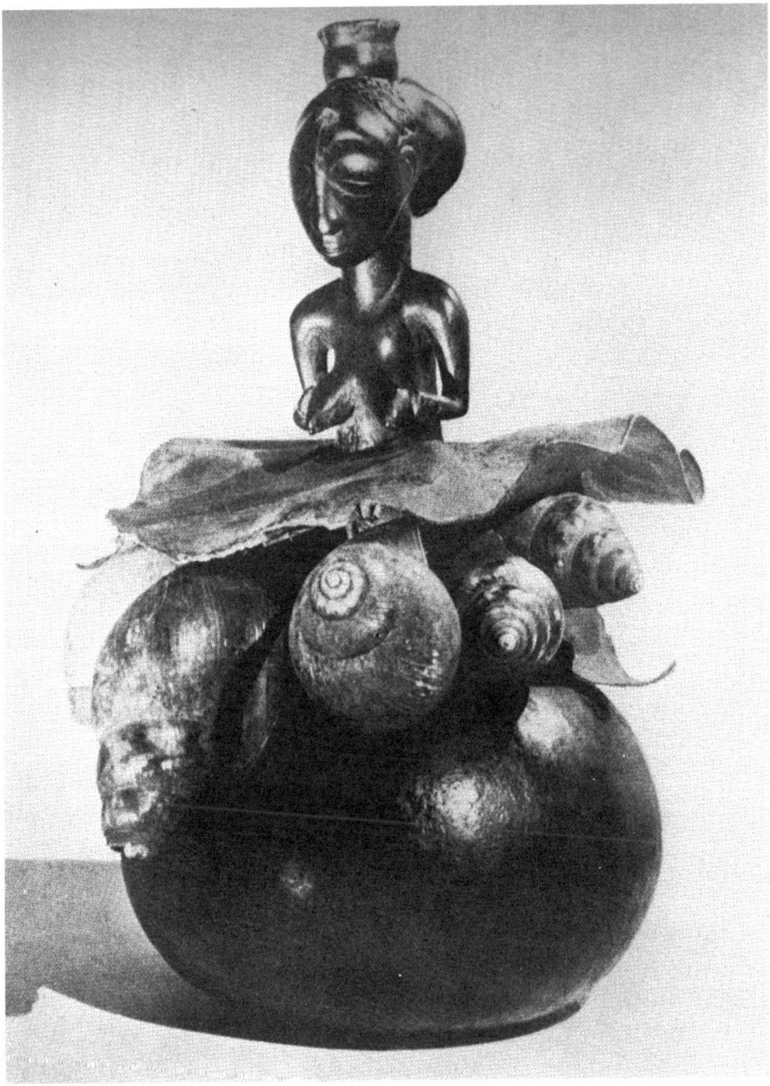

FIG. 3.2

The Artemis of Ephesus, plate LXXXVIII from volume 4 of Friedrich Creuzer and Joseph-Daniel Guigniaut, *Religions de l'antiquité considérées principalement dans leurs formes symboliques et mythologiques*, 1841

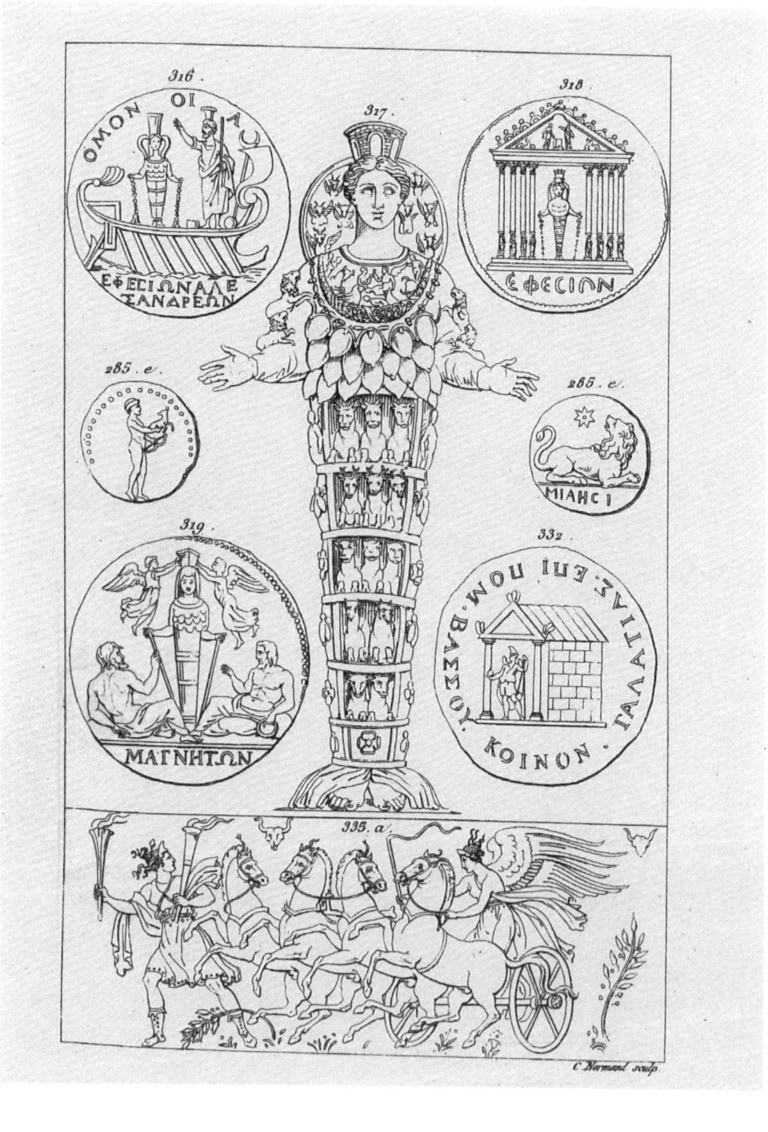

FIG. 3.3

The so-called Diana of Versailles or *Diane chasseresse*
Plate LXXXIX (detail)

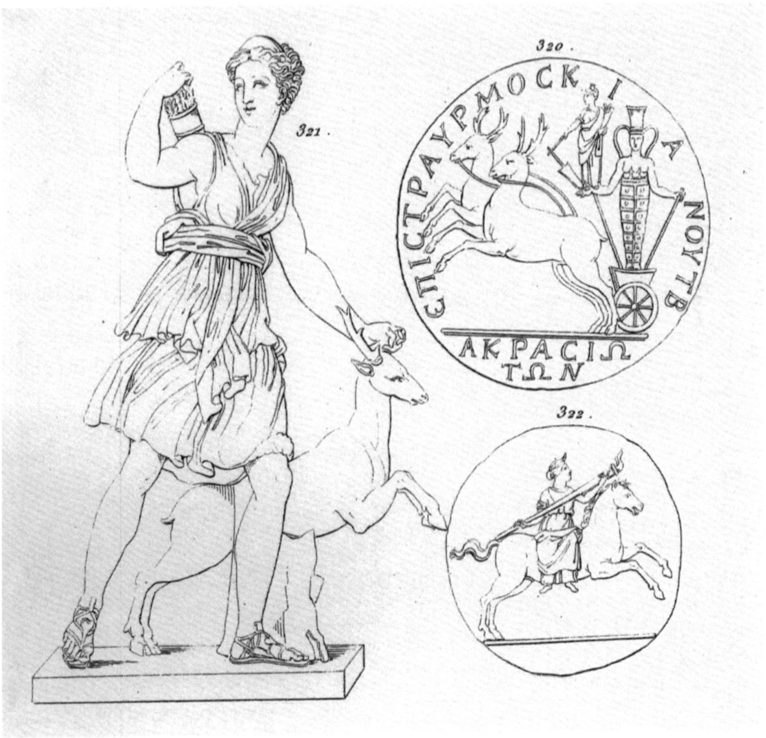

Salvador Dalí, *Objet scatologique à fonctionnement symbolique,* 1931

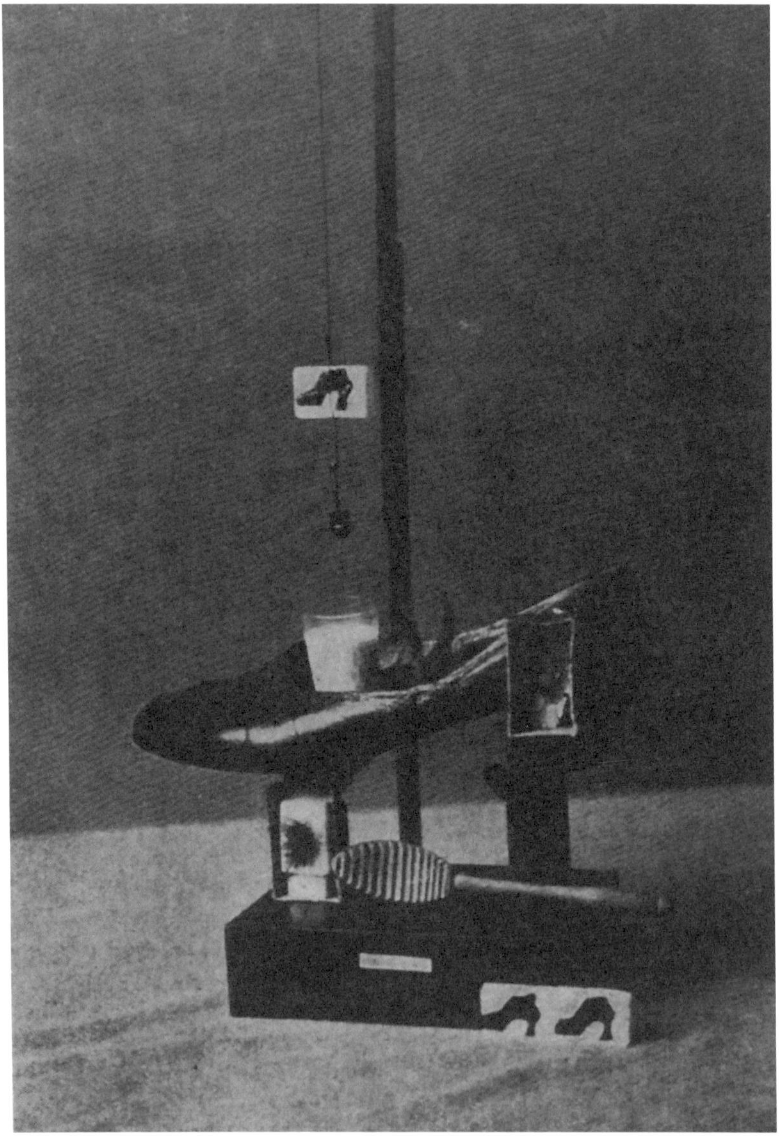

FIG. 3.5

Marcel Broodthaers, *Musée d'Art Moderne, Département des Aigles, Section Financière*, 1970–71

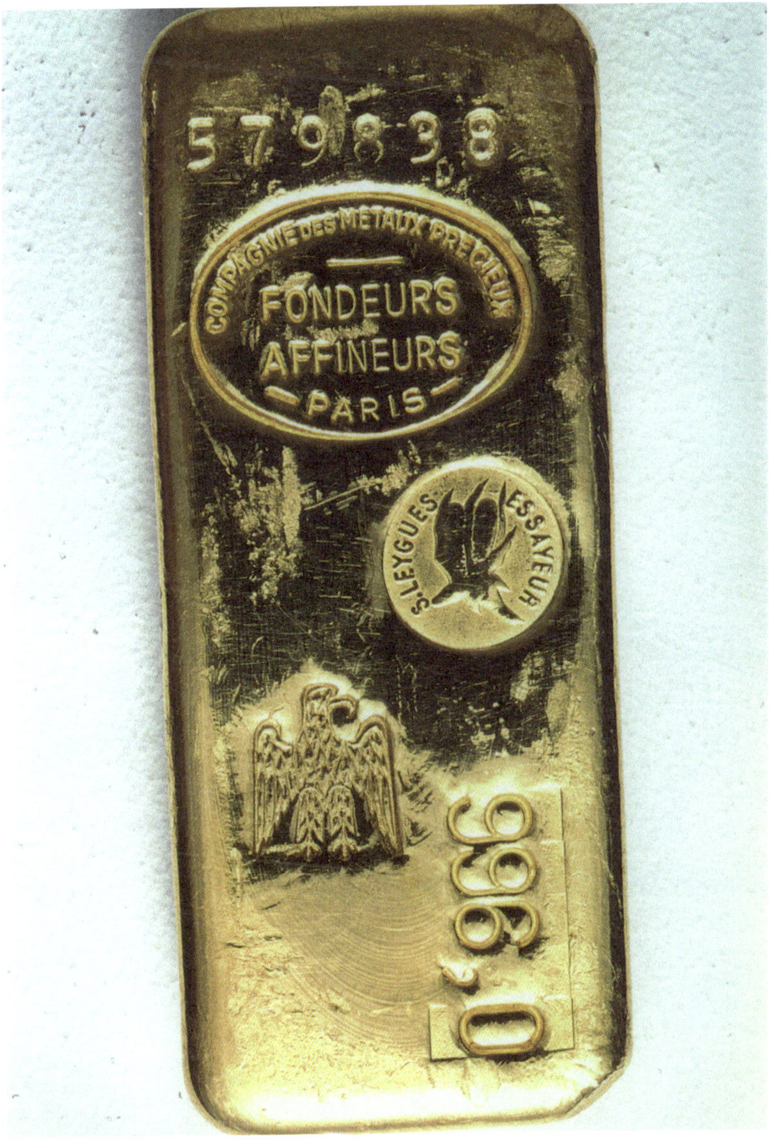

FIG. 3.6

Frank Stella, *Madinat as-Salam I*, 1973
Installation at Sears Bank and Trust Company, Chicago

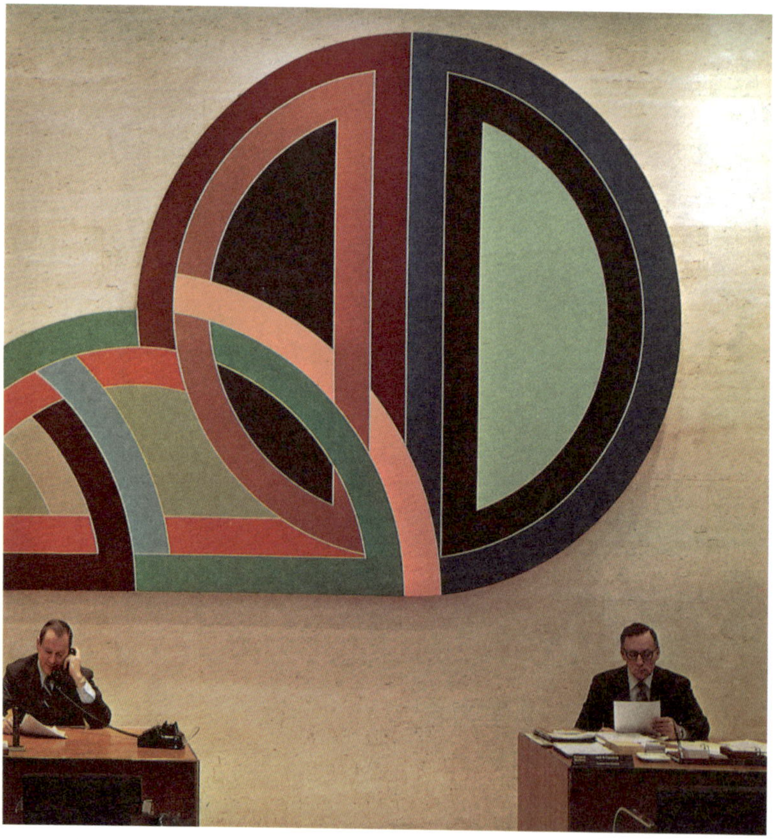

FIG. 3.7

Allan Sekula, drawing for a lecture, 2003

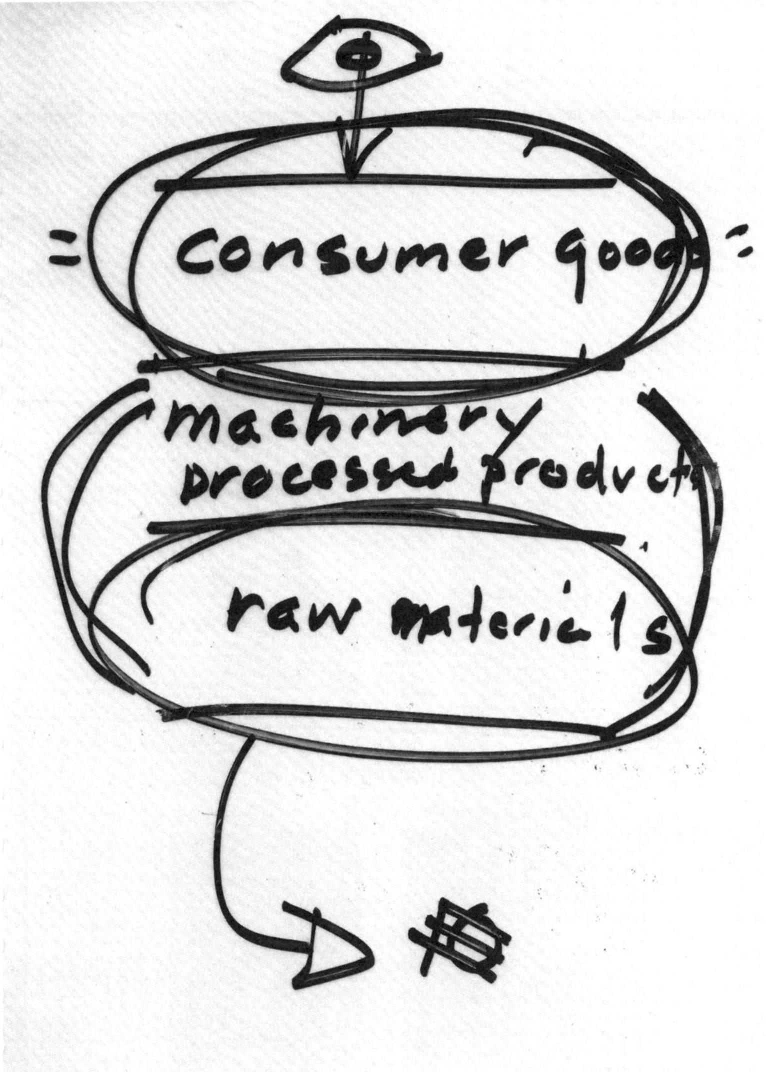

Hans Haacke, *Proposal for poster commemorating 9/11*, 2001

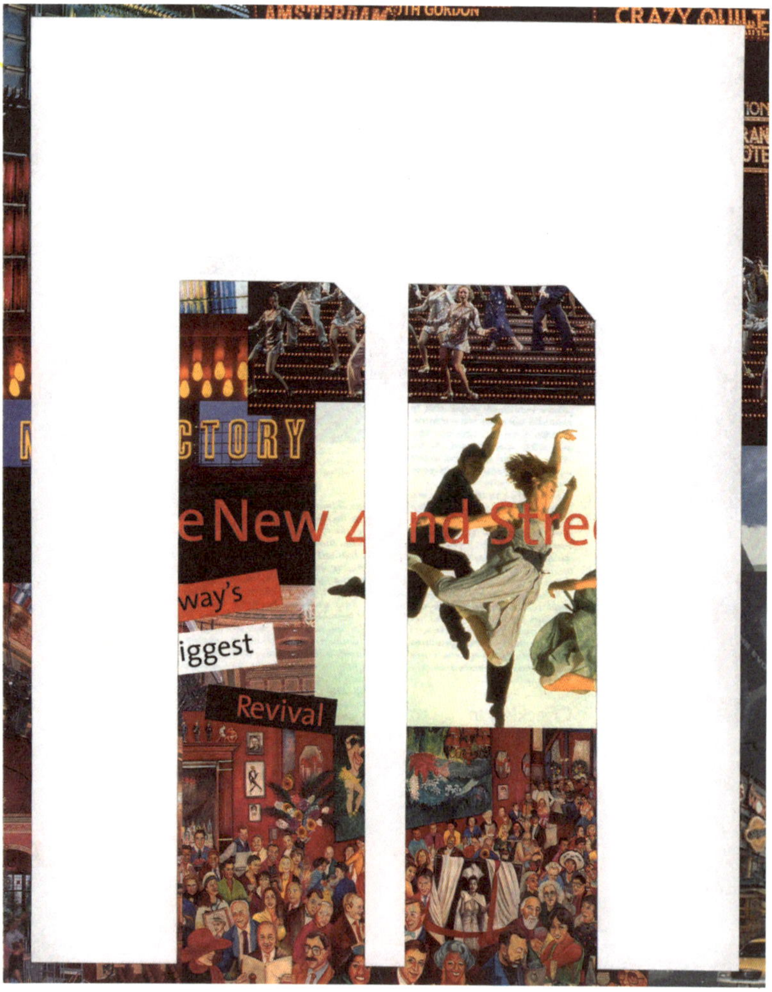

FIG. 4.1

Who's Afraid of God?, 1997

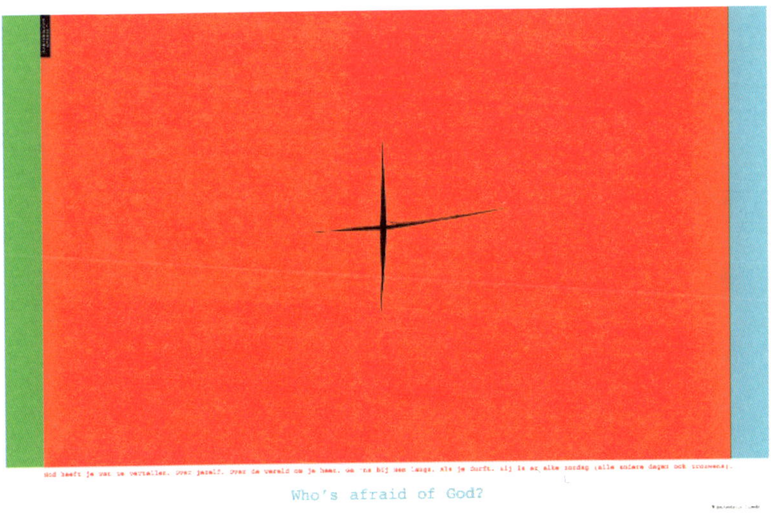

FIG. 4.2

Piet Mondrian, *Tableau-poème: textuel*, 1928

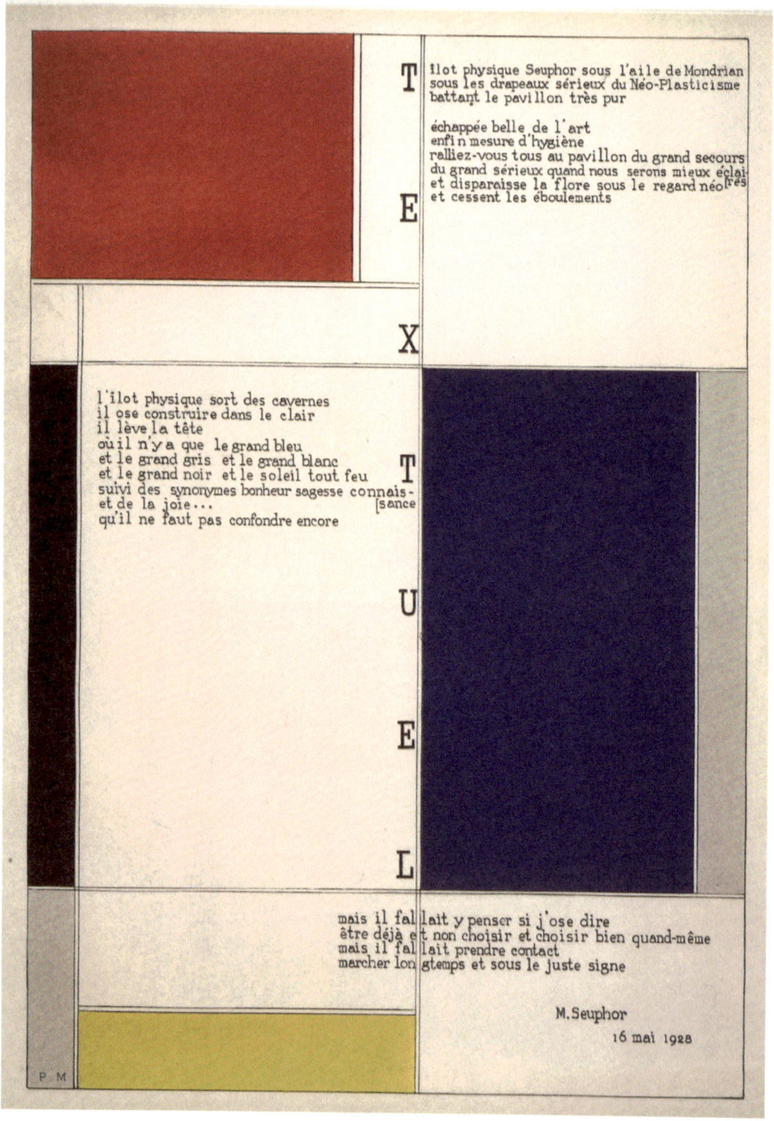

FIG. 4.3

Joseph Kosuth, *Mondrian's Work I*, 2005

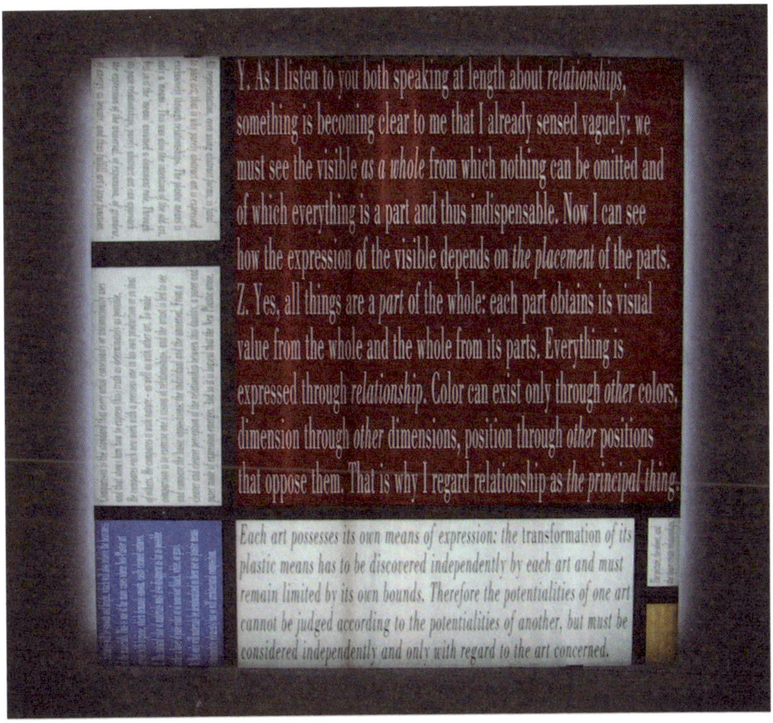

FIG. 4.4

Gerhard Richter, Cologne Cathedral Window, 2007

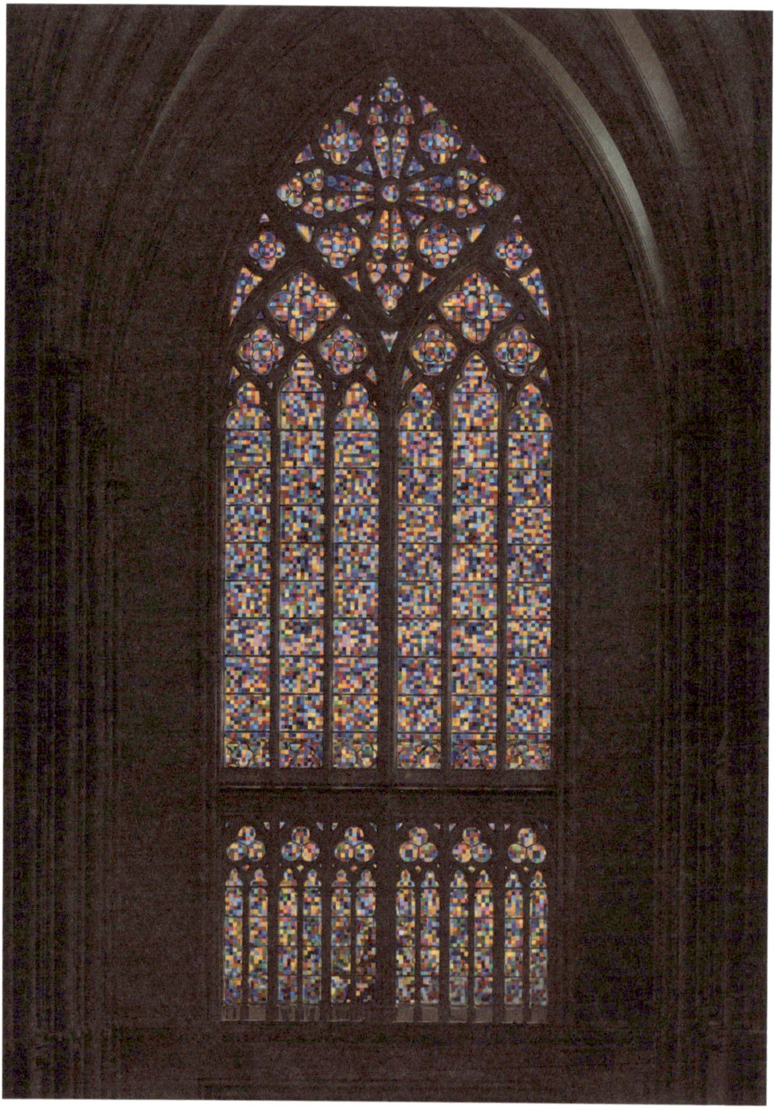

FIG. 4.5

Jeroen de Rijke/Willem de Rooij, *Bergama, West Anatolia, ca. 1850*, 2003

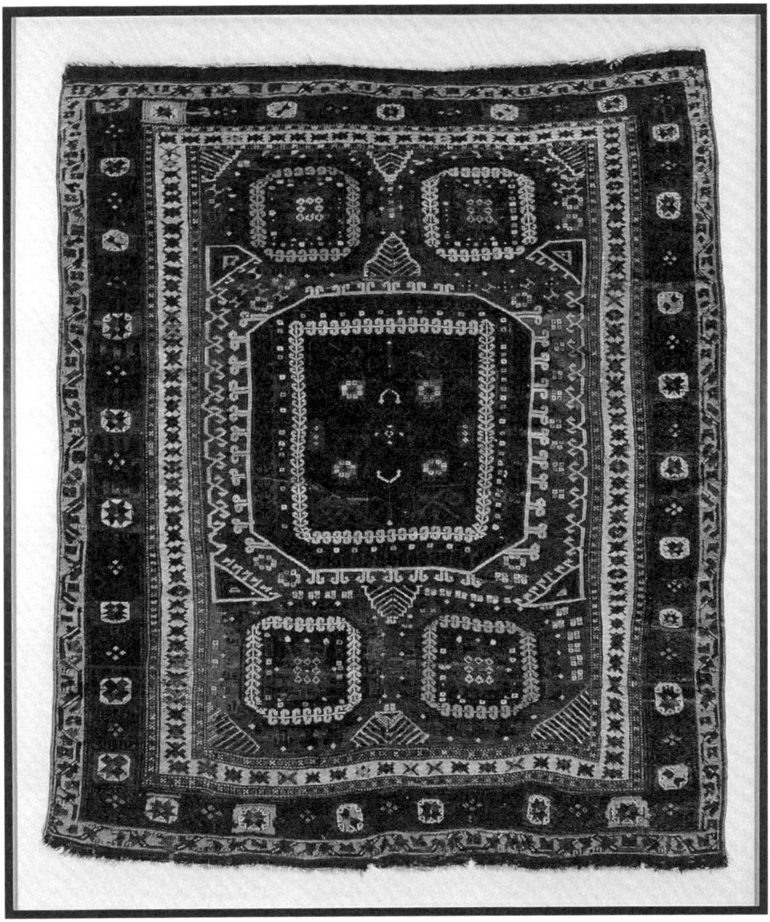

FIG. 4.6

Krijn de Koning, installation at Musée des Moulages, Lyon, 2003

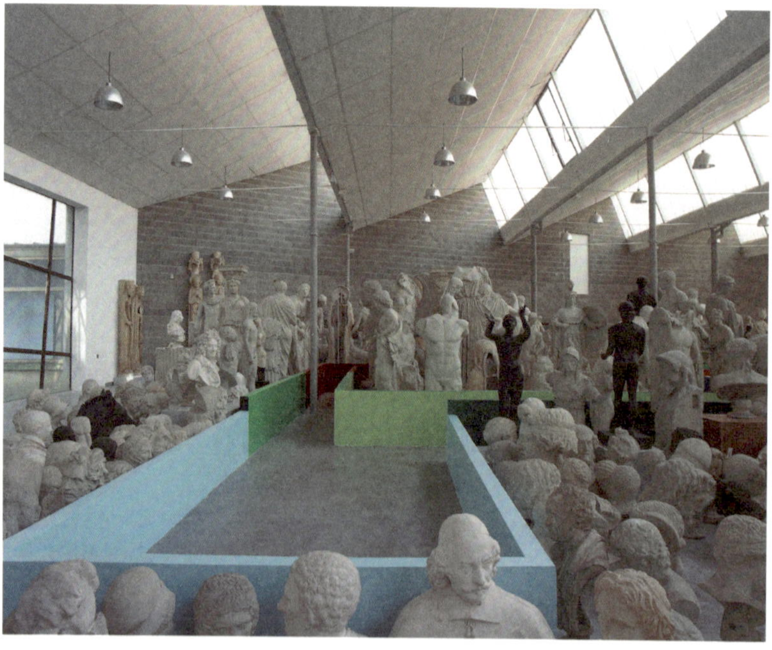

FIG. 4.7

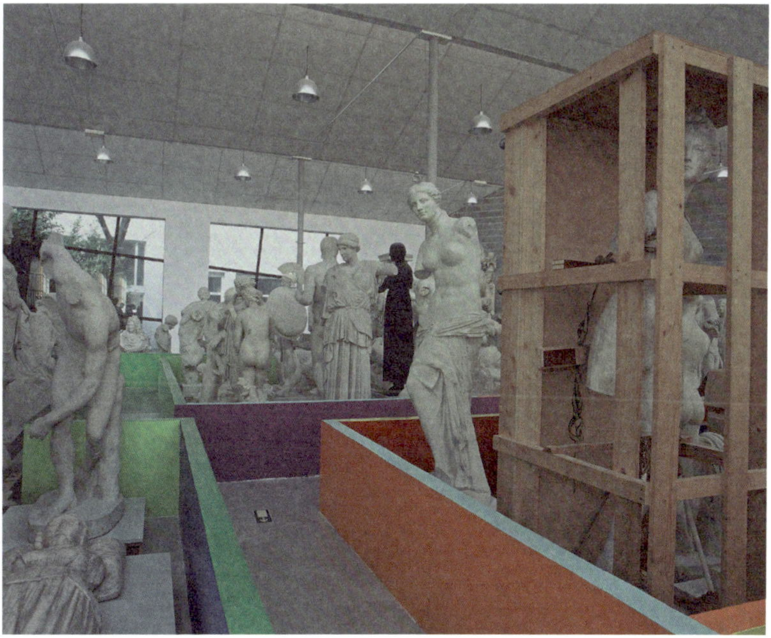

FIG. 4.7.1

Bureau d'études, *Monotheism, Inc.*, 2003 (detail)

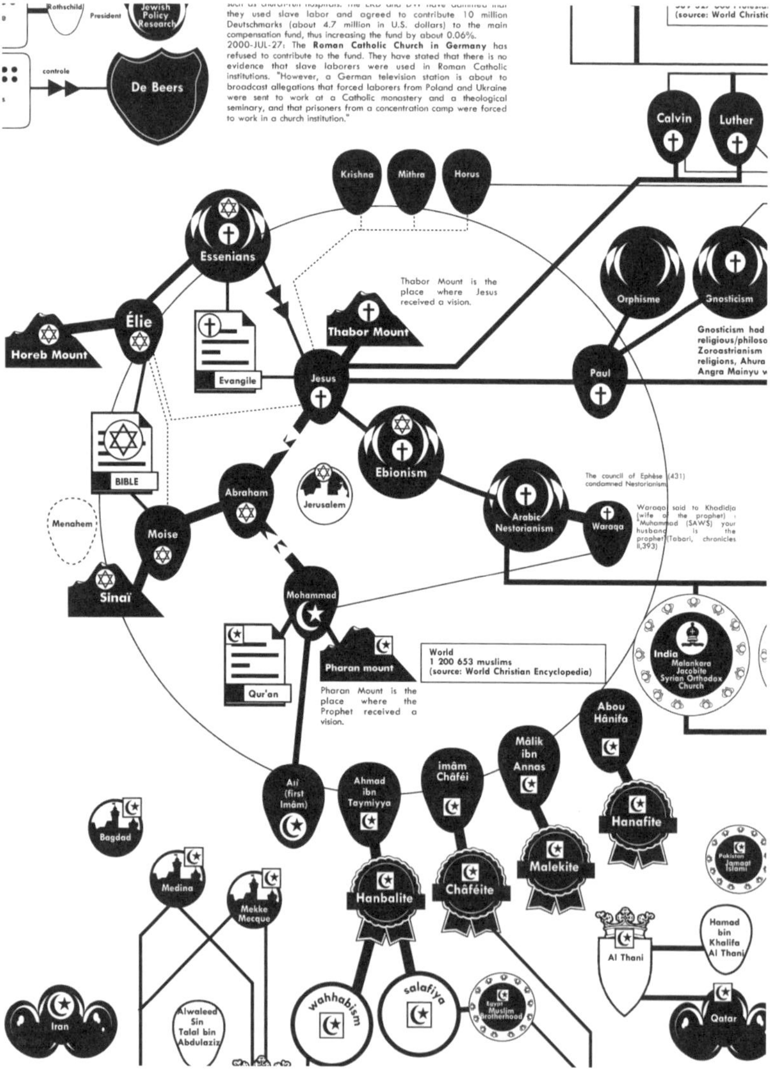

Liam Gillick, *Everything Good Goes*, 2008

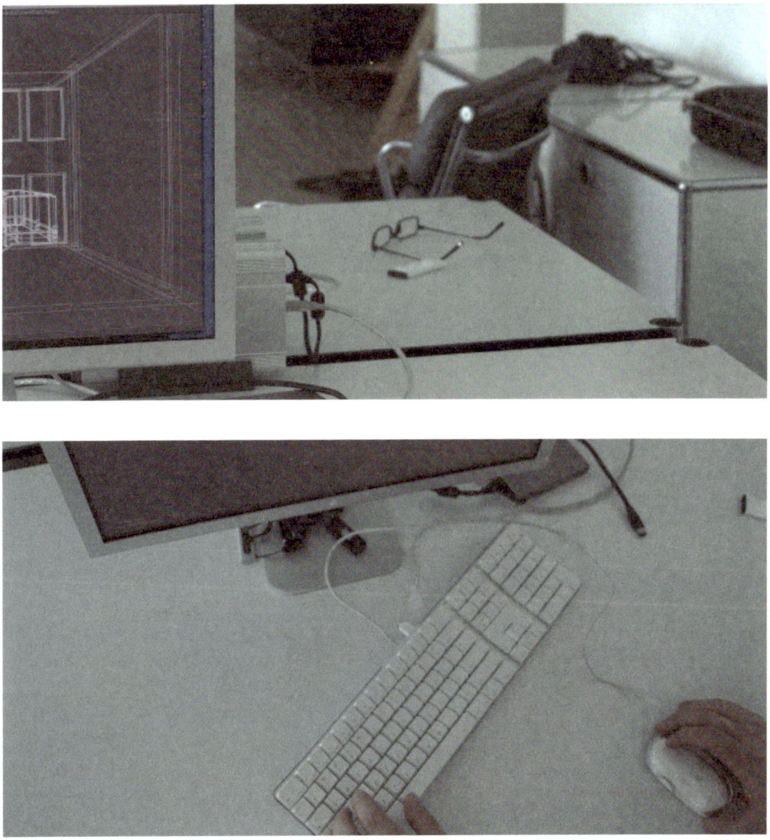

FIG. 4.9

From *The Sun*, London
Thursday, February 1, 2007

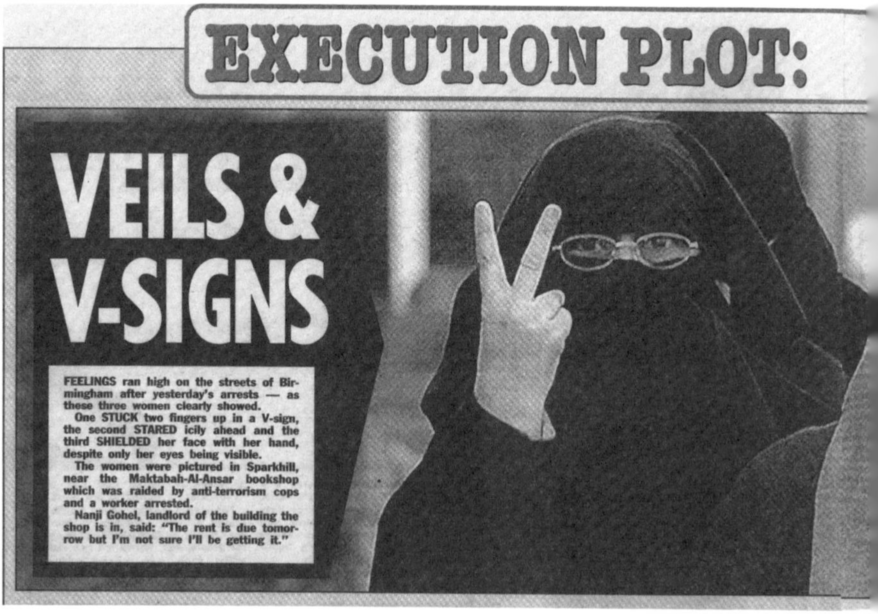

EXECUTION PLOT:

VEILS & V-SIGNS

FEELINGS ran high on the streets of Birmingham after yesterday's arrests — as these three women clearly showed.

One STUCK two fingers up in a V-sign, the second STARED icily ahead and the third SHIELDED her face with her hand, despite only her eyes being visible.

The women were pictured in Sparkhill, near the Maktabah-Al-Ansar bookshop which was raided by anti-terrorism cops and a worker arrested.

Nanji Gohel, landlord of the building the shop is in, said: "The rent is due tomorrow but I'm not sure I'll be getting it."

FIG. 5.1

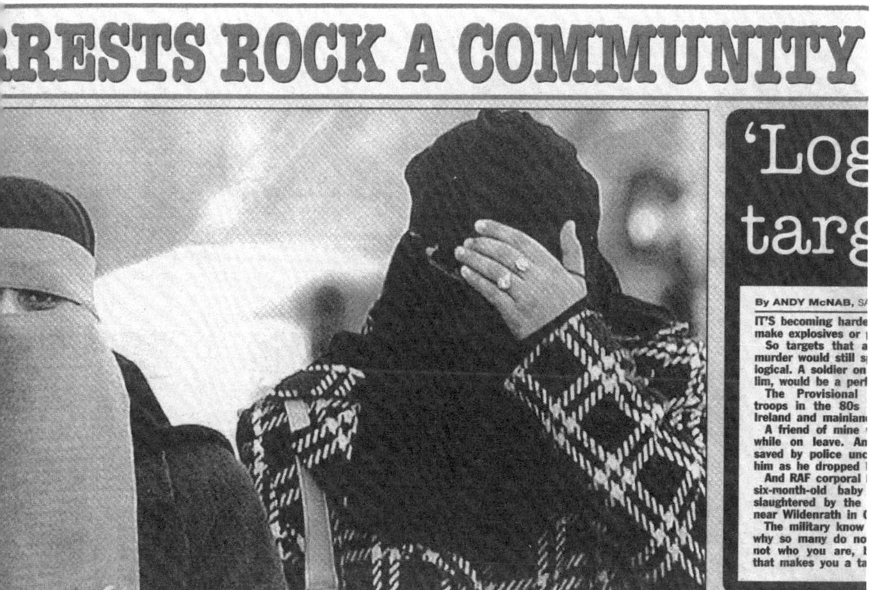

RESTS ROCK A COMMUNITY

'Log
targ

By ANDY McNAB, SA

IT'S becoming harde
make explosives or
So targets that a
murder would still s
logical. A soldier on
lim, would be a perf
The Provisional
troops in the 80s
Ireland and mainlan
A friend of mine
while on leave. An
saved by police unc
him as he dropped
And RAF corporal
six-month-old baby
slaughtered by the
near Wildenrath in
The military know
why so many do no
not who you are,
that makes you a ta

Mural in Susa, Iran

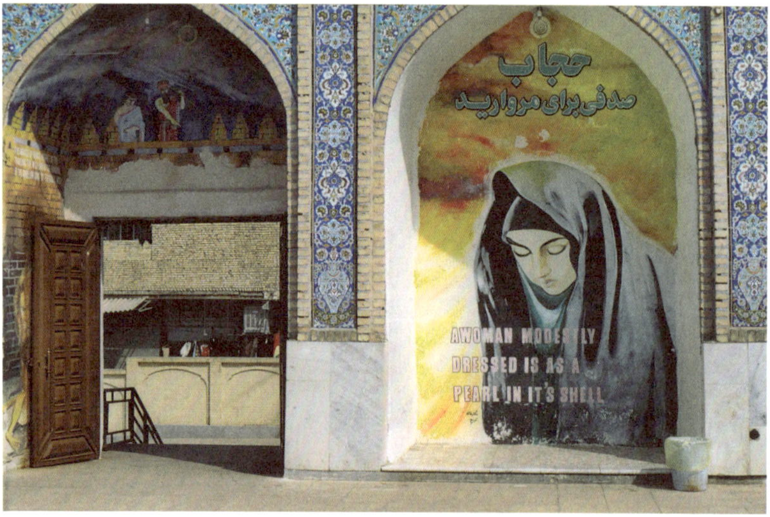

FIG. 5.2

Willem Oorebeek, *Michael in the Snow*, 2006–08

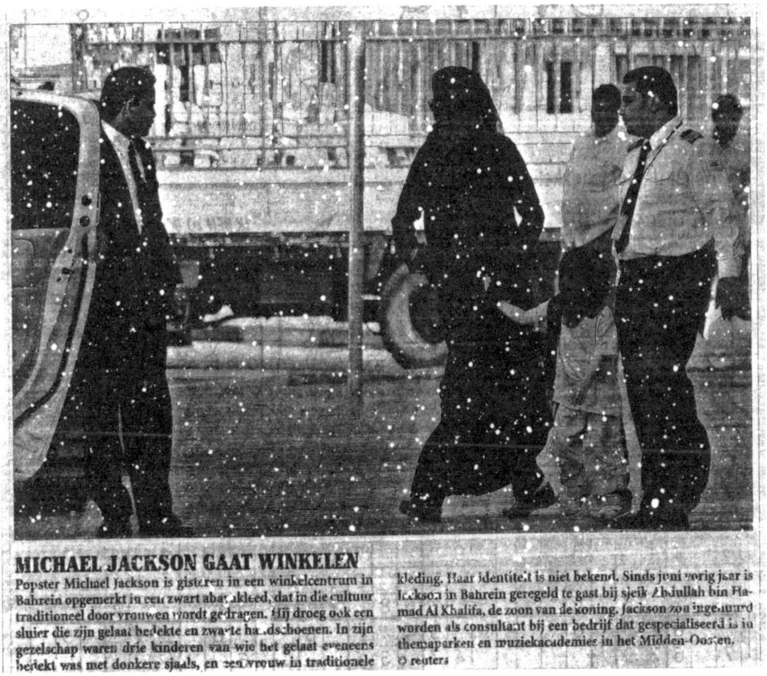

MICHAEL JACKSON GAAT WINKELEN

Popster Michael Jackson is gisteren in een winkelcentrum in Bahrein opgemerkt in een zwart abayakleed, dat in die cultuur traditioneel door vrouwen wordt gedragen. Hij droeg ook een sluier die zijn gelaat bedekte en zwarte handschoenen. In zijn gezelschap waren drie kinderen van wie het gelaat eveneens bedekt was met donkere sjaals, en een vrouw in traditionele kleding. Haar identiteit is niet bekend. Sinds juni vorig jaar is Jackson in Bahrein geregeld te gast bij sjeik Abdullah bin Hamad Al Khalifa, de zoon van de koning. Jackson zou ingehuurd worden als consultant bij een bedrijf dat gespecialiseerd is in themaparken en muziekacademies in het Midden-Oosten.

© reuters

FIG. 5.3

Fransje Killaars, *Figures No. 4*, 2006

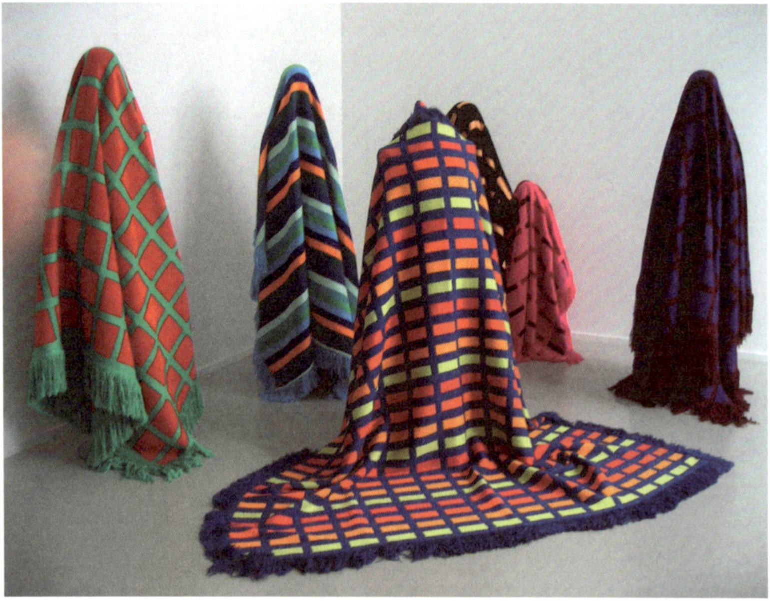

FIG. 5.4

Lidwien van de Ven, *London, 04/09/2004 (International Hijab Solidarity Day)*, 2005
Photograph and installation view

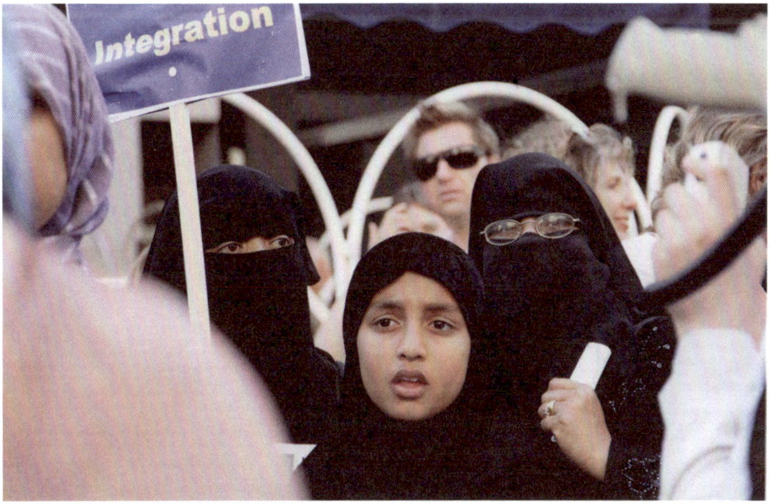

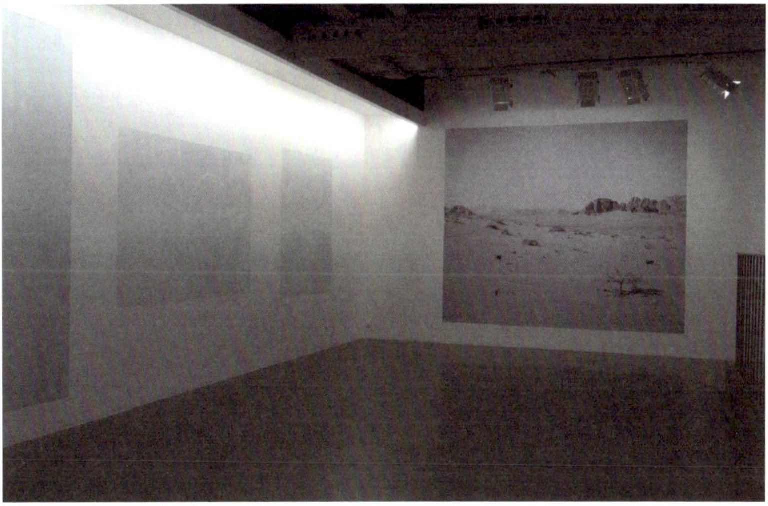

FIG. 5.5.

Loïe Fuller's Serpentine Dance
Photograph by Frederick Glasier, 1902

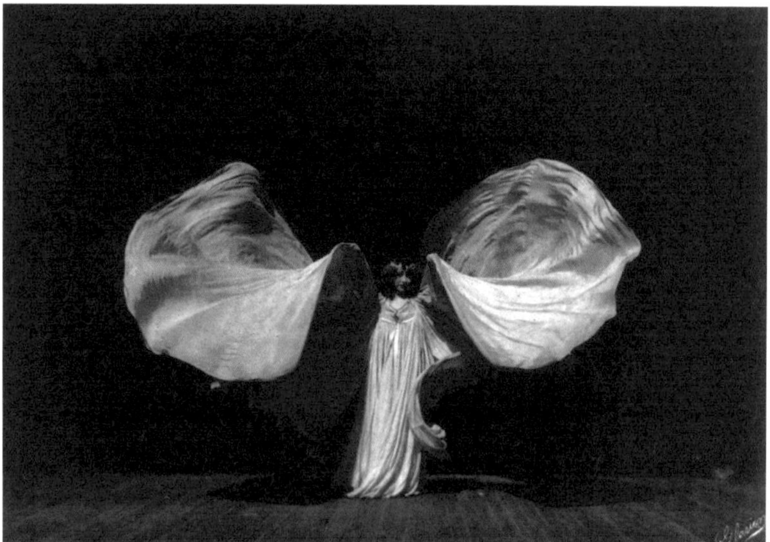

FIG. 5.6

Arnoud Holleman, *Museum*, 1997

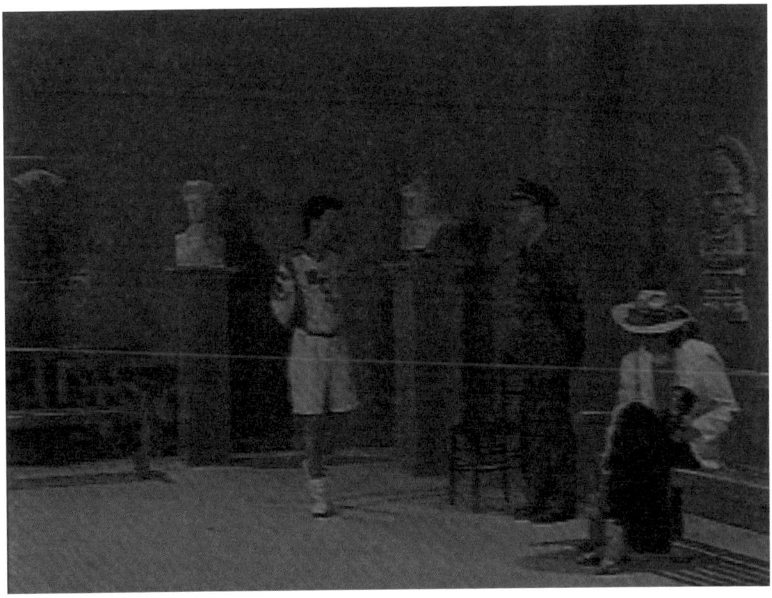

FIG. 5.7

Rod Dickinson and Tom McCarthy, *Greenwich Degree Zero,* 2006

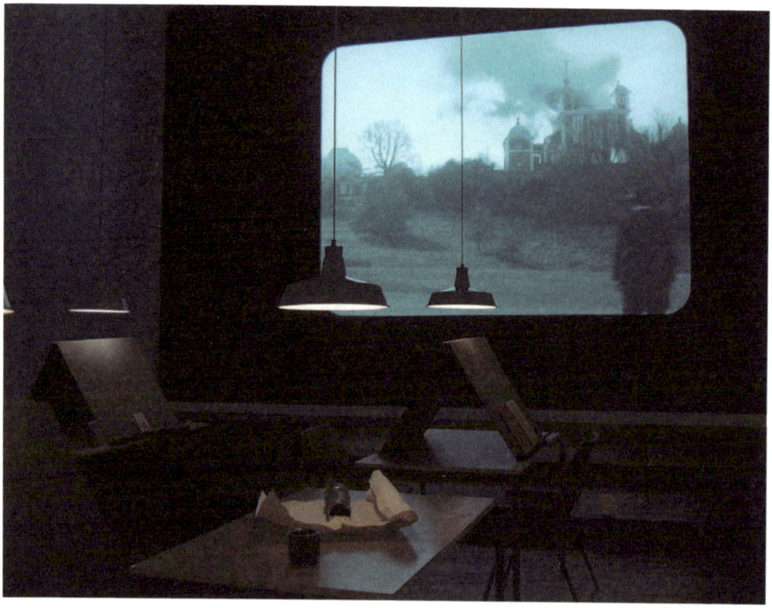

FIG. 5.8

LIST OF ILLUSTRATIONS

2.7
Natascha Sadr Haghighian
Empire of the Senseless Part I, 2006
Installation view
Motion detector, construction site spotlight, contact microphones and text by Kathy Acker
Courtesy of Johann König, Berlin

2.8
Sean Snyder
Index No. 078 (Primary Interest Component, US Department of Defense), 2007
Light Jet print, 46.5 × 66 cm
Laser Jet print, 21 × 29.7 cm
Courtesy of Sean Snyder and Lisson Gallery

2.9
Omer Fast
Godville, 2005
Video stills
Courtesy of Omer Fast and *Arratia*, Beer

2.10
Carl Andre
Untitled text piece
Art-Rite #14, Winter 1976/77
© C. Andre. Courtesy of the artist and Paula Cooper Gallery, New York

3.1
Liebig trading card depicting Muhammad destroying the idols in the Ka'aba, 1928
From a series of six Liebig Continental chromolithograph trading cards on the life of Muhammad

3.2
"Fetish" with calabash and shells, Belgian Congo
Collection Tristan Tzara, Paris
Item 489 from the exhibition *African Negro Art* (Museum of Modern Art, New York, 1935)

3.3
The Artemis of Ephesus
Plate LXXXVIII from volume 4 of Friedrich Creuzer and Joseph-Daniel Guigniaut, *Religions de l'antiquité considérées principalement dans leurs formes symboliques et mythologiques*, 1841.

3.4
The so-called Diana of Versailles or *Diane chasseresse*
Detail of plate LXXXIX from volume 4 of Friedrich Creuzer and Joseph-Daniel Guigniaut, *Religions de l'antiquité considérées principalement dans leurs formes symboliques et mythologiques*, 1841.

3.5
Salvador Dalí
Objet scatologique à fonctionnement symbolique, 1931
Reproduced in *Le Surréalisme au service de la révolution*, no. 3

3.6
Marcel Broodthaers
Musée d'Art Moderne, Département des Aigles, Section Financière, 1970–71
Gold bar stamped with the image of an eagle
Courtesy of Galerie beaumontpublic, Luxembourg

3.7
Frank Stella
Madinat as-Salam I, 1973
Sears Bank and Trust Company, Chicago

3.8
Allan Sekula
Drawing for a lecture, 2003
Courtesy of Allan Sekula

4.1
Hans Haacke
Proposal for poster commemorating 9/11, 2001
© Hans Haacke/VG Bild-Kunst, Bonn 2009

4.2
Who's Afraid of God?
Poster designed for Archdiocese of Utrecht, 1997

4.3
Piet Mondrian
Tableau-poème: textuel, 1928
© bpk/RMN/Paris, Centre Pompidou/Philippe Migeat

4.4
Joseph Kosuth
Mondrian's Work I, 2005
Silkscreen on glass, neons
200 × 200 cm
Courtesy of Simon Lee Gallery, London

4.5
Gerhard Richter
Cologne Cathedral Window, 2007

4.6
Jeroen de Rijke/Willem de Rooij
Bergama, West Anatolia, ca. 1850, 2003
C-Print, 212 × 184.5 cm
Courtesy of Galerie Daniel Buchholz, Cologne

4.7
Krijn de Koning
Installation at Musée des Moulages, Lyon, 2003
Courtesy of Krijn de Koning

4.8
Bureau d'études
Monotheism, Inc., 2003
http://utangente.free.fr/2003/monotheisminc.pdf

4.9
Liam Gillick
Everything Good Goes, 2008
Video stills
Courtesy of Liam Gillick and Esther Schipper, Berlin

5.1
Scanned douple-page spread from *The Sun*, London
Thursday, February 1, 2007, 8–9

5.2
Mural in Susa, Iran, 2005
Photograph courtesy of Frank Denys

5.3
Willem Oorebeek
Michael in the Snow
From the series "Tableaux d'hiver," 2006–2008
Lithograph on paper
Courtesy of Willem Oorebeek

5.4
Fransje Killaars
Figures No. 4, 2006
Courtesy of Galerie de Expeditie, Amsterdam

5.5
Lidwien van de Ven
London, 04/09/2004 (International Hijab Solidarity Day), 2005
Courtesy of Galerie Paul Andriesse

5.6
Frederick Glasier
Portrait of Loïe Fuller, 1902

5.7
Arnoud Holleman
Museum, 1997
Video still
Courtesy of Arnoud Holleman

5.8
Rod Dickinson and Tom McCarthy
Greenwich Degree Zero, 2006
Courtesy of Arts Council Collection
Southbank Centre, London

The publisher has made every effort to identify the owners of copyrighted material. In a few cases, this was impossible. Legitimate claims will of course be reimbursed according to the usual agreements.

BIOGRAPHY

Sven Lütticken teaches art history at VU University, Amsterdam. He is the author of *Secret Publicity: Essays on Contemporary Art* (NAi publishers, Rotterdam, 2006) and the curator of *Life, Once More: Forms of Reenactment in Contemporary Art* (Witte de With, Rotterdam, 2005) and *The Art of Iconoclasm* (BAK, basis voor actuele kunst, Utrecht, 2009).

Sven Lütticken
Idols of the Market
Modern Iconoclasm and the Fundamentalist Spectacle

Published by Sternberg Press

Copy editing: Allison Plath-Moseley, Kari Rittenbach
Design: Miriam Rech, Markus Weisbeck, Surface, Frankfurt am Main/Berlin
Printing and binding: Brandenburgische Universitätsdruckerei Potsdam

ISBN 978-1-933128-26-9

Sternberg Press
Caroline Schneider
Karl-Marx-Allee 78, D-10243 Berlin
1182 Broadway #1602, New York, NY 10001
www.sternberg-press.com